FROM CLERK
TO CONTROLLER

FROM CLERK
TO CONTROLLER

Roderick H. Fowkes

PEN & SWORD
TRANSPORT

First published in Great Britain in 2016 by
Pen & Sword Transport
An imprint of Pen & Sword Books Ltd
47 Church Street
Barnsley
South Yorkshire
S70 2AS

ISBN 978 1 47384 416 2

Typeset by Milepost 92½
Printed and bound in India by Replika Press Pvt. Ltd

Front cover:
New in 2008, 'A1' Pacific No. 60163 *Tornado,* pictured leaving Plymouth station on its return
working to Bristol on 8 August 2009, soon to be tackling the formidable climbs to Hemerdon
and Dainton banks with the 'Tamar Tornado', run by Pathfinder Tours and administered by
Gloucester-based Peter Watts.

Back cover:
A popular former King's Cross-allocated 'A4' Pacific was No. 60034 *Lord Farringdon,* seen
here entering Stirling station on 14 April 1966 with the 'Grampian', 1.30pm Aberdeen
to Glasgow Buchanan Street train. With only four months to go before withdrawal from
Ferryhill (61B) shed, the locomotive was broken up by Hughes Bolckows, North Blyth.

Signal & Telegraph staff, Bob Naylor, Fred Astle and Wilf Foulds, pose for the
photographer, from the task in hand, in a 1964-dated scene, as the 3.45pm Nottingham to
London (St Pancras) Blue Pullman service takes the 3rd Up passenger line at Trent Station
North Junction.

Going nowhere, a line-up of Domestic & Cross-Country HSTs in Laira Carriage Sidings on
Christmas Day 1993.

Typeset in Palatino

Pen & Sword Books Ltd incorporates the imprints of Pen & Sword Archaeology, Atlas,
Aviation, Battleground, Discovery, Family History, History, Maritime, Military, Naval,
Politics, Railways, Select, Social History, Transport, True Crime, and Claymore Press,
Frontline Books,
Leo Cooper, Praetorian Press, Remember When, Seaforth Publishing and Wharncliffe.

For a complete list of Pen and Sword titles please contact
Pen and Sword Books Limited
47 Church Street, Barnsley, South Yorkshire, S70 2AS, England
E-mail: enquiries@pen-and-sword.co.uk
Website: www.pen-and-sword.co.uk

Contents

Preface

This is my account of my service on the railway in the latter days of steam up until privatisation. It consists of random recollections and anecdotes, spanning almost forty years from when the London Midland Railway took me on in 1957 until I left the Great Western Region in 1996.

I describe in detail many aspects of life on the railways, and the various posts I undertook, starting as a Junior Porter, and moving on to Signal Box Lad, Telegraph Clerk, Controller, Supervisor, Traction Arranger, Duty Manager and Operations Manager.

In the book, I describe the fun it can be working with a cross section of characters, whilst the intransigence of others often led to displeasure.

The Early Years

'That's a sign of rain' – a cliché echoed by my mother on many occasions when the sounds of wheels on rail joints appeared to emanate from just across the road, instead of the half-mile or so away on the London Midland Region's Derby to London railway line. With the prevailing westerly wind enhancing the sounds of trains, it was not surprising that their passing could clearly be heard, although on occasions the prophecy must have come true.

I was born in 1941 in Breaston, a village midway between Derby and Nottingham, some 2 miles from Toton, the largest marshalling yard in Britain. At school, no sooner had we trooped in for morning assembly when, just over a quarter of a mile away, a 'Jubilee' would rattle by at 9.10am with an express for London. Scant regard was paid to the music teacher when the lunchtime freight from Toton to Chaddesden went by hauled by a mighty Beyer-Garratt 2-6-6-2T. All trains heading towards Derby, except those via Way & Works, whistled a routing at Sawley Crossing and these could clearly be heard. The Chaddesden freight trundled past with an endless stream of wagons, to be followed in the opposite direction by another 'Jubilee'-hauled express for St Pancras.

I was the youngest of three children, and the only one with an interest in the railway that began at an early age, no doubt prompted and encouraged by my mother, the daughter of a stationmaster. It was she who accompanied me for the first time to Tamworth and Crewe. Most – me included – came to Tamworth to see the largest classes of ex-LMS steam power.

I was brought up on a diet of Stanier 'Jubilee' Class 5XPs, and Stanier and later BR Standard 5MT Class 4-6-0s from Millhouses (Sheffield) Shed, Holbeck (Leeds), Trafford Park (Manchester), Kentish Town (London), Derby and Nottingham, as they were the usual first line of motive power on the expresses running to and from St Pancras.

As a young boy I often stood on the platform at Derby station, observing the driver operating the handle of the water column after his fireman had put the 'bag' in the tender of an express for London or the West Country. Now with both driver and fireman back on the footplate, any trainspotters who might have been fortunate in being allowed onto the engine during

The fireman of the lunchtime Toton to Chaddesden freight gives a friendly wave to the photographer as his train, hauled by Beyer-Garratt 2-6-6-2T No. 47996, approaches Sawley Crossing in July 1955. Some fastidious drivers objected to running bunker first and, in 1931, the Toton Local Departmental Committee submitted a complaint on behalf of men working the Garratt engines tender first, which was declined by the company's representatives. Joe Wade

the brief stop were ushered back onto the platform. After tending to his fire, the fireman would then eagerly look for the right away from the platform; a whistle from the locomotive, up would go the regulator and, often with a deafening roar, the express would move away. Those interludes, involving proud individuals with cherry blossomed boots, often with collar and tie, left me with a mounting desire to be an engine driver. But, it didn't quite turn out like that.

Left to my own devices, I can't ever remember having a conversation with my father regarding my schoolwork and he showed absolutely no interest at all regarding my future employment. He had railroaded my elder brother into wasted years on the Co-op milk round, when Ivor himself would have preferred an apprenticeship. My sister Diana (Jane), I suspect, had to make her own way in the world, such was the lack of interest shown, and it was left to mother to mend any fences.

The cosy little cottage on 'The Green', two up, two down, no electricity, with an adjoining washhouse with toilet, linked to a large two-roomed coal-house with two upper storeys, in turn joined onto our gas-lit living accommodation. There was an oak-beamed living room with open fire complete with range, oven and boiler all requiring black-leading at intervals. According to some it was a house was where illicit dealings took place.

A delightfully clean 'Jubilee' Class 4-6-0 No. 45655 *Keith* of Trafford Park (9E) passing through Trent station with a Manchester (Central) to London (St Pancras) express in 1952, one of the few trains not stopping at the station and running via Nottingham and Melton Mowbray. Joe Wade

There was no sink or running water, hence the washhouse down the yard. Rainwater from an outside water butt was fed into the boiler and this provided the necessary hot water for washing. Rainwater, according to my mother, was much better than tap water for washing the hair and a sprig of rosemary in the final rinse would produce a fine sheen. Sunday of course was bath night, ready for school the following day; this was in the form of a large tin bath in front of the fire, with two buckets of rainwater heated on the gas stove. There was no heating at all upstairs; indeed, only one of the bedrooms had a gas light, with an adjustable flame. During extremely cold weather an oven shelf wrapped in a blanket supplemented the hot water bottle. We had a selection of animals: a couple of ducks, some hens whose eggs were religiously dated by mum, and no less than five cats, all female. Two of them would take it in turns to sit on the boiler, often singeing their tails whilst turning around; usually though they had the best seats in the house. A weekly rent of seven shillings (35p in today's money) was paid to a local farmer. I well remember those heady haymaking days when *Bonnie* and *Flower* provided the necessary horsepower with the loaded hay carts and with double summer time in evidence – in those days it didn't get dark until well after eleven o'clock. Not having electricity meant no television; nonetheless there was a 'friend in the corner' which was a source of entertainment, namely a wireless. It was a huge contraption, with a large Vidor battery, big valves and an accumulator. At an early age I listened fanatically to the wireless, sifting through the *Radio Times*. The latter, I recall, was recycled, finding its way into the small room at the end of the week. The mellifluous voices of the announcers and newsreaders gripped my imagination – the revered tones of Stuart Hibberd, John Snagge, Frank Phillips and Alvar Liddell, the legendary radiomen of that era. Immediately following *Dick Barton* on the then BBC Light Programme at seven o'clock was *Radio Newsreel* with *Imperial Echoes* as its signature tune. Families made their own entertainment; although dad was out at the pub every night, the adage that television killed the art of conversation cannot be denied. My father was a warehouse foreman at the Long Eaton Co-op, and he also acted as bookie's runner for Harold Dykes who ran the Regal Club in Long Eaton. The illicit dealings referred to earlier were connected with the level of interest generated by horse racing, which was considerable, and on big race days the *Grand National* and the *Derby* produced huge amounts of stake money. Even the local policeman – 'bobby Mackay' – was not averse to having a flutter. In 1950 my brother Ivor joined the forces, his eighteen-month stint in the Royal Army Medical Corps being extended to two years because of the Korean War. He was hospitalised for a while and had a spell at Netley recuperating. When home on forty-eight hour leave, he would return to his base at Aldershot, travelling back from Derby to London (St Pancras) on the 6pm train on a Sunday evening. At mother's insistence we'd walk down the dark lane to Sawley Crossing, lit by a solitary gas lamp on each side, in the vain hope of catching a glimpse of my brother Ivor as the train flashed by in the darkness. But all to no avail, the train was going too fast.

Taken at Sawley level crossing, where the only illumination was provided by the solitary gas lights each side of the crossing, as Johnson Midland Class '2F' 0-6-0 No. 58125 heads back to Chaddesden Sidings with the local pick-up goods from Sheet Stores. It was here with Mother that we stood waiting to glimpse my brother, Ivor, on the 6.00pm Derby to St Pancras express, all to no avail.

The Way In

Like so many other boys of my generation, I wanted to be an engine driver; two boys in my class had applied successfully for the position of engine cleaner at Toton Motive Power Depot. My dreams were dashed in 1956 when I went for a medical at Derby station. So much depended upon having perfect eyesight and I was extremely nervous. Fearful of failing, I became confused over white, yellow and orange colours flashed in different sequences, gradually getting smaller in size to simulate signals at various distances. The examination comprised tests for ordinary and colour vision. There was also an ingenious book designed by a Japanese professor called Ishiara. It contained various pages incorporating a number interposed in coloured dots, the number being identifiable by someone with normal colour vision. Those with defective vision may see different numbers or no number at all. Forty-eight hours later my apprehension was realised. The caller-up from Toton was the bringer of bad news. I opened the letter with trepidation, half expecting the worst. I had not attained the required colour vision level and was therefore unsuitable for the footplate grade. It was truly the darkest period I had known; I probably wept at the time. The lifetime ambition to be an engine driver was over; I had failed at the first hurdle, and later it turned out to be all the more poignant that my two classmates, who had been successful in joining the footplate grade as cleaners, left after only a short time. The consolation of being offered the position of junior porter, which at the time I did not take up, I don't recollect why, was of little consequence. Just what type of work did I now want? Still reeling from the disappointment of a lifelong desire to be an engine driver, I went to work for Jones Stroud, a textile firm in Long Eaton.

After almost five months in the wilderness, help was at hand, and it came by way of a porter at Draycott & Breaston station. I still had a yearning for the railway and kept in touch with happenings locally in the shape of wee George Mellors at the station. A likeable fellow, George rode the station bicycle in a very uncertain manner when he was delivering parcels between trains; he was also renowned for his rendering of Draycott in his high-pitched falsetto voice when a train arrived at the station. One day, he was showing me how to knock the crank of my bicycle back into shape – it had fallen over and as

Little over three quarters of a mile from what was initially known as Breaston station, this is Draycott, renamed Draycott & Breaston in 1939 owing to the increase in housing locally. This 1958 picture looking towards Derby has an overbridge in the background, which carried a major road and was about to be replaced by a new concrete structure. Wee George Mellors, the station porter here until the station closed on 14 February 1966, was instrumental in my joining the railway in 1957. Joe Wade

a result the crank was catching on the frame – when he mentioned that there was a vacancy at Trent for a junior porter, a position I had earlier turned down. This opportunity could not be allowed to pass; I applied for the job, was successful, and began my thirty-nine-year career with British Railways on 14 January 1957.

I reported to A.W. (Tony) Smith the Stationmaster; he explained the role of junior porter general-purpose relief, rate of pay 63 shillings (£3 15p in today's money) per week and the signal boxes at which I would be relieving at as a control reporter, Sheet Stores Junction, Trent Station South Junction, Toton Centre, Stanton Gate North Junction, Ilkeston South Junction and Beeston North.

There was no shortage of characters in the signal boxes, whether regular or relief men. A spell at Toton Centre covering a vacancy was, to say the least, interesting. With contra-rotating shifts between signalman and control reporter, one either loathed working alongside the redoubtable Bill Butler, or, strangely enough, as in my case, enjoyed it. Perhaps one week in three was sufficient, for at times working side by side with Bill resembled something more akin to a pantomime. He could be a cantankerous individual and had a love-hate relationship with quite a few drivers. Bill liked nothing more than sliding open a window and thrusting out a red light to stop an engine with incorrect lamps. This was brought about when an engine off a train that had drawn onto the Up arrival line, was released for the depot or one of the Down yards. After reversing on the independent line the fireman would be too tired to get off the engine to changeover the lamps. Geoff Wall always saw it as a relief when his week with Bill ended; back to more tranquil surroundings with either Jimmy Trigger or the placid George Bailey. Bill's father had been a signalman and was also reputed to have been an obstreperous individual. Like father, like son.

After a year on relief I applied for a permanent post at Sheet Stores Junction, named after the nearby factory which manufactured and repaired tarpaulins and sheeting to protect loaded open wagons. I was no stranger to the workings of a signal box. During my latter school days at Sawley Crossing,

B.R. 14300/98

BRITISH TRANSPORT COMMISSION

R. J. POWELL
District Operating Superintendent

Telephone
NOTTINGHAM 85251
Ext.

Telegraphic Address
DISTROP MIDLAND STATION
NOTTINGHAM

BRITISH RAILWAYS

DISTRICT OPERATING
SUPERINTENDENT
LONDON MIDLAND REGION
NOTTINGHAM

Our Reference   S3

2nd January, 1957.

Your Reference

Mr. R.H. Fowkes,
7, The Green,
BREASTON,
Derby.

Dear Sir,

With reference to your application for employment with British Railways; I am pleased to inform you that you were passed fit by our Medical Officer on the 1st instant. I can now offer you the position of Junior Porter (Control Reporter) at Trent, and shall be glad if you will please arrange to report to Mr.Smith, Station Master, Trent, as soon as possible.

Yours faithfully,
for R.J. Powell,

The start of a thirty-nine-year career with British Railways.

one afternoon it started to rain and the signalman on duty invited me into the box. Being a relief signalman I followed him to signal boxes at Spondon Station, Junction and Turntable Sidings, in addition to Castle Donington, and after a time became pretty proficient in working them.

The 'KGB' was not only to be found behind the Iron Curtain, it being in evidence around the Trent district in the form of relief signalman Kenneth G. Bradford, and having worked with a variety of bobbies (signalmen) Ken was certainly one of the best. Having cut his teeth some years earlier as a control reporter, his prowess in often raising the stakes when regulation became problematic spoke volumes; his overall ability left others with some catching up to do. Little did I know that a couple of years later when I was courting a girl who is now my wife, I learned that she lived a hundred yards from Ken and used to baby-sit for him in her younger days.

The Control Office, despite its name, was not directly concerned with the regulation of trains. Being dependent on ground reports the Control only had a general overview. The detailed train regulation was in the hands of the

Sheet Stores Junction signal box, where I worked as a box lad, was a standard Midland Railway design. This view is looking south east, and LMS '8F' 2-8-0 No. 48646 is working a Beeston to Chaddesden freight on 15 July 1964, on the South curve from Trent station. The line off to the right is from Leicester.

The interior of Trent Station South Junction, with signalman Norman Dean and myself.

signalman, which was clearly right. Perceived by some as faceless individuals, those in the Control Office were only able to disseminate information which had been fed into the Control by whatever means and from information gathered internally.

Often the Section Controller would instruct Sheet Stores not to let any more freight trains off the Castle Donington branch owing to the reception roads and goods lines to Beeston or Toton being full. Some trains would then stand on the branch end for long periods and, on occasions, a relief train crew would be sent to relieve the train. Control was very well aware that some signalmen would not entertain having train crews to wait in the signal box, other than to carry out Rule 55. This was perfectly understandable, judging by the conditions that some relief cabins were left in.

Shift patterns varied from box to box, anti-clockwise at Sheet Stores as was the Control, and with that a rapport developed with Albert Jones in the Derby District Office and Freddie Pratt at Nottingham. Both were followers of Derby County Football Club and we arranged to meet one Saturday at the bus stop outside Derby station to go to the football match. Various thoughts crossed my mind of matching the voice to the individual; the only clue was to look out for two 6ft 3in men. Sure enough there were not too many of that description about and I approached a couple of likely looking gents; these were they. I wasn't sure of what to say by way of introduction. I remember saying to Fred after making myself known, 'What about this Toton standing on the branch?' Not the most topical remark to have made; fortunately the Upperdale Road trolley bus came to my rescue. I realised from this encounter that these faceless individuals were actually human. Seven years later I would link up with them in what would be a highlight of almost forty years on the railway.

When Derby County FC had a football match in London, no visit was complete without looking in at Euston, King's Cross and Liverpool Street stations. Here at Euston in 1960 are two arrivals from the north 'Princess Coronation' Class '8P' 4-6-2 No. 46252 *City of Leicester* (left) and No. 46257 *City of Salford*.

Having been watered on arrival, Norwich-allocated 'Britannia' Pacific No. 70006 *Robert Burns* will be turned prior to working back home from Liverpool Street in 1960. Norwich shed had an allocation of twenty-two Britannias.

Derby County Football Club travelled by train to many away fixtures particularly to the capital, and I used to combine a day in London with visits to the termini at Euston, Liverpool Street and King's Cross before going to the match in the afternoon. My recollection is that the 'Rams' never fared too well in the metropolis. The grandeur of St Pancras was a joy to behold. The mellifluous tones of the station announcer – it was as if he was addressing every passenger personally – his voice reverberated around the giant roof span adding to the splendour of just being present, with sights and sounds to savour. Even the 'Jubilee' on the 6.30pm departure to Derby seemed to respect the occasion by keeping its steam under control. Likewise the tank engine at the buffer stop end of the platform, as the footballers settled down in the restaurant car in readiness for their evening meal, as we waited for the right away.

'Bunking' Motive Power depots was the norm for hundreds of train spotters each weekend, Crewe North and South sheds being a Mecca. I remember writing in 1957 to the District Commercial Manager (DCM) at Derby and again three years later, requesting permission to visit Crewe Motive Power Depots. The reply to each cited 'technical difficulties in

Gerard Fiennes described these machines as 'magnificence embodied in 3,300hp under the bonnet'. D9001 (55001) *St Paddy* is leaving King's Cross station for the servicing shed, past a posse of personnel, after working an express from the North in 1964.

Reply from DCM Derby regarding visits to Crewe Motive Power Depots.

connection with works taking place at Crewe' as the reason for the refusal, although parties affiliated to various Clubs might well have enjoyed access. A further request to the DCM in 1961, whilst still implying the no visit scenario to Crewe Depots, requested that applications be submitted through my local Staff Office.

The travel facilities enjoyed by railway staff enabled those so inclined to make the maximum use of the five free passes per year, and whereas only one 'foreign' free ticket was allowed a few years earlier, the relaxation then resulted in greater diversity, this together with unlimited privilege tickets. It was the general rule to have the free tickets made out to commence at, or in the vicinity of, your local station. I saw this however as being restrictive, hence the idea of using the south coast as the starting point to maximise their usage. Various itineraries were contemplated, including French ports on one occasion, but after sampling Brighton once, I settled on Weymouth and Bournemouth where 'Merchant Navy' and 'West Country' Pacifics still held sway. Any recognised routing could be undertaken which would allow travel to Scotland to be made via the East Coast, West Coast and the Midland lines, or a combination of all three. To make the most of this facility the dating of the tickets was crucial: they had to overlap. Linked with the free and reduced travel were visits to various engine sheds across the system.

Trent station was 'last century' some might say – one of the cornerstones of the Midland Railway Empire. Of Midland Gothic architecture, with its honeycomb of cellars and interlinking upper storeys, Trent's position and importance as an interchange junction for five main railway routes, through the plethora of junctions, served London, Birmingham, Derby, Chesterfield and Nottingham. Remarkably enough, trains could depart from opposite platforms in opposite directions to the same destination. Trent could be a

Free travel tickets

most inhospitable place: biting north/north-easterly winds that chilled the bone to the marrow, the hardiest of individuals would seek shelter in the waiting rooms or solace in the refreshment room, when open.

With no real desire to be a signalman, I submitted an application to transfer to the clerical staff. A period of time elapsed before sitting the entrance examination in my own time. Early in 1960, Stan Burchell, a Telegraph Clerk at Trent, moved on promotion to Controller in the Line Manager's Office at Derby, being closely followed by John Hardaker who went to a similar position in the Nottingham Control Office. The Rest Day Relief clerk, David Shaw, took one vacancy and I subsequently filled the other vacancy.

'Well I'll go to Trent!' was an expression my mother often used to make when faced with situations surpassing belief, and there I was, back after three years. I would spend a further six years at the station – in retrospect, a few wasted ones. Over the years Trent won many awards. For example, in 1953 it gained a first prize for cleanliness and a third prize for its gardens.

Although not widely known, all manner of royalty often visited Trent, which was possibly unbeknown to them, in the form of the Royal Train that stabled overnight between Trent Station North Junction and Sawley Junction – on the North Curve.

Other well-known celebrities would also change trains at Trent; amongst those mentioned by signalman George Bailey was Ella Fitzgerald, and on one occasion I saw Primo Carnera.

Quite often, a somewhat liberal view was taken of the low 15mph permanent speed restriction through the platform by some trains, on the Down road in particular, and none more so than the Luton to Bathgate motor car train and the 'Condor', with its 27 roller-bearing fitted, and vacuum-braked 'Platefit' wagons loaded with containers, these making staccato overtures on the jointed track. Another train that often showed scant regard for the

Trent station in the mid-1960s.
Photograph by George Bailey.

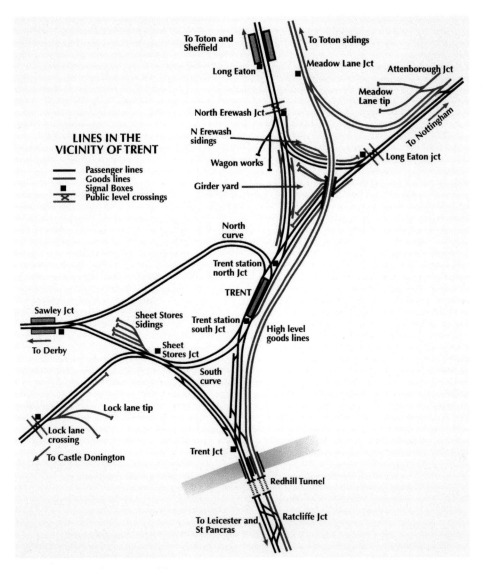

LINES IN THE
VICINITY OF TRENT

Passenger lines
Goods lines
Signal Boxes
Public level crossings

To Toton and
Sheffield

To Toton sidings

Long Eaton

Meadow Lane Jct

Attenborough Jct

Meadow
Lane tip

North Erewash Jct

N Erewash
sidings

To Nottingham

Wagon works

Long Eaton jct

Girder yard

North
curve

Trent station
north Jct

TRENT

Sawley Jct

Sheet Stores
Sidings

Trent station
south Jct

High level
goods lines

To Derby

Sheet
Stores Jct

South
curve

Lock lane tip

Lock lane
crossing

Trent Jct

To Castle Donington

Redhill Tunnel

To Leicester and
St Pancras

Ratcliffe Jct

Image courtesy of Steam World

mandatory speed restriction was the Down 'Thames-Clyde Express' until a station stop was introduced in late 1962.

In April 1966, I went for an interview at Furlong House in Nottingham for the post of Assistant Controller (Passenger) Class 3, located at Leicester. J.A. McEvoy took the interview and I was asked various questions appertaining to train running, etc. John McEvoy was a gentleman, short in stature and habitually looking over the top of his spectacles when in conversation. He always gave me the impression of being a sincere person, extremely positive and well respected by most. We talked at length of the functions of the Control Office and I asked him if he knew Jack Galletley in the Line Manager's Office at Derby, to which he replied that he did. Echoing the

The next departure on the clock from this platform is the 12.40pm for stations to Nottingham and Lincoln. Rattling through Trent station, taking a liberal view of the 15mph permanent speed restriction, is the 'Thames-Clyde Express' in the early 1960s – on a very cold day judging by the heavy frost still on the trees – hauled, according to David Shaw the Telegraph Clerk, by 'Royal Scot' Class '7P' 4-6-0 No. 46151 *The Royal Horse Guardsman*, a recent acquisition of Millhouses (41C) shed. It wasn't until 1962 that a station stop was introduced on the down 'Thames-Clyde Express', thus affording a connection into Nottingham. David Shaw

Trent station in the mid-1960s. Photograph by George Bailey.

sentiments of Jack, whereby he told me of his willingness to have me working alongside him, might possibly have worked in my favour as I received a letter dated 22 April informing me that I had been selected to fill the position at Leicester, date of transfer to be advised. It was signed by A.P. Watkinson, Station Manager, Long Eaton. This must have been one of the earlier appointments for Paul as he went on to become Director, Employee Relations, at the British Railways Board.

A letter dated 3 May from Furlong House reached me after initially being sent to Leicester, advising that I would become displaced under the Nottingham Divisional Control Organisation – Amalgamation of Nottingham, Derby and Leicester Control Rooms. Attached to the letter was a list of positions that I could apply for in the Nottingham Control Organisation under the closed list procedure. How unusual: displaced, even before being transferred to the new post. At the interview I didn't recall Mac informing me that the Leicester office would be relocating to Nottingham, although I'm pretty sure that he must have done. A further letter of 13 May informed me that I had been appointed Assistant Controller (General Assistant) Class 3 under the closed list procedure. My transfer date to Leicester was 16 May 1966. So, after just over six years at Trent, it was off to pastures new.

Trent Station, ultimately died quietly on New Year's Eve 1967. There had never been ranks of taxicabs outside, no buses passing the entrance, or no tannoys to disturb the tranquil surroundings. It was situated in a truly idyllic rural location without civilisation on the doorstep, and many no doubt enjoyed this charm, but for me it will always be particularly special, as it was the location where my thirty-nine-year career with British Railways began.

Thereafter, the five years in Control were undoubtedly a highlight of my railway career that also included subsequent supervisory positions at Toton before being ensconced at Plymouth from 1978 until retirement in 1996

British Railways London Midland Region

Station Manager.,
Long Eaton.

Mr R.H.Fowkes,
Clerk,
Trent.

Apr. 22nd, 1966

y/r
o/r Staff Pad.

Dear Mr Fowkes,

I am pleased to inform you that you have been selected to fill the position of assistant Controller (Passenger Trains) Class 3 Nottingham D.M.O. (Located Leicester) with an allocation date of 16.3.66.

Your date of transfer will be advised to you later.

Yours sincerely,

Confirmation letter to inform me that I had been appointed the position of assistant controller in Leicester.

Five years in Control

'The five years spent in the Control Office [at Nottingham] *together with the short period at Leicester were, without doubt some of the best days of my thirty-nine year railway career'.*

The LMR's Leicester Divisional headquarters functioned from its new offices in a modern block in Granby Street in the heart of the city, a couple of years before my transfer. The task of planning the organisation, finding the accommodation – which, when chosen, still had to be completed as a building – and grouping the new staff under its roof, was completed within a year. The Divisional Manager, Mr R.D. Gardiner, had taken over control of the functions previously executed by District Operating and Commercial Managers from separate offices in Leicester and by a District Motive Power Superintendent at Wellingborough. Most of the staff worked in large open-plan offices, which facilitated close contact between sections and eliminated inter-departmental correspondence.

The headquarters' Traffic Control covered 90 miles of the Midland main line from Loughborough to Sharnbrook, and from Melton Mowbray to Kettering, and its supervision also extended over other routes to Ashby-de-la-Zouch, Hinckley, Lutterworth, Theddingworth, Kelmarsh, Thrapston, Seaton and Luffenham – 192 route miles in all. There were five Section Controllers who employed the graph method, instead of train cards, to record the hour-to-hour progress and operating data of individual trains.

Having previously held the requisite 8 miles free travel allowance, it was then necessary to obtain a residential ticket for the additional 12 miles travel to Leicester. There was also a dependence on the train service to coincide with shift working. Early turn on Monday necessitated cycling almost 10 miles to Nottingham to catch the overnight Edinburgh (Waverley) - London (St Pancras) service at 5.47am. The remainder of the week with a seven o'clock start the 6.16am from Trent sufficed, returning via Nottingham Midland to Trent or Long Eaton station as appropriate. The night turn was the most time consuming, having to leave home at around 7.15pm and cycling to Trent to catch the local DMU half an hour later. This early arrival at Leicester afforded time at the local hostelry to brush up my darts playing, whereby Harry Gregory travelling from Nottingham had an alternative rendezvous, returning off the night turn by way of the 7.40am to Trent and arriving home some thirteen and a half hours later. Some Saturday night turns I would be booked off. This was fortuitous as there was no train to get me back home on the Sunday morning. Of the couple of shifts that I did work, help was at hand. My colleagues arranged a light engine move to either Derby or Toton on which I travelled to Trent and, on the other occasion, I caught a ballast train. My spell at Leicester was to be even shorter than was anticipated, even though the moving date had been deferred by four weeks, until 30 October.

I had been waiting since May to go into hospital for a hernia operation and was summoned to the Derbyshire Royal Infirmary on 8 September and was discharged three days later. At the time there were seven Railway Convalescent Homes owned by the employees of British Railways, London Transport Railways, Docks, Waterways and British Transport Hotels Ltd who contributed to the funds. A Board of Trustees and various committees, the members of which gave their services voluntarily, administered them. Being a member, the minimum contribution payable through the paybills was 3d per week; wives were also covered by their husband's subscriptions. Taking advantage of this, members were actively encouraged to make use of them, of which five were available for men. Dawlish, being the most popular, was my first choice. Not surprisingly, there wasn't a vacancy and I was allocated a two-week stay at Par.

In between coming out of hospital and going convalescing to Par, Peter Griffin, who worked in the LMO at Derby – he, along with other controllers, would transfer to Nottingham the following year when the HQ office relocated to Crewe – and myself made an overnight trip to Carlisle returning via the Furness line to Barrow. We reflected on this journey thirty years later: neither of us could recall the reason for the jaunt but an exhilarating footplate ride was long remembered. At Barrow-in-Furness we introduced ourselves to the driver of the 8.46am to Preston and, having made our interest in steam known and that we were railway controllers, were offered a footplate ride to Lancaster. 'Britannia' Pacific No. 70011 *Hotspur* was at the head of a four or five-coach train. Fog, patchy, but dense in places was still lingering as the locomotive romped away with its trifling load. The fireman offered Peter his shovel and with it he fed a hungry *Hotspur*. I had to decline the invitation owing to my recent operation. Instead, the fireman sat me in his seat with instructions to sound the whistle each time the driver nodded, on account of the number of level crossings and the prevailing foggy conditions. It may have been a long time since *Hotspur* had chimed so incessantly over such a distance. Music to the ears.

During the 1960s, diverting services to other routes was a deliberate ploy on behalf of the British Railways Board in cognisance of the Beeching Report in running down many of the lines across the country, which included the whole Great Central route. Also the fact that people were using other forms of transport including the motor car, passenger numbers were falling and closures were inevitable.

The Great Central main line lost its through workings to London, the last passenger train leaving Nottingham Victoria for Marylebone on 3 September 1966 at 17.15, hauled by Stanier Class 5 4-6-0 No. 44984. The station at Nottingham Victoria would close a year later and the remaining DMU service to Rugby Central, starting from Nottingham Arkwright Street, would cease on 3 May 1969 when the ex-GC line south of the city closed to passenger traffic, a once proud line that only a few years earlier furnished services to almost all parts of southern England, the north and Scotland and did not have a single level crossing from Beighton Junction (Sheffield) through to Marylebone.

On resuming work in the final week at Leicester it was cheerio to some and goodbye to others. Many controllers opted for working at Nottingham, a number would move home, others preferring to travel, whilst a couple would be accommodated locally to more menial posts. To coincide with the closure of the Control Office, a Train Controller (Regulator) was introduced in Leicester North signal box. A similar post had been created a few years earlier in Trent Station North signal box. And so to Nottingham, Furlong House, situated adjacent to the old steam shed in the heart of the Meadows – not the most salubrious part of Nottingham. Harry Gregory, who had travelled daily from Nottingham for a number of years, benefited more than most from the closure of the Leicester office. Living in the Meadows he then only had to fall out of bed to get to work. Some months earlier, the Derby District Control Office had closed and many of the staff transferred to Nottingham, which resulted, with our arrival, in three offices being merged into one, now controlling an area from Horns Bridge (Chesterfield) to Tamworth, Tutbury and Hinckley, Aslockton and Staythorpe to Ketton, Kelmarsh and Sharnbrook. There was also a responsibility for the line through the Peak District although freight traffic had been withdrawn from the route in readiness for its complete closure beyond Matlock.

3 September 1966 was the last day of through workings on the Great Central line. The LCGB ran a rail tour from Waterloo to Penistone, returning to Marylebone. Arriving at Leicester Central shortly after midday is Southern Region 'Merchant Navy' Pacific No. 35030 *Elder Dempster Lines*.

SECTION 'D'

MISCELLANEOUS INSTRUCTIONS

Nottingham Divisional Manager Control Organisation

As from Sunday, 30 October, 1966, the District Control Office at Leicester will be closed and all duties formerly undertaken at this office will be transferred to the Nottingham Divisional Control Office, Furlong House, Nottingham.

(WT/185/15) (10.9.66)(41)

(The first item page 3, ME. No. 37D is hereby amended)

Notice of the closure of the District Control Office at Leicester on 30 October 1966.

APPENDIX INSTRUCTIONS

SECTIONAL APPENDIX, MIDLAND LINES, DATED 1960

THE MAXIMUM PERMISSIBLE SPEEDS between RUGBY CENTRAL STATION AND HEATH Shown in the Table on page 40 of ME. 2 Notices No. 39 and 40 are AMENDED as follows :–

	Down	Up	
RUGBY CENTRAL STATION AND HEATH	60	60	MAXIMUM PERMISSIBLE SPEED.

The following to acknowledge immediately on receipt of this Notice by telegram to "TRAINS NP. DERBY" using the code "ARNC S.N. 1134" :–

M.P.D. – Cricklewood West, Cambridge St. Diesel Depot, Bedford, Wellingborough, Kettering, Leicester Mid., Nottingham Mid., Colwick, Kirkby in Ashfield, Derby Mid., Burton, Rowsley, Toton, Saltley. Rugby

D.M. – Euston, Nottingham, Birmingham, Sheffield.

D.C. – St.Pancras, Leicester, Manchester South.

Y.M. – St.Pancras, Brent, Wellingborough, Leicester Mid., Nottingham, Kirkby East, Toton, Westhouses, Colwick, Rowsley, Chaddesden, Burton on Trent, Saltley.

S.M. – St.Pancras, Bedford, Glendon & R., Corby, Oakham, Melton Mowbray Town, Market Harborough, Leicester L.Rd., Nottingham Mid., Mansfield Town, Hasland, Derby Mid., Burton on Trent, Moira, Coalville Town, Tamworth H.L., Coleshill, Birmingham New St., Kings Norton, Manchester Cen., Rugby Cen., Lutterworth, Leicester Cen., Ilkeston North, Sheffield Vic.

DERBY,
29 1966.   LINE MOVEMENTS SUPT.
SEPTEMBER

September 1966 also saw the remaining ex-LNER Gresley 'A4' Pacifics withdrawn, Nos. 60009 *Union of South Africa* and 60019 *Bittern* both joining 60007 *Sir Nigel Gresley* in preservation. The locomotives had four extremely successful years on the Glasgow to Aberdeen route. Indeed, there must have been many a doubting Thomas, when it was announced that ageing steam engines were to replace the troublesome North British Locomotive Company Type '2' diesels on the accelerated 3-hour express services. Featuring tightly-timed schedules with little to spare on intermediate point to point timings, it was to be the swansong of the 'A4s'. Credit must go to the enginemen at Aberdeen (Ferryhill), Glasgow (St Rollox) and Perth who put up creditable performances with their 'A4' locomotives not forgetting, of course, the maintenance staff at either end of the 'Caley' main line. The ex-LNER Gresley 'A4' Pacifics mainly came from Haymarket, although some had been rescued from south of the border via Peterborough (New England) when King's Cross shed closed in 1963, with other compatriots transferred from Gateshead. In addition to the decline of BR steam at the time, Glasgow Buchanan Street station was closed in November 1966 with services diverted to nearby Queen Street. Then, in September 1967, the line from Stanley Junction (north of Perth) to Kinnaber Junction was closed, a legacy of the Beeching 'cuts', leaving the communities of Coupar Angus and Forfar on the attractive Strathmore route isolated, without a rail connection.

Ex-LNER 'A4' Pacific No. 60024 *Kingfisher* backs onto its train at Glasgow (Buchanan Street) from St Rollox shed, in readiness to work the 'Grampian' three-hour service to Aberdeen on May 25 1966; four months later it would all be over for the 'A4'. In October the locomotive was scrapped at Hughes Bolckows, North Blyth.

Up 'Bon Accord', the 7.10am Aberdeen to Glasgow (Buchanan Street) waits for the right away at Stirling in 1964, with Gresley 'A4' No. 60009 *Union of South Africa* in charge. It was withdrawn in June 1966 and sold to J.B. Cameron in July 1966.

Ex-LNER 'A4' Pacific No. 60019 *Bittern* taking water at Perth station in 1965, working the Aberdeen to Glasgow (Buchanan Street) three-hour 'Bon Accord' express. *Bittern* was withdrawn by BR along with other 'A4s' in September 1966 and was bought by Mr Drury for preservation. I returned to Buchanan Street on a bitterly cold and frosty night in February 1966 to board the 11.00pm to Aberdeen, where 'A4' No. 60019 *Bittern* was simmering quietly. After exchanging pleasantries with the enginemen, I was invited on to the footplate for a maiden nocturnal trip. With eleven coaches in tow, there was much slipping on the 1-in-79 gradient through the tunnels to St Rollox, the start being very slow in consequence. With a full moon and a crisp exhaust beat, it was an exhilarating experience; a permanent way check and a dead stand at Larbert for signals, culminating with a maximum speed of 75mph before Stirling, were the main highlights. The fact that the schedule was more generous than the three-hour daytime services was academic. From that point I retired into the train, cat-napping to Aberdeen, arriving seven minutes early at 3.13am on a relatively easy schedule.

The doyen of the 'A4s', judged as one of Ferryhill's best performers over this route and a locomotive the re-doubtable King's Cross driver Bill Hoole will always be associated with; 'A4' Pacific No. 60007 *Sir Nigel Gresley*, taking water at Perth when in charge of the 7.10am Aberdeen to Glasgow (Buchanan Street) 'Bon Accord' in 1965. It was withdrawn from Aberdeen Ferryhill (61B) in February 1966 and rescued by the A4 Preservation Society in May 1966.

Predominately a Scottish Region-allocated engine, ex-LNER 'A4' Pacific No. 60024 *Kingfisher* rests between duties in May 1966. Having worked the 'Grampian' from Glasgow (Buchanan Street), the 'A4' has been serviced at its home depot ready for its next working south. Of the Gresley 'A4s' drafted onto the three-hour Aberdeen to Glasgow expresses, No. 60024 *Kingfisher* was the last to appear at Ferryhill (61B).

At this juncture it might be appropriate to include the methods appertaining to the workings of the Control Office.

TRAIN AND TRAFFIC CONTROL INSTRUCTIONS

OBJECTS OF CONTROL

The fundamental principle of efficient train and traffic operating is that the scheduled timings of trains in the working time tables, notices, etc. be maintained, the booked workings for Guards, Enginemen and engines be adhered to, and that the instructions relating to the classification, marshalling and loading of freight trains be complied with.

The main objects of Control are to maintain the booked arrangements to the maximum possible extent, to guide the working back to normal when out-of-course, and to modify the arrangements when necessary to meet fluctuations in traffic.

The Control in conjunction with other Operating and Motive Power staff engaged in train and traffic working will have the following general aims: —

(a) To ensure the expeditious working of traffic including empty stock.
(b) To plan and organise the current working of Passenger and Freight trains so as to avoid delay.
(c) To obtain the maximum work from engine power and trainmen by:
    (i) Punctual working.
    (ii) Using the fewest locomotives possible.
    (iii) Securing the maximum authorised loading.
    (iv) Incurring the minimum amount of light mileage or unrequired assistance.
    (v) Releasing engines promptly after completion of work.
    (vi) Making the best use of unbalanced engines.
(d) To regulate the working of trainmen to ensure economical working and avoid excessive hours.

All staff associated with the working of trains and the movement of traffic must carry out instructions given from the Control and must co-operate at all times to the fullest extent, by information, consultation and suggestion to overcome difficulties.

Station Masters, Yard Masters, Supervisors and the Staff under them are not relieved of their responsibility and must use their initiative in carrying out laid down arrangements.

Departures from scheduled arrangements and the provision of power and trainmen, for any purpose other than booked, must be made through the Control.

PASSENGER TRAINS MUST START AND WORK PUNCTUALLY and must not be held for connecting services, unless written authority has been issued or permission has been obtained by telephone from the Control, to which an early advice of such a possibility arising must be given. If a train arrives late at a station every effort must be made to regain the lost time.

FREIGHT TRAINS MUST START AND WORK PUNCTUALLY and must not be held, either for vehicles to be completed or off connecting services, except by permission from the Control, to which an early advice of such a possibility arising must be given.
If a train arrives late at a station or traffic yard every effort must be made to regain the lost time and the station or traffic yard staff must keep in touch with the Control so that instructions can be given to achieve this object.

TRAIN CONTROL
The detailed regulation of trains in running must be carried out by the Signalmen (or Regulators) from information received in regard to the actual running, the working at their signal boxes and their knowledge of the requirements of the line ahead, taking into consideration the margins available for each type of train.

Signalmen will, when necessary, receive instructions from the Control as to ultimate requirements, thus assisting them in carrying out the detailed regulation. In certain circumstances, however, the Control Staff will give definite instructions to the Signalmen on questions of regulation.

Signalmen or others responsible for regulation must consult the Control in all cases of difficulty.

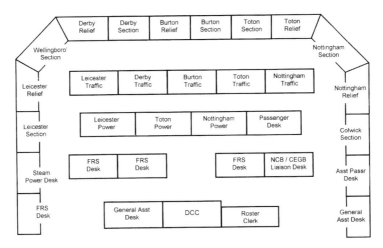

Floor plan of the Control Office at Furlong House now merged with three districts, Derby, Nottingham and Leicester. At the back of the room, in a position commanding a view of the whole area, is the head controller (DCC), who can thus see all under his jurisdiction.

The whole area now controlled from Furlong House was divided into sections. Each Section Controller had a train board that encompassed a track diagram and ran the perimeter length of three sides of the office. All traffic movements were plotted by means of pegs and small cards that had details of the train, which were moved as the train progressed as telephone reports were received from the various reporting points throughout the district. Before a train entered the area, the neighbouring Control Offices – Birmingham, London, Sheffield, Lincoln, Manchester, Stoke – from which it was being forwarded, telephoned the Nottingham Control Office with the information to be inserted onto a train card. This comprised of the home depot of the driver and guard; the time the men booked on duty; the engine number; the description and loading of the train. Different coloured cards distinguished Up and Down trains. The cards were then hung on the train board to indicate to the Section Controller from which neighbouring area it would approach. It was then affixed to the appropriate position on the train diagram board on receipt of the first signal box reporting point.

Subsequent reporting from designated signal boxes enabled the cards to be moved along the track diagram commensurate with the information received. Each Section Controller maintained a record of the train movements; they would need to be scrutinised in connection with delays to that or other trains. Some controllers preferred to use the 'graph' method of recording, although it had been dispensed with by the time I went into the Control Office. Initially at Nottingham there were twenty-five controllers on a shift, an FRS (wagon) clerk supplemented by a further two on the day shift, and a liaison officer who provided the link with the Central Electricity Generating Board and the National Coal Board.

During my box-lad days the controllers, some of whom I reported trains to some eight or nine years earlier, were often referred to, by some, as faceless individuals. But now a face could be aligned to the voice. In those control-reporting days I shared the same frustration as the signalmen and others in endeavouring to contact the Control, trying to curb my impetuousness, repeatedly pressing the red button on the telephone, wrongly assuming that a series of rings could be heard in the office, when in point of fact, all that happened was a light illuminated on the concentrator. The times I used to hear *'can't get hold of the blooming Control!'* Now it was plain to see just why.

With such a cross section of individuals there were bound to be some lame ducks; there is in every organisation. A few would do no more than what was required of them, whilst there were others who could not make a decision to save their life. The latter, it must be said, were few and far between. Reliant on telephone reports from stations, yards and signal boxes etc, the controllers were entirely dependent on this information, which had to be current for their knowledge of happenings outside. It was a far cry from today's computer system that accurately displays the state of the lines on a TV monitor. The Control Office, despite its name, was not directly concerned with the detailed regulation of trains; that was left in the hands of the signalmen and other people on the spot. Establishing a rapport with signalmen was essential: forewarned is forearmed; a train a few minutes overtime in section or running sluggish may well be a potential failure further on. Prior advice of this might expedite the situation should assistance be required. Although my position in the Nottingham office was of Assistant Controller (General Assistant), I did in fact cover the Assistant Passenger Controller's post on the corresponding shift to the one worked at Leicester, and Harry Gregory was also on the same shift, as were the two Section Controllers and the Power Controller. The Passenger Controller reported express and parcel trains on and off the area, and at principal stations, together with any delays, to the Line Manager's Office at Derby.

For the first month or two, I travelled to the office by train from either Sawley Junction (later renamed Long Eaton after the station of the same name on the Erewash Valley line closed in 1967) or Trent station to Nottingham Midland on my residential pass, although for the early turn the bus service had to be used.

On the Nottingham Traffic Section was Walter Plowright, often referred to as 'The Dog' or 'Blue Leader'. He only lived a mile away from my home, and after the first couple of weeks of getting to know people on the shift, I had a lift with him to and from the office. Walter drove an Austin A35 and on the night turn he used to be ready to go around nine o'clock to drive the 9 miles to Nottingham; I would walk the three quarters of a mile to a pick-up point. Instead of wanting to get to work in reasonable time he would amble along at around 30mph, which appeared funereally slow at the time. A ploy used when on the late turn was for someone or something to upset Walter close to change over time. He would then put his foot down on the way home, which was advantageous as the pubs in those days closed at half past ten.

In late 1966 there would have been an overall staff complement in the Control Office of around 105 personnel that included the regular controllers, on a three-shift roster, and rest-day relief and general-purpose relief controllers. Notwithstanding, camaraderie was in general friendly enough, although friction was known to build up on occasions between the traffic controllers who would, tongue in cheek, admonish the power controller. He needed to move his wagons, while others were unable to provide the necessary traction to do so. There was also an element of antipathy when the detestable 'Duke' – Stan Wiggins – came across from another shift on promotion. He was always immaculately dressed, aloof with more than a degree of arrogance, ate alone, always taking his break before anyone else, and never lowered his dignity to ask for a lift home should the need arise.

The first of my children, Alan, was born at the Derby Nightingale Maternity Home on 5 May 1967, and the following month I bought my first car, a Ford Cortina 1200cc. From then on Walter and I would take it in turns with transport to and from Nottingham.

As time progressed, I became quite satisfied with my performance in the Control Office, albeit as a mere Assistant Passenger Controller, going to great lengths to try and remedy some of the anomalies that occurred with overcrowding, late running and missed connections. It must be said that at the time the office was to some extent overstaffed, with most of the controllers working their rest days with a full shift on duty on the Saturday night turn. There was obviously a transitional period with the amalgamation of the three offices, which was later addressed.

The summer of 1967 saw the three remaining Leeds (Holbeck) 'Jubilees' having their final fling of working over the Settle & Carlisle route: nos. 45562 *Alberta* and 45593 *Kolhapur* being the first line choice for hauling the Saturday relief trains; the 06.40 Birmingham-Glasgow (10.17 ex-Leeds) and the 09.20

My first house, which cost £2,750 in 1965, and this was my first car.

'Jubilee' Class '6P' 4-6-0 No. 45593 *Kolhapur*.

St Pancras-Glasgow (a relief to the 'Thames-Clyde Express') which didn't call at Leeds station, but changed locomotives at Engine Shed Junction. The other 'Jubilee', No. 45697 *Achilles*, was the standby engine for the two turns. In point of fact the two summer Saturday extras – the swan song for the Holbeck Jubilees – had virtually become enthusiasts' excursions, some of whom supported the Holbeck shed staff in keeping their external condition exemplary, such was the drawing power of steam. The previous summer, an overnight relief to the St Pancras-Glasgow sleeper was also booked for 'Jubilee' haulage. The first of three trips in 1967 was somewhat disappointing. On Saturday, 29 July, the 09.20 from St Pancras had arrived at Leeds Engine Shed Junction on time, hauled by a Peak class diesel, which hooked off and went onto Holbeck shed. Usually the replacement locomotive would have been in the siding alongside, but not this day. The

Leeds (Holbeck) Passenger Engine & Men Working, June 1967.

14.11 departure time had long since passed before No. 45562 *Alberta* put in a belated appearance, the net result being a fifty-two minute delay. As to whether the enginemen had already given up the ghost as a result of the lateness remains a matter of conjecture; suffice to say that a further twenty-eight minutes were dropped to Carlisle, the only significant delay being an unscheduled stop for water at Hellifield. Having said that, who are we to know what problems might have been encountered up front? It was, though, a pretty lacklustre performance.

The following week saw another punctual arrival of the train at Engine Shed Junction; what then transpired was beyond my wildest dreams. On the adjoining line was the replacement locomotive, 'Jubilee' No. 45593 *Kolhapur*. I was in the leading coach as the guard being relieved had made his way from the rear brake through the train to join the diesel to Holbeck Depot. As he was alighting, I inquired who the enginemen were on the replacement steam locomotive, and would he ask the driver if there was any chance

At Leeds Engine Shed Junction, the 9.20am London (St Pancras) to Glasgow relief to the 'Thames-Clyde Express' is about to change locomotives as the train did not call at Leeds station. The 'Peak' diesel will be off to Holbeck shed, whilst 'Jubilee' No. 45593 *Kolhapur* waits in the siding to work the train forward with me on the footplate.

of a footplate ride, careful to point out to him that I was a controller at Nottingham, which just might sway the decision. Imagine the sheer delight when the guard gesticulated to me that my request had been acceded to. Without further ado, complete with my Halina 35x camera and a super 8 cine camera with two reels of fifty-foot silent film, I jumped down onto the ballast making sure that the coach door was fully closed, and clambered onto the footplate. Exchanging pleasantries and with formalities completed, the locomotive backed onto the train of nine coaches and, after the mandatory brake test had been carried out, the Carlisle Kingmoor crew quickly had *Kolhapur* into its stride. I might not have been so fortunate the previous year when Holbeck enginemen had the turn. Supposedly, for some time 45593 had been running with a middle piston gland blowing, a feature that might not have endeared it to some pernickety lineside photographers. The penalty for passing Shipley Leeds Junction two minutes early was a dead stand for one minute at Cononley. Recovering from the signal stop, and with nose to the stable, the train was on time by Skipton, the impetus being the need for an unscheduled stop for water at Hellifield. This afforded the onboard enthusiasts and photographers on the station platform a closer look at the

'Jubilee' Class '6P' 4-6-0 No. 45593 *Kolhapur*, taking water on the unscheduled stop at Hellifield.

immaculately turned out locomotive; it also enabled the fireman to build up the firebox in readiness for the 'Long Drag'. The six-minute stop for water put the train nine minutes late through Settle Junction on a clear sunny afternoon. The enginemen had now swapped duties, the beat of *Kolhapur* lengthening as the train crossed the magnificent twenty-four arch Batty Moss viaduct before plunging into Blea Moor Tunnel. Across the high tableland around Ribblehead and Ais Gill, the adjacent fields were littered with scores of enthusiasts all vying for the perfect photographic shot. Then came a further opportunity to replenish the water tank at the highest troughs in Britain – Garsdale.

On the long descent to Carlisle there were one or two lively stretches and the arrival there was seven minutes late. The engine some years earlier would have been worked considerably harder than on this occasion. Nonetheless it had been a most memorable journey and by way of appreciation a ten shilling note was left on the driver's seat. All eight minutes of the silent super 8 cine film were later transferred to video and onto DVD, augmented with sounds from an Argo recording of *Newfoundland heads the Waverley*.

A week later No. 45593 *Kolhapur* was again allocated to the 14.11 departure from Engine Shed Junction, and a special stop for a minute at Keighley to set down put the train through Skipton seven minutes late. A two-minute stop at Hellifield for water, which for some reason was not forthcoming, meant a five-minute stop at Settle to take on water; the net result was twenty-five minutes late passing Ais Gill. There were three permanent way slacks on the route including one over Garsdale water troughs, which was inconvenient to say the least, and Carlisle was reached thirty-two minutes late. An even

One of Holbeck's longest-serving 'Jubilee' Class '6P' 4-6-0 locomotive No. 45562 *Alberta*, heading north over the Settle & Carlisle line, with the 6:40am Birmingham-Glasgow in 1966.

earlier run behind *Kolhapur* from Leeds station on the 06.40 Birmingham-Glasgow had a relatively easy schedule with a booked sixteen-minute stop at Skipton for traffic purposes and water; this was to allow the following 10.25 Leeds-Glasgow to proceed. A signal check at Gargrave before being brought to a stand at Settle Junction probably winded No. 45593 and a stop at Horton-in-Ribblesdale for eight minutes for a blow-up put the train twenty-seven minutes late over Ais Gill. The two minutes recovery time, with a couple more picked up at Appleby owing to smart station work, reduced the arrears at Carlisle to twenty minutes.

The Anglo-Scottish expresses over the Settle & Carlisle line had produced a varied selection of motive power including BR 'Britannia' Pacifics and for a short spell in 1960 Gresley 'A3s' were drafted in before being moved away following dieselisation of the Leeds-Glasgow-Edinburgh services. The 'Royal Scot' stud based at Leeds Holbeck dominated the workings via Ais Gill in the 1950s, seldom found working south of Leeds into St Pancras. This leg was diagrammed to one of the eighteen allocated 'Jubilee' engines, which also worked over the S&C and shared the cross-country workings with Bristol Barrow Road shed. During my box-lad days it was noticeable that Holbeck must have been hard pressed at times in providing the rostered 'Jubilee' locomotive for the Up 'Thames-Clyde Express'. Odd this, one would have thought that this prestige train would have had preference over others working out of Leeds. Instead, the substitute, a Stanier 'Black 5' could not be expected to keep time and often acquired a pilot – usually another Class '5' – from Leicester to St Pancras.

Holbeck shed was no doubt short of power on this day in June 1959, as Stanier Class '5' 4-6-0 No. 44849 was deputising for the rostered 'Jubilee' on the up *'Thames-Clyde Express'*, seen here coasting towards Trent station. In view of this, a pilot engine was probably attached at Leicester in order to maintain time. Joe Wade

At a Passenger Services Progress meeting held on 8 January 1968, chaired by the Divisional Operating Superintendent J.A. McEvoy, the deterioration in performance during December was highlighted and in an effort to correct this the Divisional Inspectorate, including Running Inspectors, were to be intensively employed on Class 1 passenger services, a programme having been worked out with the Birmingham and London Divisions.

Included in the minutes of the meeting was a discussion held regarding the communications between the stations at Leicester, Nottingham and Derby with the Control and vice versa, and the Chairman said he would nominate a member of the Control staff to discuss these issues with the Area Managers concerned, especially the requirements for improved telecommunications between the points mentioned. I had the privilege of being the nominated controller to visit the various locations in an attempt to sort out the difficulties. It was an interesting exercise as communication with the main stations was on occasions a problem, the people on the ground often being unable to contact the relevant controller for a decision.

Also in 1968, the Line Manager's Office at Derby (known as Regional Control) was merged with the Crewe office; some staff in the various sections of the Derby LMO relocated with the transfer whilst others would travel daily; there was even a 07.44 staff train laid on from Derby for a period to cater for those travelling personnel. The remainder were accommodated locally as positions became vacant; some of the controllers then found positions at Furlong House. Amongst them was Peter Griffin who lived at Burton-on-Trent. He then had an increase in journey times, and later used to convey some of the ex-Derby District Controllers to Furlong House.

W. Banks.
Passenger Services.

Copy to :-

S. Hall.
A. Kemp.
D.C.C.'s.
R. Fowkes,
Pass. Controller.

PASSENGER PUNCTUALITY.

A report has been submitted on the control procedure which highlights our deficiencies in carrying out the plan.

Summarised they are :-

(1) The Control rostering must take into account a man's proficiency to do the job. While this applies to the Passenger Assistants, it equally applies to any other position in the Control.

(2) Current reporting by Signalmen. This ends up in a dispute – no attention to Control telephone. A practical suggestion that All Signalmen should record in T.R.B. train delays, e.g. Distant check, Brought to stand, cautioned because of equipment failure in addition to the times the trains are actually at a stand. The T.R.B. should also indicate reported to Control or Regulator so that we have a check on no explanations on the Bulletin sheets.

(3) Lack of consultation main stations/Control stations. This is particularly applicable to D.M.U's and other failures at Etches Park, Leicester and Nottingham. Also on their known stock shortages each day.

(4) Telecommunications with Leicester – Derby. Suggestion that Derby A Box to be on Trent Regulator circuit and to include Chief Inspector, Derby. Leicester Station Inspectors to be on Leicester Regulators circuit and answered by Passenger Controllers. (Check on alterations already in hand with Thornton of the D.M.s. Works Section)

(5) Proposed altered seating arrangements for Passenger Controllers.

(6) Suggestion that X.P's. should be reported before Sheffield.

I have arranged for Mr. Fowkes to be detached from Monday, 5th February to visit you in remedying these deficiencies. Please arrange a meeting with the main stations to discuss the improvements necessary and for positive action to be taken towards a permanent improvement in our day to day arrangements.

Please arrange to report to me on progress by Monday, 19th February at the latest.

Nominated by J.A. McEvoy to visit outstations in connection with the Passenger Punctuality scheme.

From June 1968 the control of the Etches Park-based Diesel Multiple Unit fleet was devolved upon the division, together with the control of non-passenger carrying rolling stock. *'All work previously performed in the GM's. PRS. Section will be passed to the Divisional Passenger Controller in Nottingham Control'*: this was the wording of a letter issued in connection with the Control of Diesel Multiple Units. As it happened, the Passenger Controllers didn't want anything to do with the DMU working; it was shunted over to the assistants' desk. Together with my other two colleagues and rest day relief man, we took on board the control of the DMU fleet and ran with it. A system was already in place, whereby each morning the Assistant Depot Engineer at Etches Park advised the GM's PRS Section which DMU sets were required for exam that night. He would continue with this arrangement and advise us of the requirements at around nine o'clock in the morning. I soon put a stop to that; the units were already allocated into diagrams, some of which would not finish at Derby that night. It meant breaking down the diagrams and doing unscheduled changes in the stations, and in those days there was a significant amount of GPO traffic being carried which would require transhipping; it also caused inconvenience to the passengers having to change trains unnecessarily. The control of DMUs was now a Divisional responsibility! The DMU fleet had an 'A' exam at Etches Park every 1,250-1,500 miles and a table of subsequent exams was produced in a document issued in February 1969 by the General Manager Crewe. It also contained a procedure for recording mileages by extracting them from the template DMU diagrams and not by taking the mileometer readings. I emphatically resisted this, and had from the start placed a degree of faith in the mileometer readings obtained despite the fact that on occasions the readings of the two power cars often varied considerably.

The arrangement was particularly useful when the units were working off the division at the weekends, particularly in East Anglia and on the Birmingham division when no one bothered to advise us that the Etches Park sets were being utilised. An amendment to the GM's document was issued by the Divisional Manager to the various Area Managers for their respective depots to furnish the Control Office with daily mileometer readings. We made our own arrangements with the Control Office at Lincoln for receipt of these details from the sets stabled there overnight. With the control of Diesel Multiple Units now firmly established on the Assistant Passenger Controllers' desk, I submitted an application for re-grading on behalf of my colleague (there was at the time a vacancy on the other shift), although my allocated position was still that of General Assistant. As expected, management turned down the application; the next step was to put it forward to the Transport Salaried Staff Association union, and it was placed on the agenda for the next meeting of the Staff Side of Sectional Council No.1, where it was deferred. The elected staff representative worked on the passenger desk, and the controllers then were claiming overall responsibility for the control of DMUs as they thought that a regrading was now a possibility for them, having wanting nothing to do with it initially. A representative from the TSSA union came to interview me regarding the case and it was subsequently listed for discussion with Management at the spring 1970 series of Sectional Council No.1

CONTROL OF DIESEL MULTIPLE UNITS.

Commencing Monday 00.01, 24th June, 1968, the control of Diesel Multiple Units will be devolved upon the Division.

All work previously performed in the G.M's. P.R.S. Section will be passed to the Divisional Passenger Controller in Nottingham Control.

Requirements will be three fold :-

1. To allocate D.M.U. sets to meet traffic requirements.

2. To allocate and adjust sets and circuits to accommodate A exams (i.e. 1,250 - 1,500 miles) and other exams to requirements of Maintenance Department.

3. To allocate and adjust sets and circuits to meet D.M.U. failures and defects.

Nottingham Control will be responsible for D.M.U. sets allocated to Derby Etches Park starting at the following points :-

> Derby, Nottingham, Leicester,
> Birmingham Division,
> Stoke Division,
> Lincoln, Cambridge,
> Rugby Central.

1. At 03.00 information should reach my Passenger Control by telephone, strad, wire giving details of sets at finish of work.

2. Based on this information a forecast will be made of the allocation of sets for start of work in conjunction with Maintenance Foreman at Derby Etches Park. This will be adjusted up to approximately 07.00 in accordance with availability of sets off maintenance depots.

   N.B. Special attention should be given to planned and accumulated mileage. Template D.M.U. programmes will be provided giving mileage details.

3. Form 2 and Form 1 should be completed when final allocation is made.

4. 10.00 hours - Complete and submit information to G.M., Crewe, as per Form 3.

5. Continual liaison should be maintained between Passenger Controller and Maintenance Foreman at Derby Etches Park with reference to vehicles under maintenance and repair.

6. A special note of defective vehicles and deviations should be maintained on Form 2.

7. Information concerning D.M.U. defects should be immediately passed to the Passenger Controller at Nottingham to enable speedy transpositions to take place.

Instructions concerning the control of DMUs and non-carrying passenger rolling stock being devolved upon the division, work previously undertaken by the Passenger Rolling Stock Section at Derby Line Manager's Office.

Continued/...........

Although the Castle Donington line didn't have a regular passenger service, it proved to be a useful diversionary route. With ongoing civil engineering works on the main line at Draycott, involving the removal of two overbridges, all traffic was diverted over the Castle Donington branch on Sunday, 25 September 1959. A 'Cravens' diesel multiple unit has just passed Lock Lane crossing with a Nottingham to Derby service. Joe Wade

meetings. The discussions that took place at the meeting of Sectional Council 'A', however, did not rule in my favour. Management continued to adhere to the line that the Passenger Controllers assumed full responsibility for the work of the appellants. A Joint Enquiry was then held in order to establish the facts in dispute. The protracted application, first submitted on 16 July 1968, was finally resolved on 10 October 1970 when, at the LMR Sectional Council 'A' Sub-Committee 'A' meeting, it was conceded that the position of Assistant Controller (Passenger) be re-classified as Controller Grade 'A'. It just goes to show that persistence does pay off, never having any doubts, although at one time it didn't look all that promising. During that period I had been working on the Leicester section for a spell and getting the higher rate of pay; nevertheless the arrears were appreciated.

As a diversion to working in the Control Office, Peter Griffin and I used to turn out at the weekend as casuals on the permanent way. It all came about when a fellow out of the engineers department, also located in Furlong House, came into the Control Office for whatever reason and during a conversation the idea was adopted, the rate of pay being that of the permanent way staff. We spent one or two Sundays on the Old Dalby test track south of Edwalton, de-stressing long welded rails. Lifting and packing could be particularly wearing, especially after a heavy Saturday night at the local. Nonetheless it was an interesting experience, and usually there was a pub not very far away where two or three pints at lunchtime went down extremely well.

≡ **British Rail**

to Mr. R. H. Fowkes, Assistant Controller, NOTTINGHAM D.M.O.	**from** Divisional Manager, Furlong House, NOTTINGHAM. **ext.** 057-2279

y/r		o/r SC1/8/317
date		date 28.10.70.

L.M.R. Sectional Council "A".   Sub-Committee "A" Meeting.   14.10.70.

I am pleased to inform you that at the above sub-committee meeting your position of Assistant Controller (Passenger) was re-classified as Controller Grade "A" with effect from 16.7.68, and arrangements are being made to enter you arrears of salary as under, as soon as possible.

It wasn't unusual to go out on the length on a Sunday morning to various locations in the Nottingham division, as far away as Sharnbrook near Bedford on one occasion, and after a full day working on the permanent way I took up my normal duties in the Control Office that same night. Arranging the manpower for the weekend engineering work was Eric Smith, he was timekeeper at Trent some years earlier during my time there as telegraph clerk. We often reminisced about those repetitive haircuts, when he would slope off down the town to the nearest hostelry. That acquaintance augured well in that Eric would allocate us to the less strenuous jobs at the weekends, some work being hard but interesting. I would continue with the double shift working when appropriate until leaving the Control.

Each weekday morning the head of the Passenger Services section would come into the Control Office and scrutinise the log on the Passenger desk, enquire of the early morning services and the running in general. Not long after, in would troop the nine-to-five wallahs one after another, have a read of the passenger controllers log with a 'how's things this morning?' before retreating when challenged over outstanding issues, which in our opinion had not been previously addressed. A right bunch of clockwork toys they were! On one occasion, when the Passenger Services section should have been more proactive in an attempt to alleviate overcrowding, they failed miserably. I was on the night turn in August 1969 when a relief train, the 1V35 22.55 Sheffield-Plymouth, ran and wasn't booked to call at Derby or Birmingham. When it passed through Derby station there were only two passengers on the train from Chesterfield to Bristol. A few minutes earlier, the 1V41 20.45 Bradford-Paignton had left the station full and standing. The information was passed to the Deputy Chief Controller who advised RHQ Crewe for them to decide whether or not to route 1V35 via Birmingham New Street station as it was booked to run via Camp Hill, so avoiding New Street. I wrote to Stan Hall, the Operating Officer, acquainting him of the situation, and suggested an alternative for the succeeding Friday to the Passenger Services section, who, as expected, did absolutely nothing about it. The next Friday, two trains of empty coaching stock were shown to run from Leeds to Paignton and Plymouth after working relief trains out of the West Country that morning. The rolling stock was required back for the Saturday workings from the Western Region, but I contended arrangements should be made to use one of the sets to run as a relief to 1V41 which had previously been grossly overcrowded – after all it was the peak holiday season for goodness sake. Nothing was forthcoming. I was furious at this inaction and wrote to John McEvoy, Divisional Operating Superintendent, frustrated by the lack of a positive response. Although no special arrangements were put in place for that Friday, the following week was covered in the form of a wire issued by the Passenger Services section, and a letter signed by Stan Hall, no doubt prompted by Mac.

Another service that was often over-subscribed on Friday nights during the summer months was the 1M10 21.30 Bradford (Forster Square) to London (St Pancras), although loading to nine vehicles (eight from Leicester), only four of which were passenger coaches with seating for 24 first and 138 second class passengers. Scant regard had been paid to the fact that this service was regularly full and standing from Leicester; it seemed to be accepted for what it was. One Friday night I asked David Winckle, Chief Inspector at Derby station, to advise me on how 1M10 was loading, having already primed the Leicester relief controller for a spare train crew if required, which on that occasion was available. A relief train was then arranged when advice was received that 1M10 was full. The express was booked at Leicester for twenty minutes and a DMU was laid on after connecting out of 1M10. The railcar then returned empty from St Pancras to Wellingborough to form the 07.05 to Nottingham. As a consequence of this the 05.30 empty DMU from Leicester to Wellingborough (diagrammed for 07.05 to Nottingham) would not run. Out of interest I contacted the Station Inspector at St Pancras to ascertain the loading of the additional DMU; he estimated 100/150 passengers off the 3-car unit whilst 1M10 was full on arrival. The relief DMU would run on subsequent Saturday mornings if required, subject to train crew availability. This level of involvement was most satisfying and demonstrated just what could be achieved. It was unfortunate that the weekend rostering in the Control Office did not take cognisance of having a Passenger Controller on duty, or one with a semblance of that position, as overrunning Engineering Work would often be an issue with missed connections.

Drink was a powerful driving force for a few when on the late turn. Depending on who was in the Deputy Chief Controller's chair, several of us would disappear for half an hour or so on the five-minute hike to the local for a couple, the desk being taken care of by a colleague who would have provided relief at food time. This situation would not be tolerated today, and quite rightly so. The Crocus Inn, situated in a particularly rough area of the city, was a typical spit and sawdust establishment; the clientele were friendly enough, including Mick the landlord who had a gammy leg. On

To: R. Fowkes,
NOTTINGHAM CONTROL.

From: Passenger Services Section.

Ref: Q.

Extn: 2237.

Date: 11.8.69.

RELIEF TRAINS. WORKING OF EMPTY STOCK.

I thank you for your letters of 1st and 6th August, regarding the provision of relief trains on the North East/South West route.

I agree that it seems ironical that empty stocks are running back from Leeds to the West, but as you obviously appreciate, the stock is required back for use on Saturday. The relief trains shown are sponsored by the Western Region, and so far as programming is concerned, the Movements Organisation has booked the stock straight back.

The provision of relief trains is initially the responsibility of the Passenger Commercial who base their requests on known information. They are aware, as we all are, that some overcrowding is unavoidable during the peak holiday weeks. It is very difficult to forecast the passenger flow to a greater degree of accuracy because there are so many factors which can influence it. It has been noted in the press that this year the exceptionally good weather has attracted more people away, and that many resorts have been unable to accommodate the people, similarly our services have been fully extended.

The N.E./S.W. route is a difficult one to assess, so far as this Division is concerned. Whilst we have had reports from the Control of overcrowding on some trains, there have been no reports from Area Managers and no request for relief or strengthing. The information is being noted in the proposals for next year, and I have drawn the General Manager's attention to the anomalies of these empty stock workings, and suggested that they could have been run back as reliefs. You will appreciate, of course, with inter-regional working this raises numerous problems, and in any case, the sponsorship of relief and seasonal trains is a complicated procedure.

With regard to the overcrowding of 1M10, arrangements were made last week for the 02.13 Leicester - London to run. Also with regard to the Sheffield - Plymouth relief train not booked to call at Derby or Birmingham, I suggest that this could have been stopped by Control Arrangements, and I would certainly support any such action on your part.

Thank you for your interest.

47

In the marshalling of Passenger Trains c1966/67, the 9.30pm Bradford to St Pancras had an additional SK vehicle on Friday, with seating for forty-eight passengers. This was discontinued in the 1969 timetable booklet.

After a protracted and unnecessary delay, no doubt prompted by a letter addressed to J. A. McEvoy, District Operating Superintendent, expressing my annoyance at the lethargy in dealing with overcrowding, the Passenger Services Section finally woke up and issued the telegram.

one hot evening, an elderly lady – Maisie – decked out in slippers, pinafore and headscarf shuffled in from across the courtyard carrying her usual large jug and exclaimed, 'Ain't it F*****' 'ot!' Mick then filled the jug and off she went. Unusually, on this particular evening, and possibly the only time that he ever visited the Crocus, was controller Harry Bagguley, a likeable fellow with a voice like a foghorn, who I first came across during my days as box lad at Sheet Stores Junction when reporting train times to him at Derby District Control. Here, he was about to meet his match. For, twenty minutes later, in sauntered Maisie again. Bagguley remarked laughingly, 'You've soon downed that;' Maisie glowered at him, and then promptly threatened to wrap the jug around his head, and just for once 'Bag' was left speechless. His remark was inoffensive enough but it obviously touched a raw nerve; perhaps her old man had a thirst on that evening.

The control of DMUs continued to provide an interesting diversion; the 'Cravens'-built units had been transferred to Newton Heath, whilst Etches Park had acquired ex-Western Region Class 120 units to work alongside the 'Birmingham Railway Carriage & Wagon'-built railcars. After the twenty-two ex-WR DMUs had received maintenance at Etches Park for a month or two, their availability improved, which was more than could be said of the Manchester-based twin sets working the Nottingham service. Barely a day went by when one of the units wasn't in trouble and was frequently replaced by an Etches Park set. The delinquent unit was often hauled back to its home

Tony Smith took this photograph from the signal gantry on the North Curve. A 'Cravens' unit working the 6.27pm Leicester to Nottingham service is leaving Trent station on 18 June 1959.

Froggatt Edge isn't so very far away in this picture of a BR/Sulzer 'type 4' at Grindleford on the Hope Valley Line, with a stopping train for Sheffield

depot, either in service or dead, usually via Crewe. There were many occasions when DMUs were not released off Etches Park when estimated. Indeed, during a conversation with one of the maintenance supervisors regarding the slippage he revealed that staff were being deployed on BR/Sulzer Type 4 diesel locomotives whose availability was around 80% in 1970 and that the Peaks were their 'bread and butter'. That admission was passed on to the Divisional Maintenance Engineer at Furlong House (A.S. Parker), on his usual morning visit into the Control Office, after which there was then an immediate improvement in the DMU position. Despite the initial problems with the ex-Western Region sets and the difficulties encountered with the Newton Heath units, seldom was a service cancelled. On occasions during poor availability, diesel-hauled coaching stock was resorted to. After Nottingham Victoria station closed, all that remained on the truncated ex-GC line was a DMU service from Rugby Central to Nottingham Arkwright Street. Punctuality was abysmal, with services at the Rugby end subjected to cancellation owing to flat batteries and various other problems with the units.

The advent of Derby Power signal box, commissioned in July 1969, together with the introduction of Trent Power Box in December of the same year, had a marked effect in the Control Office. The new box at Derby alone had replaced thirty-seven conventionally operated mechanical signal boxes in that area, and this brought about the demise of the Section Controller. Some would find their way into either of the power signal boxes, those who had previously travelled to Furlong House from the Derby area having found their way back home.

Beeston, some 3 miles west of Nottingham, had a freightliner depot built on the site of the redundant sidings. Applying for the position of supervisor at the terminal, the interview, where I did particularly well, was held at Leeds. Being in the frame I felt somewhat uneasy about the post, thinking how long Beeston might be operational, and then declined the opportunity. It did close some years later along with other terminals.

Freightliner had their own fleet of diesel locomotives varying from Class 47, 57, and here a Class '66', No. 66524, runs through Derby station with a westbound train. Beeston, near Nottingham, had a freightliner depot that opened in 1969 and closed in 1987.

We had a further addition to the family in August 1969, a daughter, Janet; it had been a difficult birth and for a while we were both apprehensive as to the outcome. She was transferred almost immediately from the Queen Mary Hospital in an incubator to the Nightingale Maternity home in Derby and remained there for several days. Fortunately everything turned out for the best and there were no further problems, much to our relief.

The spring of 1971 heralded a further Control Office reorganisation; future promotion within the office was extremely slow. Now that the power signal boxes were up and running the fundamental operation of the Control Office had, to some extent, been eroded.

The power signal boxes had created a void, from the small intimate surrounds of the Leicester office, homely and self-contained with its own individuality, to the vast openness of the Nottingham office, which had earlier realised twenty-five controllers on each shift.

There were, however, still the traffic, power and relief controllers, together with the passenger side. They came in all sorts of shapes and sizes, and differing temperaments, which on occasions resulted in a clash of personalities. As intimated earlier, there was often tension between the traffic and power controllers, the former wanting to clear his traffic and the latter being unable for whatever reason to provide the necessary traction. Vociferous exchanges were all part and parcel of the daily routine in the operation of the railway, being put aside during times of disruption whatever the cause, and it was there that the Control Office came into its own, with the contingency plans and amended and altered workings for train crews and traction and rolling stock. Obviously, in any walk of life, there are those who were prepared to sit back and let the job come to them; the Control Office was no exception. Out of all this though, job satisfaction could be guaranteed. Just down the corridor from the Control Office was an open-plan office. This housed the passenger and freight sections, together with the commercial side and other oddments. Often referred to as the supermarket, word had it that an individual could go to the pictures in the afternoon and not be missed. But that was not what I enjoyed most about it. Those five years in the Control Office at both Leicester and Nottingham were without doubt some of the best days of my thirty-nine years on the railway.

In the autumn of 1971, the post of Yard Supervisor at Toton appeared on the vacancy list. I applied for the position and was interviewed by Allan Casey, Assistant Area Manager, and appointed to the position in November. I was now 'Getting out of Control' and needing to brush up on my rules and regulations, even though a few years earlier I had taken a correspondence course on the subjects.

British Railways London Midland Region

Furlong House

Middle Furlong Road

Nottingham NG2 1AL.

Nottingham 48531 Extn. 2279.   R. D. Gardiner   Divisional Manager

Mr. R.H. Fowkes,
Passenger Controller,
Nottingham D.M.O.

'r
/r SS2/SALVAC/33/M1286.   19th November, 1971.

Dear Mr. Fowkes,

      Advertising of Salaried Vacancies, List
No. 33, Vacancy M1286, Relief Supervisor
(G.P.) Grade B, Toton A.M.

    I am pleased to inform you that you have been
selected to fill the above vacancy with an allocation
date of 29.9.71, and hope that you will be happy and
successful in this position.

    Will you please arrange to transfer to commence
training for your new duties on Monday 22.11.71,
reporting to the Area Manager at 14.00 hours.

             Yours sincerely,

Appointed Relief Supervisor, Toton.

Toton Marshalling Yard

Toton Sidings originally developed in the 1850s, getting its name from the small village of Toton to the east of the yard. During the years up to the turn of the nineteenth century there was unprecedented growth, principally in coal output, leading to the expansion of Toton Sidings as a major marshalling yard. Being a 'flat type' yard, the wagons were shunted into place, not only by locomotives, but also using horses.

Frederick S. Williams, a minister in the Congregational Church, and renowned nineteenth century railway historian, best known for his books on the early history of the railway, wrote in his 1883 version of *Our Iron Roads*:

The amount of business done at Toton day and night is enormous, but it varies with the season. In a summer month 18,000 wagons will be received and despatched; in winter as many as 26,000. The staff required also depends on the season and the work. In summer perhaps thirty or forty shunting horses would suffice, but in a severe winter the grease in the axle box will freeze hard, the wheels instead of turning round will skid along the rails, and two or three horses will be required to move a wagon. It is very interesting to see their sagacity and to watch them picking their way among the moving wagons, especially at night. After being suddenly unhooked from a wagon they will be perfectly still where there is just room for them to stand between two lines of rails, while a squealing engine and a shunt of wagons passes on each side of them. It used to be said that there were a great many accidents. Sir Beckett Denison, in one of his kind speeches, called Toton sidings the Midland Company's 'slaughter house' – didn't he?

Toton, with its large railway depot and marshalling yard, was situated on the southern fringe of the Nottinghamshire and Derbyshire coalfield on the Trent-Chesterfield (Erewash Valley) line about 2 miles north of Trent. It was an important section of the former Midland Railway and formed part of one of the main trunk routes between London and the north. In addition, Toton became the largest freight engine shed on the London Midland & Scottish Railway. The sidings comprised of two traffic yards, the Up on the east side and the Down on the west side of the main running lines extending over a distance of nearly 2 miles between the closed Stapleford & Sandiacre and Long Eaton passenger and goods stations. At both yards, incoming trains were broken up and the wagons sorted for different destinations and directions. They were then made up into trains for forward despatch. The Up yard was used as an assembling point for wagons conveying coal from Nottinghamshire, Derbyshire and South Yorkshire collieries – those going south, west and east – and as a sorting and despatching point, mainly to London and the south, Birmingham and the West, Peterborough and the eastern counties. The Down yard was used principally for sorting empty mineral wagons going north in the reverse direction, en route to the collieries. Passenger trains over this route were in the minority, one exception being the 'Thames-Clyde Express'.

Local operations were initially supervised by a Yardmaster, responsible to a District Operating Superintendent at Nottingham. There was also a District Motive Power Superintendent whose headquarters was at Toton, and the area embraced a District Wagon Repair and Maintenance depot and a Civil Engineering store.

The Down side was converted into a hump yard at the time that the high-level goods line from the south at Trent Junction was opened into the Down yard in 1901. This allowed the intensive goods workings to avoid Trent station and also the two busy level crossings on the Erewash Valley line at Long Eaton; the high-level lines carried the heaviest freight traffic in the country and

DOWN SORTING SIDINGS AND CONTROL TOWER

UP SORTING SIDINGS AND CONTROL TOWER AS SEEN FROM HUMP

WAGON IN RAILBRAKES

UP YARD HUMP AND HUMP ROOM

UP YARD ARRIVAL LINES

OPERATING PANEL IN UP HUMP ROOM

ILLUMINATION AT OUTGOING
END OF UP YARD

Interior of Upside control tower

Up sidings and control tower from hump

Right
Down sidings as
seen from
control tower

Centre
Wagons being
shunted to
Down sidings

Bottom
Diesel shunting
engine on
Down hump

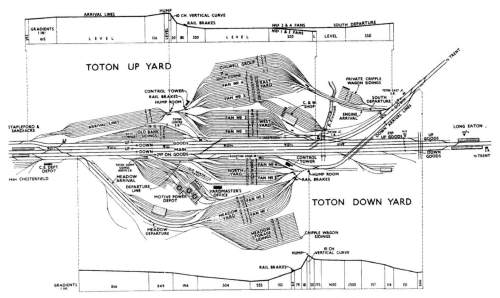

Single line diagram showing layout of Up and Down yards at Toton and gradient
profile through arrival lines, sorting sidings and departure lines.

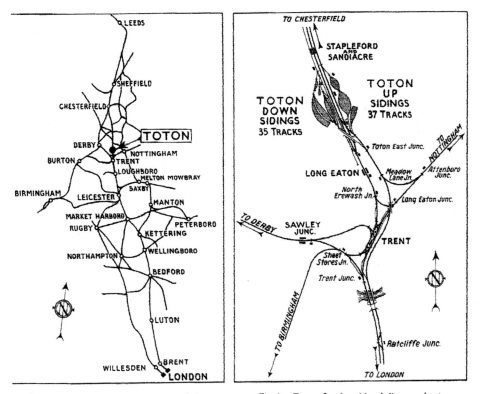

Fig. 1. *Toton—Positional diagram in relation to main lines*

Fig. 2. *Toton—Local positional diagram showing junctions in vicinity*

Used with the permission of the editor of *Railway Gazette International*.

Entrance to High Level arrival lines (on left) from Toton East Junction, showing train entering West arrival line

The lines on the right of this picture are the continuation down the Erewash Valley of the high level goods lines that avoided running through Trent station and over the two level crossings in Long Eaton. On the left is the entrance to the Down side taken from Toton East Junction signal box, showing a train entering the West arrival line. The building on the extreme left is the Toton Lodging House for train crews. Used with the permission of the editor of *Railway Gazette International*.

remain in use today. There were also many through trains conveying mostly mineral traffic and empty wagons which avoided either yard, and passed over the running lines, of which there were five: two in the Up or southbound direction and three in the Down or northbound direction.

Toton Down yard, the ingoing end of which was modernised in 1939, incorporated the 'hump' principle, whereby incoming trains, after being uncoupled into the necessary 'cuts', were propelled by one of the two 350hp 0-6-0 diesel-electric locomotives towards a hump, from which the wagons ran down a decline into one or other of thirty-five sorting sidings, each classified for a different destination.

Lunar-white position-light signals, repeated alongside the arrival lines, displayed for the guidance of the hump engine driver one of three aspects: vertical— 'hump at normal speed' (which is about 1.75mph); oblique — 'hump slow' (about 1 to 1.25 mph); and horizontal — 'stop'. The signals were operated by switches on a panel in a structure at the apex of the hump, known as the 'hump room'. Before the wagons reached the hump, a shunter, having read the ultimate destination on the labels on loaded wagons, chalked on the

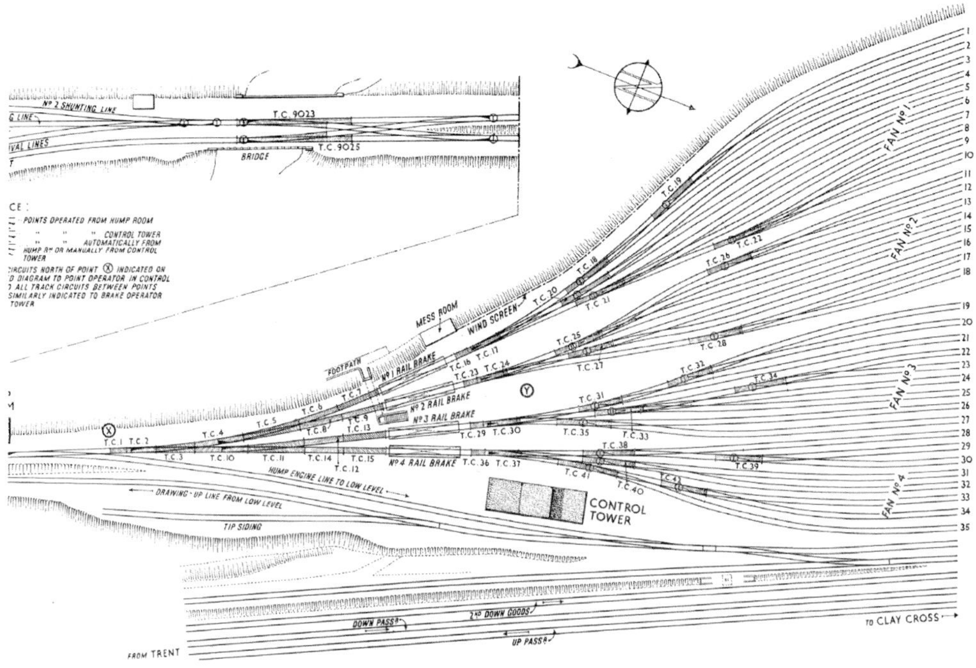

THE RAILWAY GAZETTE

August 18, 1939

Fig. 5. *Plan of layout in hump and point areas, Toton Down Marshalling Yard*

Layout of Toton Down Marshalling Yard, No.1 FAN 1-10 sidings and FAN No. 2 11-18 in the Meadow, and No. 3 FAN 20-27 and FAN 4 28-35 in North Yard. No. 19 line was to the depot. Used with the permission of the editor of *Railway Gazette International*.

The last of the wagons of the train are being propelled towards the Hump by one of the 350hp diesel-electric humping locomotives. Used with the permission of the editor of *Railway Gazette International*.

View from interior of hump room showing operator working at panel

The chalked number on the wagon (35), denoting the nominated siding for the wagon, is clearly identifiable to the panel operator in the Hump Room. Although the siding button number would have been
depressed, sidings beyond the 'Jack' points would be operated by the panel operator turning switches in
the control tower. Used with the permission of the editor of *Railway Gazette International*.

leading end the number of the siding to which that destination was allocated.
As it approached the apex, an operator in the hump room set the route for
the particular siding by depressing the appropriate button (there being one
for each sorting siding) on a panel in front of him. He also depressed a button
on a smaller bank to indicate the number of vehicles in the cut. That caused
the first three successive sets of points, known as 'King,' 'Queen' and 'Jack'
respectively, to turn for the particular route, as soon as the cut immediately in
advance had moved clear of each set. In other words, it put part of each route
into electrical storage.

All the points were electro-pneumatically operated, but those beyond the
'Jack' points were moved as required by turning switches on a panel in an
elevated structure at the side of the point area, known as the Control Tower.
The depression of the buttons in the hump room simultaneously indicated
on teletypewriter tapes in the Control Tower the number of the siding and
wagons in each cut. That enabled the operator responsible for turning the
points beyond the 'Jacks' to have before him a list of cuts on the move from
the hump. The teletypewriter tape was duplicated on a panel in the Control
Tower, from which hydraulically operated railbrakes (one set in the lead to
each of the four fans of sidings) could be applied to retard wagons travelling
too fast, and ensure they did not overtake others prematurely.

LMS   COPY   RECORD OF HUMP SHUNTING, TOTON DOWN SIDE   E.R.O. 52915

Weather — Fine and warm   Turn of duty { 6 a.m. – 2 p.m. / 2 p.m. – 10 p.m. / 10 p.m. – 6 a.m. }   Mon day   Date 3rd July 1939

Train	Time arrived	Time train engine liberated	Arrival line E. or W.	Time signal given to start humping	Time first wagon over hump	Time last vehicle over hump	No. of Wagons	No. of cuts	No. of non-retarders	Hump Engine No. or Target No.	Time left hump	To
7.42 a.m. ex Wellingboro (Contd.)	(Contd.)		West	2/9	2/15	2/9	35	22		7082	2/9	Low Level
Ex Low Level	2/0	2/33	East	2/33	2/35	2/23	55	33		7084	2/23	Yard - 20 Rd.
7.42 ex Kettering	2/30		W	2/49	2/51	2/48	78	25		7082	2/49	L.L.
Ex L. Level	2/42	2/49	E	3/0	3/6	3/0	53	28		7084	3/0	"
8.40 ex Wellingboro	2/48		W	3/19	3/23	3/19	78	40		7082	3/19	"
Ex L. Level	3/7		E	3/32	3/36	3/32	56	32		7084	3/32	"
Ex Up Side	3/34	3/45	W	3/34	3/48	3/45	29	18		3753	3/45	19 Rd.
Ex L. Level	3/38		E	3/45	4/6	3/58	57	40		7082	3/58	L.L.
2/55 ex Beeston	3/59	4/0	W	4/3	4/19	4/17	69	43		7084	4/17	"
Ex L. Level	4/16	4/17	W	4/19	4/29	4/29	59	30		7082	4/29	"
8.40 ex Wellesden	4/46	4/48	W	4/33	4/36	4/46	63	43	1	7084	4/46	Yard - 20 Rd.
2.20 ex Brent	5/10	5/40	W	4/48	4/51	5/8	90	58		7082	5/8	L.L.
12/1 ex Romiley	5/40	5/42	W	5/30	5/33	5/40	28	19		3079	5/40	"
12/10 ex Holwell	5/42		W	5/42	5/45	5/59	75	48		7082	6/20	18 Rd.
Ex L. Level			E	5/42	5/45	5/59	62	42		7084	5/59	Yard - No 1 Rd.
Ex 18 Rd. Coryo	6/27		E	6/44	6/30	6/44	67	36		7082	6/44	L.L.
1/4 ex Northampton	6/20	6/22	W	7/2	6/47	7/1	80	33		7084	7/1	Yard - 66 & 9 Rd.
12/35 ex Peterboro	7/1	7/2	W	7/2	7/5	7/21	69	49		7082	7/21	L.L.
Ex Up Side	7/11	7/35	E	7/22	7/26	7/35	45	31		7084	7/35	Yard - 2 Rd.
Ex No. 2. Various	7/43		E	7/43	7/45	7/55	60	45		7084	7/55	Toton East
2/4 ex Peterboro	7/21	7/22	W	7/55	7/58	8/7	48	25		7082	8/7	L.L.
12/35 ex Wellesden	8/6	8/7	E	8/7	8/10	8/17	45	25		7084	8/17	"
Ex L. Level	8/14		E	8/17	8/20	8/28	36	25		7082	8/28	Toton East
1/53 ex Wellingboro	8/32	8/30	W	8/32	8/35	8/44	48	23		7084	8/44	"
8/8 ex Beeston	8/57	8/58	W	8/44	8/46	8/57	59	28		7082	8/57	"
6/30 ex Knighton	9/10	9/11	W	8/58	9/0	9/10	56	32		7084	9/11	Yard - 26 Rd.
Ex L. Level	9/25		E	9/17	9/19	9/31	80	43		7082	9/31	" 20 & 23 Rd.
"	9/55		E	9/31	9/33	9/45	53	23		7084	9/45	L.L.
				9/55 (Contd.)			—	—				

HOURLY SUMMARY

Time From	To	Cuts	Wagons
2	3	108	221
3	4	130	220
4	5	145	236
5	6	90	135
6	7	117	222
7	8	125	174
8	9	126	236
9	10	98	189
TOTAL HUMPED		939	1633

GRAND TOTAL WAGONS   1633

REMARKS.—
Complete trains:—

2/23 - 2/31 Ballast movements
5/10 - 5/30 Meals
6/20 - 6/27 Drawing Coryo (DH)
7/35 - 7/43 Drawing No. 2 Rd.
9/45 - 9/55 Waiting

Shunting Engines:-
7082 - No.15
7084 - No.16

(Signed) G. W. King

Fig. 13.   Specimen of daily humping record

Interior of control tower showing operators at brake and point panels

View of yard from control tower showing artificial lighting

View from control tower at night looking towards hump

Used with the permission of the editor of *Railway Gazette International*.

The yard was open continuously on weekdays and some sixty or seventy trains arrived each twenty-four hours. The traffic consisted of goods, mineral and empty wagons, the latter requiring sorting according to type. The throughput varied round about 3,000 wagons daily in cuts averaging about 3 vehicles, but on occasion up to 4,000 a day were sorted in twenty-four hours. From 1939 up to the end of 1966 up to a million wagons had been handled each year.

Toton Up yard was remodelled completely and enlarged in 1949-50. Arrival lines capable of accommodating the longest trains were provided. The hump principle was maintained but, as at the Down yard, the former manual method of operating the points leading into the sorting sidings from a series of cabins was abandoned in favour of power operation, and remotely controlled railbrakes were installed to replace the previous practice of controlling the speed of wagons by handbrakes on the side of vehicles during shunting.

In general the process of operation was similar to that at the Down yard, with certain exceptions, as described below, which were improvements rendered possible partly as a result of the experience of mechanised yard practice and partly from the fact that nothing short of the 100 per cent alteration to the layout of the entire yard would have enabled the benefits desired to be achieved. There were ten arrival lines and a separate hump engine run-round line, all provided with position-light humping signals, repeated as necessary. To economise in their number, some were double-sided, and also had a unique system of applicability indication in the form of wing lights, since the signals were only installed between alternative arrival lines. The arrival lines and all other sidings in the yard were, as far as possible, laid dead straight. When the Up side was remodelled in 1949/50, the panel operator in the Hump Room was able to set the route throughout into the 37 sorting sidings. On the Down side it was only possible to set the route as far as the 'Jack' points; from there the Control Tower took over. The great bulk of traffic at the Up yard consisted of loaded mineral wagons and the gradients from the apex of the hump were not as steep as at the Down yard. The teletypewriter system transmitted cut information from the hump room to the Control Tower, where there was an illuminated panel diagram of the track-circuited point area leading into the sorting sidings. From the panel, which was normally set for automatic working, the points could be turned to correct an overtaking shunt during humping, or when it was necessary to send an engine into the sidings to correct a wrong shunt, or close wagons together.

Railbrakes remotely controlled from the Tower were provided similar to those at the Down yard but with a subway and deeper pits to facilitate maintenance. Electric lighting had replaced the former gas, and a comprehensive loudspeaker installation permitted instant communication between all key operating positions throughout the yard. All the operating and staff buildings were new and equipped on modern lines, including four main line signal boxes, which it was necessary to rebuild. Both shunting engines were 350 h.p. 0-6-0 Diesel Electric and each day some seventy trains arrived from the colliery areas and the north of England, and about a similar number departed for destinations in the south, west and east of England.

The yard dealt with up to a million wagons a year which were sorted into

November 23, 1951   THE RAILWAY GAZETTE   57

Modernised Marshalling Yard at Toton—2

Hump room building as seen from descent from hump, Toton Up yard

View from interior of hump room, showing operator at work during humping operation

Used with the permission of the editor of *Railway Gazette International*.

Modernised Marshalling Yard at Toton—3

Control tower operating room, showing point panel on left, and railbrake operator to right, with telephone concentrator on desk

Point operating panel in control tower

Railbrake operating panel in control tower

Shunting in full flow on the Up side showing the railbrake operator. Photo courtesy Geoff Griffiths

cuts averaging between two and three wagons. An average of 3,500 wagons were shunted each day although this was not maximum capacity. 4,156 had been sorted in 24 hours and 1,716 in one 8-hour turn of duty.

Radio telephones were provided linking the hump room and the Control Tower and the diesel shunting drivers. This communication was particularly useful in adverse weather, in particular dense fog, facilitating the working of the shunting engines on the arrival lines and yard area.

When I was appointed Yard Supervisor at Toton in 1971, Ray Pattison was the Area Manager, responsible to the Divisional Manager at Nottingham. A member of the Salvation Army, he was perhaps the finest boss that I worked for during my railway career. There were a number of occasions when I was summoned to the inner sanctum to explain my utterances; a feeling of apprehension prevailed when walking down the corridor to his office. He wasn't revered by some. He seldom paid a visit around the yards; neither for that matter did his assistant. They were, however, kept fully informed of proceedings by an overseer on each shift: the Area Freight Assistant (AFA), housed in the Toton Centre signal box from where there was a good overview of the yards. Allan Casey was Ray's assistant, a season ticket holder for Derby County Football Club, a very down to earth individual who didn't mince his

B.R. (L.M. Region). **RECORD OF HUMP SHUNTING, TOTON ~~DOWN~~ UP YARD.** E.R.O. 52915

Weather: Rain COPY. Turn of duty: ~~6 a.m. — 2 p.m.~~ 2 p.m. — 10 p.m. ~~10 p.m. — 6 a.m.~~ Tues-day Date: 26-6-1951

TRAIN						HUMP-SHUNTING								OTHER PERIODS		
Train	Engine No.	Time ~~RAT. Jcn~~ ~~ATTEN. Jcn~~ S. Gate	Time Arrived	Time train engine liberated	Arrival line	Time signal given to start humping	Time first wagon over hump	Time last vehicle over hump	No. of Cuts	No. of Wagons	Hump Engine No. or Target No.	Time left hump	To	Time From	Time To	Remarks
11.30 Mapperley	43979	1/25	1/40	1/42	5	2/13	2/15	2/21	15	47	12046	2/21	Yard	2/21	2/36	Pushing 36, 32.
ex Down side	7551	—	1/45	OFF S & S	4	2/23	2/26	2/35	22	50	12045	2/35	Sandiacre	2/50	3/15	2 wrong wgns. 37 Rd. 36, 34
6.0 Normanton	48618	1/36	1/53	1/55	7	2/41	2/43	2/50	39	70	12045	2/50	Yard	3/3	3/17	Pushing 20, 25
ex Mapperley	44136	1/45	2/4	2/7	8	2/51	2/54	3/3	43	57	12046	3/3	Yard	3/54	4/13	" 25
12/5 Sleights	48184	1/55	2/8	2/10	3	3/18	3/20	3/25	21	35	12045	3/25	Sandiacre	4/4	4/8	Clear 31 road
1/15 Coates Pk	43850	3/5	3/10	3/12	7	3/27	3/30	3/34	18	31	12046	3/34	Sandiacre	4/43	4/49	Pushing 36
1/30 Heanor	48636	3/15	3/25	3/26	8	3/36	3/38	3/43	28	60	12045	3/43	Sandiacre	4/58	5/38	Pushing 20, 26, 19
12/20 Kirkby	48000	3/10	3/28	3/35	5	3/44	3/46	3/54	33	48	12046	3/54	Yard	5/40	6/0	Food
1/25 Spl. Portland	44206	3/40	3/50	3/56	7	3/58	4/0	4/4	14	29	12045	4/4	Yard	6/30	6/52	Pushing 36, 35
6.15 Wath	48661	3/50	4/0	4/5	4	4/14	4/16	4/21	11	51	12045	4/21	Sandiacre	7/43	8/10	" 36, 21
10.53 Staveley	48185	3/55	4/7	4/9	8	4/24	4/26	4/30	11	30	12046	4/30	Sandiacre	7/56	8/10	Ex 21 assisting. Southend engine in rear.
2/55 Tibshelf	44407	4/15	4/20	4/23	5	4/34	4/36	4/43	31	62	12045	4/43	Yard			
10.50 Spl Masboro	44036	4/15	4/30	4/33	7	4/50	4/52	4/58	31	46	12046	4/58	Yard	8/38	8/55	Pushing 26, 23, 22
7.38 Carlton	48412	4/10	4/40	4/45	4	5/0	5/2	5/6	13	36	12045	5/6	Sandiacre	8/53	9/11	" 36
8.25 Wath	48152	4/35	4/47	4/48	8	5/10	5/12	5/17	18	55	12045	5/17	Sandiacre	9/26	9/50	" 36
12/40 Staveley	48010	4/55	5/7	5/9	5	6/0	6/3	6/9	28	60	12045	6/9	Sandiacre			
3/30 Mapperley	43810	5/8	5/18	5/20	7	6/10	6/14	6/21	17	43	12046	6/21	Sandiacre			
12/30 Woodhouse Mill	47978	5/30	5/35	5/45	8	6/22	6/24	6/30	23	72	12045	6/30	Yard			
Lock Lane Ballast	58169	—	6/35	6/40	4	6/36	6/37	6/40	1	23	58169	6/40	Sandiacre Ballast			
4/15 Heanor	48075	6/25	6/30	6/32	5	6/41	6/44	6/50	31	59	12046	6/50	Sandiacre			
6/50 Cossall	58176	6/35	6/45	6/54	7	6/58	7/0	7/8	17	43	12046	7/8	Sandiacre			
ex Down side	4136	—	6/55	OFF S & S	4	7/16	7/18	7/23	21	36	12045	7/23	Sandiacre			
3/0 Avenue	58146	6/50	7/6	7/10	5	7/26	7/28	7/33	17	27	12046	7/33	Sandiacre			
3/48 Kirkby	43305	6/55	7/12	7/15	8	7/36	7/38	7/43	28	46	12045	7/43	Yard			
Spl Westhouses	48357	7/15	7/22	7/25	7	7/44	7/46	7/56	32	63	12046	7/56	Yard			
5/20 Mapperley	43990	7/15	7/30	7/35	3	8/15	8/17	8/22	26	44	12046	8/22	Sandiacre			
Various ex 21	12045/6	—	8/10	—	6	8/26	8/28	8/38	47	83	12045	8/38	Yard			
2/10 Roundwood	48759	7/39	7/55	8/0	4	8/41	8/43	8/53	13	55	12046	8/53	Yard			
Sandiacre shtr	47551	—	8/10	8/12	7	9/0	9/3	9/10	25	37	12045	9/10	Sandiacre			
6/20 Tibshelf	48280	7/50	8/20	8/25	8	9/14	9/17	9/26	43	77	12045	9/26	Yard			
6/2 Sleights	48400	8/15	8/35	8/40	9	9/27	9/29	9/37	41	74	12046	9/37	Slip			
88 trip Stanton G	44371	8/25	8/45	8/56	5			See	10/0	p.m.	sheet					
5/5 Shirebrook	48176	8/30	8/50	8/57	3			"	"	"	"					
7/30 Langley M	58173	8/45	8/55	8/59	2			"	"	"	"					
7/37 Swanwick	3817	9/5	9/25	9/40	4			"	"	"	"					

HUMP ENGINES

Nos.

12045

12046

BRAKES

Trains 26

Spare —

Total 26

HOURLY SUMMARY

Time From	Time To	Cuts	Wagons
2	3	76	167
3	4	143	231
4	5	98	218
5	6	31	91
6	7	100	257
7	8	115	215
8	9	86	182
9	10	109	188
TOTAL		758	1549

(Signed) E. SIMS

Fig. 15—Reproduction to approximately half size of an actual hump shunting record

words and usually appeared on duty complete with bowler hat and a rose in his lapel. As General Purpose Relief Supervisor, I relieved at the following points: Centre Up Side (Up Hump), South End Down (Down Hump) and two departure yards – Meadow and East yard (the West yard was covered by a chargeman and the North yard and Old Bank by a senior railman).

Located alongside the AFA was a Quality Services Supervisor (QSS) whose duties included monitoring the departing services with details of late starts, and each train loading was critically examined with a reason obtained from the yard concerned of any train having left under-load. Punctuality was usually attributed to 'waiting power', there being no sense of urgency at the traincrew depot as I was to find out three years later. At two-hourly intervals, a count of traffic on hand in both yards was obtained from the clerk in the hump rooms; this information was also given over to the Control Office at Nottingham. An hourly record of the number of trains and wagons shunted was also maintained, and in the case of the Up side, the number of trains still to shunt. Relieving the QSS was an interesting experience to say the least, if only to listen to the Area Freight Assistants during their handover. Talk about trying to emulate one another – the four of them hadn't a good word to say about each other. What was discussed at morning prayers or 'children's hour' was nobody's business. As to whether management saw through the charade, or even encouraged it, remains a matter of conjecture; even the most trivial matter was given an airing at 'the Kremlin' each morning. Certainly some character assassination took place at that time. During my training I observed closely the rapport between supervisor and shunter, often reflecting later something I picked up at Webb House, Crewe – *'that the obstreperous individual should be studied rather than fought.'*

It may have been deliberate to have been nominated so soon for Stage 1 of a Supervisors Course at Crewe but it was appreciated. Although some students that were together on Stage 2 treated the introductory stage lightly, I considered it most beneficial. The transition from controller to supervisor was an interesting experience, and, as in the Control Office there were those who would require a different approach, including some who

Raymond Pattison, Area Manager at Toton, a member of the Salvation Army in full regalia – a fine boss!

67

would resist the positive instruction and turn plain bolshie. A fresh face is often treated with some scepticism and mine was no exception. One evening, approaching shift changeover time on the Down Hump, a train of coal from the Kent coalfield was being shunted into the Meadow yard. The designated road for Tees traffic was becoming full and there was little option of where to put the remainder of the wagons. I remember telling the panel operator to drop the coal behind the brakevan in a particular road; it would then be straightforward for the Meadow shunters to get at when the train of empties had departed. With one eye on the clock, the panel operator had other ideas: he deliberately dropped the wagons into another fan. After the brakevan of the train had been shunted he set the points for the engine slip, and was just about to tell the Control Tower 'that's it' when I intervened and told him to send the shunt engine down the yard to pick up the wagons and put them where he had been instructed previously. This obviously didn't go down well. Having said that, he would pay heed in the future. As I had worked at both the Meadow and East yard departures, I looked for consistency.

Although the Down side (SED) dealt predominantly with empty wagons for the collieries, there were coal flows off the Leen Valley for destinations via the yard at Tinsley, and from the Kent coalfield destined for the north-east. The normal procedure when a train arrived via Toton East (from the Nottingham or south direction) onto the High Level (East & West) arrival lines was for the loco to be released to the depot as soon as the guard had joined the engine. Quite often, the driver on a train from the south would be asked to draw his train of coal over the hump into the North yard. Some would, whilst others refused point-blank. Trains arriving 'on the bottom' from Chaddesden, the south and west, would run onto one of the two reception roads. From there a diesel shunt engine, or possibly two if the train was particularly heavy, would draw the train back over the avoiding line past the hump onto the East arrival road in readiness for shunting. Should there have been a train also on the West arrival, and the train off the 'bottom' was a double draw, most of the drivers on the leading diesel would cut off to Toton East to go around the train on the West arrival.

The comparison was often drawn between the regular shift supervisor and the RDR/GPR units. The panel-operators in the hump rooms normally had a free reign in how they set the yards out. Often, when designated roads were full, traffic was run into adjacent roads in the same fan. What the relief supervisors did not accept was that the wagons that went wrong were automatically fetched out at the departure end. There was no fun in pulling a road of fifty-odd wagons in order to get the wrong wagon out, when it ought to have been done from the hump end. The principle of hump shunting was similar in both yards.

Once the train engine had been released the chalker and uncoupler would proceed along the train. Wagon destination labels would be read, the wagons chalked with a number corresponding to the relevant siding number;

Built at Doncaster Works in October 1985 is No. 58034 *Bassetlaw*. Allocated to Toton along with the rest of the class, it is seen here behind the control tower with a raft of empty MGR wagons about to run onto one of the two reception roads. The lines in the foreground are from the engine slip and the draw back from the reception roads.

Approach to hump showing train being humped off East arrival line

Colour-light running signal with bracket arm, and position-light humping signal

The chalker and uncoupler are dealing with a train being humped off the East arrival line approaching the hump. On the right is a colour-light running signal with bracket arm, and position light humping signal. Used with the permission of the editor of *Railway Gazette International*.

although most empty wagons did not carry labels, each type had its own nominated road. Whereas on the automated Up side, shunting into all four fans was permitted, the constraints on the Down side of only being able to use two out of the four fans at any one time was often time consuming and restrictive; an additional panel operator would be required in the Control Tower to shunt into all four fans. The signalling system for hump shunting was uniform on both sides except that on the Up arrival lines a left or right wing, when illuminated, indicated which line the signal applied to.

Of the two yards, the New Bank (CUS) was always regarded as the more important, certainly by the supervisors working there. Gone, however, were the days when trains had to be put off at Stanton Gate as a matter of course, when Toton was chronically on the block. With ten reception roads and the Old Bank to fall back on, decisions were pretty straightforward. The Up yard primarily dealt with coal traffic from the pitheads in Nottinghamshire, Derbyshire and South Yorkshire, destined for town gas plants, industry and for domestic hearths, London and the south east having an insatiable appetite for coal. The steelworks at Corby and locally the CEGB installations at Castle Donington, Repton & Willington and Drakelow were serviced daily. Trains arriving on the New Bank were shunted through four fans into the West yard 1 to 8 and 9 to 18 roads, and the East yard 20 to 28 and 29 to 35 roads; number 19 road was for wagons for the C&W shops, and 36 & 37 for Chilwell Group. The CUS Supervisor, in conjunction with the Traffic Controller at Furlong House, arranged the traffic for originating services. Around that time the timetable was divided into two sections, mandatory and conditional, the latter giving the flexibility of diverting a booked train to another destination to cater for traffic fluctuations, whereas with a mandatory service, if no traffic was available, the resources should be sent for the return working, which in effect did not always apply, shortage of power often providing an excuse for not doing so. During

A view from Long Tom Bridge shows a Class 58 diesel locomotive with a train of empty MGR wagons from Didcot Power Station and a DMU bound for Nottingham. Immediately behind the railcar are the C&W shops.

A montage of workings on the Up side at Toton. Photo courtesy Geoff Griffiths

This elevated picture above the up side control tower, looking across the Old Bank and over the main and goods lines towards the Traction & Maintenance Depot, was formed of the spoil when the Up side was modernised in 1950.

the summer months when the collieries were on holiday, only one shunt engine was manned on the New Bank (CUS) on a 09.00-17.00 turn and the night turn. During those few weeks it was essential to double up on the arrival lines. This was achieved when a comparatively short train was hauled onto the New Bank – or a cross-road trip out of the Meadow was pushed down as far as possible – with a trip off the Leen Valley being backed up behind it.

Congestion was caused by a variety of reasons, the most common being shortage of power and lack of traincrew. Traffic then built up in the departure yards and on the Up side in particular. It wasn't unusual to show a train on one of the ten reception roads a 'keep off'; this train would then be shunted as and when yard space permitted. Block trains, comprising of traffic for the same destination, would normally be accommodated on the Old Bank. On the Down side, where, with only two reception roads on the low level, and an east and west high level arrival line, a degree of head scratching was called for on occasions to prevent incoming trains from standing out awaiting Yard acceptance.

Empty merry-go-round trains from Didcot CEGB were backed off in the North yard, from where they would be examined before being worked forward to the designated collieries.

Almost all of the departures from the North yard comprised of empty wagons of varying types, worked mostly by Eastern Region engines and crews. The Meadow and Stowage sidings had a mixture of loaded and empty traffic going north. Edge Hill and Garston traffic went via Rotherwood with a maximum trailing load of 750 tons. This traffic also passed via Crewe where a higher loading would be achieved.

At Toton we operated according to the Working Manual for Rail Staff, which set out the criteria for the 'Preparation and working of freight trains – Assessing the train.' Before any freight train starts its journey, the following information has to be known about it:

(a) Its total tonnage (including locomotive and brakevan) – to ensure that it is not too heavy for the locomotive or the route to be taken.

(b) Its total brake force (including the locomotive but not the brakevan) – to ensure that it can be stopped within safe limits.

(c) The route availability of the locomotive and of individual wagons – to ensure that the train does not contain any vehicles with too heavy an axle loading for the route.

(d) The maximum speed at which the train may run.

(e) Its length in standard wagon length units.

Routes were classified A, B, C, and D for brake force purposes. Class 8 trains would run up to the maximum speed of the slowest wagon on the train. References in the loading pages included Assistance in rear and also AWB (apply wagon brakes) between specific points. Class 9 (loose coupled) freight trains ran as authorised in the Working Timetable, Trip Notices and Special

Notices, or by the Divisional Manager. They were confined to trains of a local or trip nature and to certain scheduled mineral services. The loading of Class 9 trains was quoted in tons inclusive of the weight of locomotive(s) and train brakevan. Two of the longer distance Class 9 services from Toton to Rugby and Coventry (Three Spires) were formed with a brakevan at each end owing to the reversal at Nuneaton Trent Valley. With a length limit of =50, preparation of these two services was straightforward, no need to shunt out and marshal fit-head wagons. To attain the maximum loading of 2,034 tons, 84 x 16 ton (=22 ton when loaded) wagons for Wellingborough and (Stewarts and Lloyds) Corby services worked by 2x20 locomotives, a total brake force of 212 tons was required. With 35 tons for each of the Class 20

TOTON DOWN SIDINGS

12TH OCTOBER TO 2ND MAY, 1970/71

14.00-22.00 HRS.

POWER	CODE	RUNS	TIME	TRAIN	PREVIOUS WORK		Booked To Load Bk.From	LOADING
	8QT	SX	1400	St. Gate	9T89	St. Gate	MS	
	8E82	SX	1405	Mansfield	6062 1050	Bilsthorpe	N.Yd.	
	8D72	MO(SX)	1422	Sherwood			N.Yd.	
	8D80	SX	1445	Clipstone	9D55 1037	Rufford	N.Yd.	
	8E38	D MC	1514	Seymour	9M23 1234	Seymour	M	
	8E51	SXMC	1525	Mansfield	8M80 1226	Mansfield	M	
	8E85	D	1540	Scunthorpe	8M38 1042	Wath	M	
	8E77	SX	1548	Shirebrook	8MO2		N.Yd.	
	8E59	SO	1555	Wath	8M33 1200	Manvers	M	
	8M88	SX	1615	Edge-hill		Depot	M	
	9D30	SX	1620	Riddings	9D64 1251	Pleasley	N.Yd.	
	8D93	SX	1625	Sherwood	8M23 1340	Shirebrook	N.Yd.	
	8E53	SX	1640	Welbeck	8012 1348	Welbeck	M	
	8D39	SX	1650	Rufford	9D25 1220	Clipston	N.Yd.	
	9E78	SOMC	1654	Parkgate	8M34 1355	Barrow Hill	M	
	OD73	SX	1745	Clipstone	9D32 1531	Mansfield		
	8D61	SX	1800	Tibshelf	9D86 1630	Tibshelf	N.Yd.	
	8E55	SX	1817	Worksop	8M23 1340	Shirebrook	N.Yd.	
	8E70	MO	1910	Scunthorpe	9M33 1450	Manvers	M	
	8E60	SX	1920	Mansfield	8M88 1605	Mansfield	N.Yd.	
	8D68	SX	1950	Tibshelf	8D06 1720	Avenue	N.Yd.	
	8D69	SX	2020	Tibshelf	9D42 1850	Riddings	N.Yd.	
	8E91	SX	2030	Worksop			N.Yd.	
	8E65	SX	2100	Welbeck	8082 1730	Bilsthorpe	N.Yd.	
	9T90	SX	2110	St. Gate		Depot	MS	
	8E88	SX	2115	Shirebrook	8D21 1830	Sherwood	N.Yd.	
	8E61	SX	2120	Mansfield	8022 1800	Welbeck	N.Yd.	
	9T89	SX	2140	Stanton Gate		Depot	MS	
	8E98	SX	2143	Worksop			N.Yd.	
	8E40	SX	2150	Tinsley	8M00 1821	GreaseboroRd	M	
	8E89	SX	2020	St.Gate-Park gate.	8M48 1608	Wath		

TOTON DOWN

22.00-06.00 HRS.   4TH MAY – 4TH OCT., 1970.

Power	Code	Runs	Time	Train	Code	Time	Prev. Wkg.	Loading
	8D83	SX	2200	Kirkby	8M59	1806	Dinnington	
	9M50	SX	2216	Garston	8D67	1845	Tibshelf	
	9M21	SX	2221	Mottram			Depot	
	8E24	SO	2230	Scunthorpe	8M61	1706	Scunthorpe	
	8D95	SX	2245	Kirkby	9D06	2042	Bentinck	
	8E49	SX	2250	Scunthorpe			Depot	
	8D84	SX	2310	Kirkby	8M36	2030	Shirebrook	
	8E48	SX	2325	Seymour	6M49	1940	Worksham	
	8E62	SX	2358	Mansfield C.S.	8M77	2100	Shirebrook	
	8E63	MX	0025	Shirebrook	9D73	2132	Rufford	
	8M46	MX	0145	Garston				
	8E34	MX	0204	Seymour	8M03	2315	B. Hill	
	8E33	MX	0233	Seymour	8M99	2326	Seymour	
	8E05	MX	0300	Tees			Depot	
	8D68	MX	0305	Tibshelf	8D22	0125	Tibshelf	
	8E94	MX	0315	Mansfield C.S.	8M44	0005	Mansfield	
	8D79	MX	0325	Kirkby	8M22	0001	Shirebrook	
	8E36	MX	0335	Manvers	9M26	2315	Carlton	
	8D74	MX	0343	Blackwell	8D13	0203	Tibshelf	
	8E37	MX	0420	Tinsley			Depot	
	8E95	MX	0430	Creswell	8M46	0110	Mansfield	
	8E64	MX	0445	Bilsthorpe	8084	0130	Bilsthorpe	
	8E05	MO	0500	Tees			Depot	
	9M22	MX	0500	Mottram			Depot	
	8D13	MX	0510	Kirkby	8M16	0307	Shirebrook	
	8E71	MX	0522	Dinnington	8D03	0335	Kirkby	

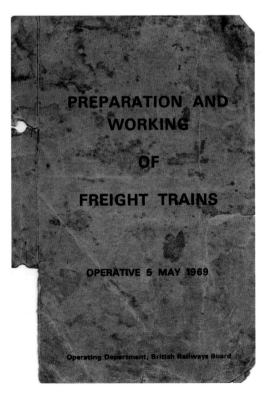

Toton Down Sidings. Late turn departures from the Meadow/Stowage sidings and the North Yard.

73

Leaving Toton East Yard with a freight for Wellingborough are two English Electric Type '1' (Class 20) diesel locomotives. They could operate single-manned (driver-only) when coupled bonnet to bonnet.

locos, a further 142 tons was required from the MCVs – (16 ton mineral fitted). Some wagons were equipped with double cylinders and counted as 11 tons brake force whilst the normal MCV was rated as only 4VB force. Although extremely rare, it could mean that 35 MCVs would be required to provide the necessary brake force of those only rated 4VB force. Often there would be a mix of the two types of fitted wagons; even so the head shunter would deem it prudent to shunt out a couple more fit-head in case one of the cylinders was found not to be working.

Insufficient fitted wagons were a problem on occasions. Slack for the furnaces at Stewarts and Lloyds – they also owned a large number of their own unfitted wagons – had to be supplemented by empty tube wagons, which were destined for Corby as part of the fit-head, this, however, increased the length of the train. Care had to be taken to ensure that all the fitted head was working and the brake blocks were fully applied on each wheel; often some didn't and the load had to be reduced accordingly.

Train preparation for many loaded trains leaving from Toton had been introduced. This effectively reduced traincrew costs, as the guard on single-manned turns would act as second man to the driver from the depot to the yard on the light diesel movement. Locomotive diagrams appertaining to services emanating from Toton were for Type '4' Class 44, 45, 47 and Type '1' and '2' – 20 and 25 locomotives, the latter two often operating in multiple. The problem was that the diagrammed traction could not always be depended upon, as, apart from a Monday morning, there was a general shortage of power throughout the week. Specific services could be relied upon to provide the correct type of traction, such as the 17.10 Toton-Lloyds, the

The other 'Lickey', this one between Toton Junction and Toton East Junction. In 1969 BR/Sulzer Type '4' diesels, later known as Class '45' are in evidence working Up and Down freight trains.

BRITISH RAILWAYS

A.T. Casey
J.E. Langford
Area Freight Assistants
Yard Supervisors, East Yard
Chargemen, West Yard
Yard Supervisor, Up Hump
Train Preparers, East Yard
Train Preparers, West Yard
Snr.Railmen, Old Bank
Secretary, L.D.C. 'C' Toton
Area Freight Centre (TOPS Shift Leaders)

From: Area Manager,
TOTON.

Ref: OP1/0/50

Date:

Train Preparation – Toton Up Sidings

Commencing Monday, **5th January, 1976**   Train Preparation arrangements as shown on the attached sheets will apply.

It should be noted that :-

1. All trains worked by Guards from other Depots will continue to be prepared by these guards, except all services from Old Bank, which will be prepared by Senior Railman, Old Bank.

2. When a booked train is <u>diverted</u> to another destination (whether the locomotive headcode is altered or not), train to be prepared by the Train Preparer who would normally do so, except those trains listed above for preparation by Guard (or Foreign Guard), in which case Guard would remain responsible for preparation.

   E.G.   21.10 Toton – Lloyds diverted to Northampton to be prepared by afternoon Turn Train <u>Preparer</u>, East Yard.

   03.05 Toton – Eastleigh diverted to Bescot to be prepared by <u>Guard</u>.

   Special trains run as such (i.e. <u>additional</u> trains) to be prepared by Guard working same.

3. Train Preparers, East Yard and West Yard, will be responsible for checking TOPS Train Lists as instructed by Supervisor/Chargeman.

A.J. Casey
R. Pattison.

The introduction of Train Preparation – Toton Up Sidings, which significantly reduced train crew diagram hours for both enginemen and guards.

After emerging from Derby Locomotive Works in 1959/60, D1-10 (44001-44010) did their proving runs on the Midland Main Line before being transferred to the Western Lines working out of Euston. In 1962, all ten were shifted to Toton and confined to freight work, their train heating boilers having been removed.

return working being from Corby to Spring Vale, a two-day diagram for 2x20 class locomotives. Very little notice was obtained from the train crew depot particularly when waiting power, and frequently a Class 44 diesel would arrive for the train that was booked for 2x20 locos, and then the task of having it reduced by 434 tons often resulted in a late start to the service. Another everyday problem was a wagon side door cotter not fully home, which was remedied by the train drawing down to the cabin, and the cotter seated by use of a crowbar and a sledgehammer. On the theme of train preparation, there was an occasion, when as supervisor in the East yard I sent a train out for Wellingborough which was over the load for the route. Considering that the services to the steelworks at Corby and those to Wellingborough took anything up to eighty-four wagons, it was often impossible to form each train up with a brakevan behind. On that occasion it was a breakdown of communication between the train preparer and me. I was given to understand that the train would be formed up in No. 20 road where there was a brakevan behind the wagons. This, however, was not the case: the wagons for the train were in No. 20 road but the guards van was in the brake slip. It wasn't until the train had left the yard that it became apparent that it was incorrectly loaded. The Wellingborough service was 200 tons overload for the route classed as 'B' brakeforce. The line to Leicester had an 'A' brakeforce category and the higher loading could be taken over that section. Detected early, the train was put in at Loughborough to reduce, so no harm was done, except the surplus traffic would have to be cleared when convenient. Only once did I receive a 'please explain' – from Allan Casey, no doubt engineered by the Area Freight Assistant, Jim Pass, regarding traffic for the private sidings at Corby, which only amounted to perhaps half-a-dozen wagons a week. The wagons were serviced via Humberstone Road (Leicester) and were tripped to Corby. 'German Joe', the head shunter in Chilwell, had left the traffic off the train for whatever reason; truth be known he was too tired to shunt the wagons out.

Not only was there a continual shortage of equipment for guards vans, shunting poles, brake sticks (the latter always a problem as they were regularly purloined by other depots and yards), and side and tail lamps – some with vessels and burners missing – but more often than not it was the brakevans themselves that were at a premium. Each morning at 08.00, a count would reveal the numbers of brakevans on hand at each location throughout the complex, the information being passed to the Control Office. On more than one occasion a departing service from one of the Toton yards would be awaiting the brakevan off an incoming train. Assistance would often be requested from other divisions to alleviate the shortage and RHQ Crewe would liaise with other regions.

The Area Freight Assistant, whilst maintaining a general overview of proceedings, was very much involved in the movement of traffic from the Up side to the Down side and vice versa. The 'cross-roaders' were worked with a Class 08 shunt loco on 46 stower and a Class '20' locomotive on 47 stower. Jim Pass often donned his trilby and proceeded to catch the road on (couple the wagons) for the guard in an effort to expedite the movement between the two yards. 'Passy' kept a tight reign on his shift, so much so that the supervisors in the East yard and the Meadow were often intimidated by his vociferous manner, both over the telephone and in person. Nevertheless he achieved possibly more than his other two colleagues with his hands on approach, although this did not endear him to some of the staff, housed in the centre signal box, where a good all round view could be had of the complex as to what shunting was, or often wasn't, taking place.

For collecting, storing and producing information about the movement of freight traffic, Toton yard used a computer-based system called TOPS – Total Operations Processing System. In computer jargon, it was an on-line, real-time system, which means:

Four condemned English Electric Class '20' locomotives (a type used on 47 Stower), 20179, 20147, 20086 and one other, in the Sandiacre dead-end of Toton TMD in June 1989, awaiting disposal to M.C. Metals scrap yard, Springburn.

(1) that it was based on permanently-open circuits between the central computer and all its outstations — the TOPS offices in stations and yards.
(2) that it worked instantaneously, and every item of information stored in its bank was immediately updated as necessary by each message as it came in.

The information bank started with the 'permanent' information about every locomotive and wagon on BR – its fleet number, its weight, its capacity, brake force and so on. Then, for each single one of them, it recorded:
 its position
 whether it was in service or down for repair
 whether a wagon was loaded or empty
 if loaded, what its load was and where consigned

From then on it recorded every change in any of these details, and could produce the latest information about any one of them at the press of a key.

Obviously a computer cannot 'know' anything unless it is told – by the people who do know, that is, the operating staff – or in some cases our customers, so the whole system relied completely on prompt and accurate reporting by staff, through the TOPS offices (now called Area Freight Centres), of every change of 'state' by every vehicle – every movement, every loading or offloading, every new destination, every cripple. Given this steady flow of information, the computer could report, in seconds, not only where each vehicle was and what was in it, but also how many wagons there were, and of what types, in any given marshalling yard or on a particular train.

Anyone who knows anything at all about freight operations can see what tremendous advantages such a system could give us. For instance:

(1) empty wagons could be directed to where they were needed, instead of waiting around to be matched with any orders that might happen to come in.

(2) marshalling could be planned in advance, instead of waiting until each fresh train came in to see what was on it.

(3) trainloads could be more closely matched, on every outgoing service, to the locomotive capacity available.

(4) customers could be told, if they asked, precisely where any consignment was – and when it was expected to arrive at its destination.

These were just a few of the more obvious benefits. There were plenty of others – particularly in movements planning and the wider matching of supply and demand for wagons. In spite of the reductions made in the wagon fleet, we still hadn't got too few wagons – only too few at the right places at the right times. The knowledge TOPS made available ensured that supply matched demand more closely: result – more satisfied customers, and more loads carried by each wagon. But TOPS was no magic wand. By itself, it would not turn a wheel, or move a load a single inch. It was only by making full use of it that its benefits could be brought about: if managers used it to make the right movement decisions; if yard supervisors used it to plan the work of their yards to maximum effectiveness; if guards and shunters made sure that every wagon movement was promptly and accurately reported; and if wagon movement instructions were always obeyed. Freight movement by rail was very much a team job for train staff, yard staff, supervisors and managers. TOPS made the carrying out of that job vastly more efficient and economical – and easier, too, for every member of the team – if fully and properly used.

In the old Toton Centre signal box, acquaintance had been renewed with Jim Barnes, Quality Services Supervisor, last seen some five years earlier when he was District Signalman's Inspector at Trent. Also a QSS was ex-stationmaster Jack Henshaw, accommodated following the widespread closure of stations under the Beeching Axe. Jack, although extremely hesitant, went on to the post that I had always coveted, that of Chief Trains Investigator on the north-east/south-west axis. A couple of signalmen, Dennis Walters and John Turley whom I had been box-lad to, in addition to George Bailey, were made redundant as a result of the commissioning of the Trent power signal box in 1969. They found their way into Toton yard as Train Preparers. They would go around the train, with a TOPS list, which would calculate the loading, after the head shunter and his mate had shunted out the fitted-head and marshalled the train. The problem was, of course, that the diagrammed type of motive power could not always be guaranteed; indeed waiting power was often the order of the day.

A lone Class '08' shunt diesel is at work on Toton Old Bank, whilst in the foreground the lines into the East Yard have been lifted, leaving only the two fans into the West Yard. Behind Toton Centre signal box (where I was a control reporter in 1957) is the compound full of condemned diesel locomotives.

I learnt how to rerail wagons with ramps and packing without resorting to calling out the maintenance staff. Derailments usually occurred on the bends of the roads, often buffer-locked caused by impact during times of poor visibility or when a slow-running wagon was being overtaken by one less retarded. Impact also caused the bottom doors of hopper wagons to open, the contents being deposited on the ground. This was recovered by hand on a Sunday, being loaded by volunteers into five-plank wagons, which were then moved to the Old Bank where the coal was tran shipped into a more suitable wagon.

Although now a supervisor, I still continued with the weekend permanent way work, despite an incident in October 1972 while on a Saturday night turn at Nottingham station, when a rail fell onto my foot at 6.30 one Sunday morning. Treated at the General Hospital I spent the next few days hobbling around.

Having completed Stage 2 of the supervisory course at Webb House, Crewe, the next stage involved the writing of a 5,000-word project on a topic given by the local manager. This was usually something associated with a problem area which required being resolved. The first week included a briefing on the Monday morning, and then it was out in the field for the remainder of that week gathering information in readiness for the writing up of the project the following week. Introduction, main theme, conclusions and recommendations were how the report had to be set out. The project selected for me was set by a relief area manager, Ray Pattison being away at the time.

It was a lacklustre one; even the tutor at Webb House admitted that there was very little 'meat' in it. The remit read:

Stores Levels — Shortages of the articles listed below often arise with very little warning. Investigate the causes of this problem and suggest remedies, including improvements to the system for the ordering and supply of these items to Toton yard and all points in the area bounded by Castle Donington, Ratcliffe, Trent and Stanton Gate. List of articles referred to: Yard stationery, brake sticks, shunting poles, oil, side and tail lamps, firelighters and coal for signal-boxes, cabins and brake vans.

Visiting the various locations, only to be told the same, always short of shunting poles and brake sticks, I set about producing what I thought was a reasonable finished project. Summoned to Faverdale Hall at Darlington, the two-week course there comprised of a revision of stages 1 and 2 at Crewe and also included a written and oral examination, culminating with the project being scrutinised by a local assessor.

The students were advised '*that the projects from this course were subject to further examination by the national assessor and that this more rigorous inspection may result in some projects being deemed unsatisfactory. This happens from time to time and we could consider ourselves a little unfortunate in being on the course this particular fortnight.*'

A notable feature at Faverdale concerned the general-purpose fellow. In addition to his various tasks of house duties he would make available the questions for the written examination to some students. I was actually given a hand-written version some months earlier by one of the Area Freight Assistants at Toton.

Some considerable time elapsed before the result came through from Darlington, and when it did it wasn't good. The national assessor had not passed the project report. After an interview with Ray Pattison, arrangements were made to re-sit the National Examination of Supervisory Studies stage IV. The remit selected for this project was:

Merry-Go-Round working - Ratcliffe Power Station.

Examine the effectiveness of Coal Train Working at Ratcliffe Power Station and make recommendations to reduce train detention and improve Operating performance.

So it was off again to Webb House at Crewe for a further attempt, and this time there could be no room for failure. Ratcliffe Power Station was chronically on the block; merry-go-round trains with thirty wagons from the Eastern Region and forty-two from the Nottinghamshire pits had no structured timings allowed into the coal circle. Trains were channelled into the power station at cleaning down and changeover time with obvious consequences. This resulted in some trains having to be recessed on Toton Old Bank whilst others stood out in the power signal box territory. An in-depth analysis was undertaken into the workings inside the power station, together with interested parties who were involved in the servicing of the station. The writing up of the project was in itself most interesting, for unlike the previous remit, there was an abundance of material in this one.

The tutor overseeing the writing up stage was John Hare; he was a signalman's inspector whom I met during my short period at Leicester. John would breeze into the Control Office, vehemently defending the signalman after I had apportioned delay to a passenger train, showing on the sheets as 'distant at Oakham...' which had not been furnished by the signalman, but obtained via the driver when challenged over the loss of time. That apart, John was extremely helpful; his phraseology was much appreciated during the compilation of the project. An endearing colleague, sadly he died a couple of years later from a brain tumour.

Crewe, a railway town, boasted an excellent park, and on all of my visits to Webb House, I never failed to walk across the road and around the park after lunch.

A week before going back to Crewe, I received a letter from the Divisional Manager at Nottingham advising me that under the Territory Organisation Concept I would become displaced. I delayed replying to the list of options offered under the closed list arrangements. These were for posts away from Toton, which was just as well, as the following week, a further letter arrived, this time from the Area Manager offering me the post of Yard Supervisor, should it become available, at South End Down (Down Hump). The post had been vacant for some time owing to long-term sickness and this is what I opted for. Yet another reorganisation – something that Gerard Fiennes was thoroughly bored with.

The giant 2,000 MW Ratcliffe-on-Soar Power Station under construction in 1965. Pictured here is a 'Peak' Type '4' on the Up main line, with a southbound mineral train.

A busy scene at Toton Junction in 1969. A BR/Sulzer Type '2' waits for the road with the returning BDVs, whilst the 6D48 Bentinck to Ratcliffe Power Station, hauled by a Brush Type '4', passes the C&W shops. Extreme left is the Down Hump Room, and waiting for a reception road to be cleared is a freight train from the west.

I made a further visit to the School of Transport at Faverdale Hall following a letter from the Principal, Dewey Gibson, who wrote: '*It is unfortunate that you have to take the examination again for you will probably know that the last time you were here your written work and oral examination were completely satisfactory and it was only your project report which was found less so. Perhaps even more disappointing is the fact that we, and the local Assessor, considered your report to be satisfactory and it was only the National Assessor who was not satisfied. However, we now have copies of your new project and I hope that this will not suffer the same fate.*' He went on: '*I trust that even though you passed the written examination comfortably last time you will not have neglected to work for, of course, you will need to reach a satisfactory standard once more.*'

Allocated number 1 on the hymn sheet at a desk set slightly aside from the other students, one had the feeling of being in the naughty boys' corner. During the two-day resit I won the 'putting' challenge at the Hall, and recalled that on the previous visit the gardener introduced me to two types of winter cauliflower that produced huge heads, Armado April and Armado May from W.J. Unwin, one curd being sufficient for a score of students. Shortly afterwards advice came through that I had been successful the second time round and was presented with a National Examination Board of Supervisory Studies (NEBSS) certificate with the customary award of £20. With supervisory training now complete, much of what had been learnt at both Crewe and Darlington I had endeavoured to put into practice, and by and large had benefited from each course.

Effective planning and maximising resources were two key areas which had always been a priority for over twenty-five years, whenever possible executing the theory both at work and also at home of, 'don't put anything off 'til tomorrow that you can do today.'

Of the two yards at Toton, the gradient was steeper on the Down side apex hump, empty wagons needing the extra impetus to travel the same distance as a loaded wagon. That though, did not persuade some empties emanating from the Carriage & Wagon shops at Chaddesden and Wigston or Claye's wagon works in Long Eaton to run beyond the 'King'

points. I well remember regularly taking duty on the late turn, to find on Nos. 1 and 2 reception roads the Chaddesden and the Humberstone Road freight trains. Invariably this was a deliberate ploy, the early turn being selective in hump shunting and yard work.

Whilst 8-12 minutes may have been the norm for humping a train, the Chaddesden and the Humberstone Road could take up to half-an-hour, owing to the brake gear having been adjusted to the point of binding. Many of the wagons needed little if any retarding and often went wrong. Planning was the essence of running the shift effectively. I hadn't given this a lot of thought until going to Webb House on Stage 1, when the groups were told to build a tower out of Lego. Some rushed straight in and built the tallest in no time at all, only to see it collapse through instability. It may have seemed a trivial exercise, but it certainly brought home the need for adequate planning.

Often maintaining a liaison with the power controller at Nottingham, offering information on the whereabouts of incoming trains in case he wished to have the diesel(s) re-manned for outgoing services, this was always appreciated particularly when short of power. Making the best use of available resources, however, was not always possible. One evening, whilst working on the Down side, traffic for the Eastern Region was gradually building up for the three services:

8E75 21.58 Toton-Scunthorpe
8E40 22.05 Toton-Tinsley
8E49 23.10 Toton-Tees

Traffic on hand was 73 wagons for Tinsley and 49 wagons for Tees (including 11 wagons of steel on bogie bolsters). 8E75 was to load to Hexthorpe with 40 empty plate wagons – some 400 tons. The traction available for the three trains was a Class 47 and two Class 25s. The Power Controller, Norman Acton, had allocated the Class 47 to 8E75 (the lightest train of the three!) with a single Class 25 allocated to the other two services.

There was a calamity at Claye's wagon repair works in October 1959, as LMS '3F' 0-6-0 No. 43650 derailed as it was leaving the yard. In doing so it blocked the footpath that ran from North Erewash Junction signal box (in the background) to Trent station. Joe Wade

No amount of badgering would get Acton to change the allocations, he was totally intransigent. That he was the Traffic Controller on the Toton section before moving onto the power desk made no difference whatsoever. This wasn't making the most of resources available! A detailed report was submitted to Allan Casey.

In addition to the Class 08 shunt diesel on 46 stower, each shunt loco was identified with a target number in each location: 49 and 50 the CUS (50 only used on a 09.00-17.00 shift); 51 in the East yard; 52 in the West yard; 53 also in the East yard-Chilwell Group; 54 and 55 SED; 56 in the Meadow yard; 57 in the North yard; and 58 in the Meadow Stowage; 49, 50, 54 & 55 being radio-telephone fitted. A source or irritation on the late turn was the appearance as regular as clockwork of the repaired wagons from out of the C&W shops. At around tea

Reply from Allan Casey regarding the under usage of power.

break the move would be ready to leave the shops, the shunter asking the signalman at Toton East box for the release to propel the wagons onto the hump arrival line and for the shunt loco to return to the East yard to take the cripples back to the C&W shops. The request to leave the wagons on the arrival was usually refused by the panel operator, the C&W shunt loco being required to shunt its own train.

The underneath of the Down Hump-room provided a haven for a number of felines. One afternoon, a cat was returning to its home from across the hump avoiding line, during which time a train was being shunted. Safely across one rail between the wagon wheels, it then had the other one to negotiate, a move which the animal had done on many occasions. Alas it was now to lose one of its nine lives. As the cat was about to clear the inside rail the flange of the wheel severed one of its hind legs. What happened next was extraordinary to say the least. I watched aghast as the feline turned half circle and laid its head on the rail for it to be severed by the next wheel. It was a most bizarre and harrowing incident to have witnessed.

Working at the varying locations in the Toton yard complex was always interesting. Often under pressure as operators frequently are, I recalled those early days as a supervisor in the East yard when trying to coax the guards in getting their backsides into gear and to get underway off the premises with their train. Punctuality with maximum loadings was closely monitored and any deviation had to be explained. In general the working relationship with both drivers and guards had been one of mutual respect. There was always the exception of course, the odd well-known hammer of management from both grades. For the most part the pilot drivers would take their meal break when the shift did, instead of between the third and fifth hour. The obstreperous individual would often insist on taking his physical needs break at a different time; this obviously did not help when both pilots were required to haul a train from the reception road to the high level arrival line, uncouple and then proceed to Toton East signal box to come back round the train on the west arrival. It was the general practice that those drivers who did not work with you did not get away early. The animosity between Harold Cooley, the hump room panel operator, and Bert Lyon in the Control Tower surfaced on occasions and a calming influence was then required, as it was on occasions between Harold and the shift clerk Alan Rose. Alan had come to the Down Hump from Trent Station North signal box where he had been displaced as Train Controller (Regulator) on the opening of the power signal box at Trent. He was a man of few words, often gaunt looking, married to a Spanish lady. He enjoyed his pipe and was a conscientious individual although I suspect that his position paled in relation to his previous post, and the one before in the Control Office at Nottingham. Another clerk who I worked with on the Down side, Brian Johnson, went on to become Business Manager with InterCity CrossCountry; it was patently obvious at the time that his talents were being wasted as a clerk.

Hump room on left, humping line in centre, and (on right) drawing-up line from Low Level

The underneath of the Hump Room was a haven for a number of felines, one of which met an untimely end when it misread a shunting movement. The humping line in the centre with the coaling stage at Toton shed in the distance, and (on right) the drawing-up line from low level reception roads. Used with the permission of the Editor of Railway Gazette International.

A June 1988 close up of the now-disused East Yard/Chilwell Group amenity block, which housed the supervisor, shunters and carriage and wagon staff.

Now a distant memory from June 1988 of the departure line from Toton East Yard, once the busiest marshalling yard in the UK.

Traction Arranger at Toton TMD

Whilst covering the vacancy on a semi-regular basis on the Down Hump (SED), I had an interview for a TOPS clerk that would have meant promotion, although I preferred something more hands-on. After three years in the Yard (not long before hump-shunting ceased on the Down side), I was walking in the Meadow yard one day with Reg Yeowart, the AFA on my shift. We discussed the various options open to me including a vacancy that had just arisen for a Traction Arranger at Toton Traction & Maintenance Depot.

Reg advised me to apply for the post, which I did and was successful. I was appointed Traction Arranger – Running Foreman – at the largest installation in Western Europe, Toton TMD, and took up my new duties in the autumn of 1974. It was an interesting decision, presumably taken at Board level, to introduce the supervision of traincrews to staff not in the line of promotion. Someone from the Operating Department was now occupying territory which had previously been regarded as sacrosanct to the footplate grade. Being regarded by some as interference did not bother me unduly. If there was a penalty to pay for effective supervision, then so be it. That resolve has over the years produced dividends. Having surmised for some time that there was no sense of urgency in the 'loco' department, suffice to say that it was considerably worse than had been envisaged.

The situation was not helped by, as some described, an Assistant Area Manager (Traincrews) whose wait and see attitude was mirrored, it was suggested by others, in a pastime

TOTON
DIESEL MAINTENANCE
DEPOT

British Rail

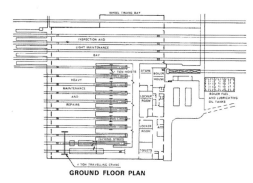

WHEEL TRUING BAY

INSPECTION AND
LIGHT MAINTENANCE
BAY

1 TON HOISTS

STORE

HEAVY
MAINTENANCE
AND
REPAIRS

BOILER
HOUSE

LOCKER
ROOM

LOCKER
ROOM

BOILER FUEL
AND LUBRICATING
OIL TANKS

JACKING STRIPS

TOILETS

4 TON TRAVELLING CRANE

GROUND FLOOR PLAN

PLAN OF DEPOT

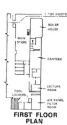

1 TON HOISTS

BOILER
HOUSE

MAIN
STORE

CANTEEN

LECTURE
ROOM

TOOL
LOCKERS

AIR PANEL
FILTER
ROOM

**FIRST FLOOR
PLAN**

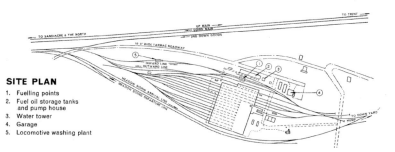

TO TRENT

UP MAIN
DOWN MAIN
2ND DOWN GOODS

TO SANDIACRE & THE NORTH

10' 0" WIDE TARMAC ROADWAY

INWARD LINE
OUTWARD LINE

MEADOW SIDING ARRIVAL LINE
MEADOW SIDING DEPARTURE LINE

TO DOWN YARD

HUMP

SITE PLAN

1. Fuelling points
2. Fuel oil storage tanks
   and pump house
3. Water tower
4. Garage
5. Locomotive washing plant

Heavy maintenance
section

The fuelling plant

A general view of Toton Diesel Maintenance Depot

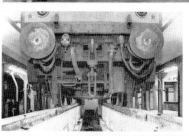

An inspection pit

The ground wheel lathe
for profiling wheels
in position

TOTON DIESEL MAINTENANCE DEPOT

Toton Diesel Maintenance Depot is situated adjacent to Toton Marshalling Yards on the west side of the Attenborough-Chesterfield (Erewash Valley) line about two miles north of Long Eaton.

The depot has been built for the heavy maintenance and servicing of approximately 400 main line and 50 shunting locomotives operating on the Midland lines of the London Midland Region of British Rail.

There are fifteen roads in the depot together with an amenities block and wheel profiling bay. Four of the depot roads have access from both ends, whilst the other eleven roads have access from one end only.

The four through roads each with a pit 230 feet long, are used for the light maintenance of locomotives, and are capable of holding three type '4' diesel train locomotives. The eleven dead end roads each with a pit 154 feet long, are used for heavier maintenance and unscheduled repairs, and will hold two type '4' diesel train locomotives.

The majority of the roads in the heavy maintenance section are provided with elevated platforms over half the length of each road, the depot floor being below rail level under these platforms. The platforms are joined together at one end to form a working area on the same level as the platforms and the main stores.

Folding doors which can be operated either manually or electrically are provided where each road enters the depot. The whole depot is centrally heated and a ventilation system has been installed to deal with the diesel fumes emitted by the locomotives.

Full use is made of natural light wherever possible and artificial lighting is provided by means of fluorescent tubular units, supplemented as required by tungsten fittings. Throughout the depot, service points are provided for electric power, compressed air, new and used lubricating oil, coolant water and battery charging services.

Three roads in the heavy maintenance section are equipped with a 4-ton capacity overhead travelling crane for removing heavy items of equipment from locomotives, including carriage heating boilers and traction motors. In

addition, two of the roads are fitted with specially reinforced concrete jacking strips on which two sets of four 20-ton capacity electric screw jacks are used. Both sets of jacks are used for lifting the diesel locomotive bodies off the bogies, one set being employed so that the bogies and body undersides can be cleaned at regular intervals, while the other set is used to enable repair work to be carried out.

The remainder of the roads in the heavy maintenance section have one-ton capacity hoists over the centre of the road, enabling the maintenance of the internal parts of the locomotives to be undertaken.

In addition to the fixed equipment in the depot, mobile maintenance and servicing equipment is provided to enable routine examinations and minor repairs to be carried out. These include lubrication equipment, compressed air operated hand tools, carriage heating boiler servicing equipment, welding equipment, vacuum cleaners, floor cleaning machines and ultrasonic axle testing equipment.

A two-storey building contains workshops, stores, offices and amenities to cover not only the maintenance requirements of the depot, but also those of the footplate staff. There are 70 supervisory and clerical and 440 workshop staff employed at the depot and in addition facilities for signing on and off duty exist for 455 footplate men. Included in the accommodation is a fully equipped classroom where the training of both maintenance staff and locomotive crews is undertaken. Special workshops are provided for the plant and machinery staff and apprentices, maintenance of batteries, air panel filters, oil filters and injectors, together with the testing of lubricating oil samples taken from the locomotives. Stores are provided on both floors.

Adjacent to the four through roads is the wheel profiling bay. This houses a ground wheel lathe which is able to reprofile the tyres of not only diesel locomotives but also other rolling stock, without the wheels being removed. This machine is used, in conjunction with others on the Region, to provide the overall in situ *tyre* turning requirement. Vehicles can be hauled into this bay and positioned on the machine by means of a capstan. Locomotive road testing facilities are also provided on this road.

Adjoining the depot are the various auxiliary services including a fuelling plant. This has a storage capacity of 150,000 gallons and two locomotives can be fuelled simultaneously.

Appointed traction arranger at Toton Traction Maintenance Depot, the largest installation in Western Europe.

of ornithology. The lack of general direction, together with the traincrew supervisors, who were still living in the steam days, only served to deflect any sense of urgency in that department. Operators are very different individuals; they have to be, as they have targets to meet. More's the pity that the Traincrew Supervisors did not show the same impetus as the Area Freight Assistants in the yard complex, or indeed as some of the enginemen. Never before or since had I worked with such an indolent bunch of individuals. The Traincrew Office at Toton comprised of a Traincrew Supervisor (TCS) and a Traction Arranger (TA) on each shift supplemented by a shift clerk round the clock. There was also another clerk on the day turn, although I never did really understand why, and later the shift clerks subsequently incorporated that duty. At the weekend the TCS and the TA alternated on the Saturday night turn, and there was no Traction Arranger on the Sunday early and late turns. The Traction Arrangers were, however, rostered to cover the late turn on a Sunday vice the TCS; the latter worked the early turn and the night shift on that day. The rest day relief post to the Traction Arranger (or Running Foreman as it was then still referred to) ran parallel with the relief unit to the TCS which was occupied by Les Matthews, who, before coming to Toton was Shedmaster at Colwick Motive Power Depot until its closure and was management grade now covering the TCS position, albeit lower graded.

Les was a man of few words and gave me the impression that in his previous role as Shedmaster he controlled proceedings and he strongly resented the lackadaisical approach to matters by the Traincrew Manager. He was also critical of the way that road learning and route refreshing was undertaken by one of the nominated TCSs, together with the amount of time spent on 'special duties' by Bill Jacques and, to a lesser extent, Harry Smith. Quite rightly, he considered that as obscene; it was totally unnecessary over such long periods and didn't do the budget any good either. The apparent weakness of the Assistant Area Manager (Traincrews) in dealing with Local District Council (LDC) 'B' (footplate reps) was licence for Bill Jacques to manipulate matters, and in so doing was paid his enhancements, loss of earnings, night rate, etc. It didn't stop there though; the Traction Arranger on Bill Jacques' shift was upgraded to cover the TCS position whilst a driver (deputy), was utilised to cover the resultant TA post on a higher rate of pay. What a waste! It ran contrary with what had been impressed upon us at Webb House, Crewe, during the supervisory training. Encouraged to look for the uncontrolled overtime, we spent the best part of one afternoon dealing with supervisor and costs, and endeavouring to put this into practice at the workplace was a different matter. Don't get me wrong, LDC 'B' – the three drivers and a secondman – required more than keeping an eye on. From time immemorial, it was the responsibility of management to draw up the links with LDC approval. That seldom happened, the reverse being the case; the plain fact was that management at most depots could not, and did not, and took the easy option and left it to the drivers' and guards'

'Peaks'-a-plenty feature in this undated BR London Midland Region publicity photograph, showing the heavy maintenance and repairs section of the depot, with D160 prominent in the centre foreground. Beyond the 'Peaks' can be discerned various shunt diesels, Type 2s, and Brush Type 4s receiving attention.

representatives to do as they pleased. Every twelve weeks the link working was evaluated in conjunction with the supplementary changes to the working timetable, and although there may not have been any significant changes, special duties were the norm. At the summer and winter timetable change, in addition to Jacquey being off with LDC 'B', the third regular TCS, Harry Smith, was detached to work alongside the guards' reps, LDC 'C', and it was on such occasions that all three TCSs would find themselves detached on special duties. The annual publication check for drivers and guards was the responsibility of the TCS who looked after the road learning. My arrival in the traincrew office was viewed with some suspicion. Bill Jacques also lived in Breaston; I first came across him at Trent station some ten years earlier when he was travelling back home after being transferred to Toton from the Birmingham area. Now, however, an outsider had appeared on the scene who was not prepared to go along with the lethargic method of working which was rife in the train crew office.

Being Traction Arranger at the largest maintenance depot in Western Europe was a thrill. Wherever possible I insisted on every diesel locomotive being put through the wash plant, the only deviation to this being congestion on the fuel lines. Toton had an allocation of 272 diesel locomotives including all 50 of the ETH-fitted Class 45s, which monopolised the Midland Main Line services for more than twenty years until the introduction of HST sets in 1982.

Toton TMD is a fifteen-road shed where stabling room at the weekends was at a premium with often over a hundred locomotives on the depot.

Saturday lunchtime was particularly busy: locos released off exam and repair had to be moved out, and the shed set up for the next shift before incoming diesels could be stabled on the shed front. This then caused a build up on both fuel lines, with some fifteen engines standing back to the ringing-on signal – this was not surprising as many wanted to 'get done' on a Saturday. Later in the shift, to relieve congestion on the depot, all available Class 44s – assuming none were required for P/Way work and pending if there were any under maintenance – this could then amount to eight or nine of the original Peaks being out-stabled on Toton Old Bank. They would then be allocated to Monday diagrams on the Sunday night turn. Class 47s were not considered for out-stabling as they were prone to losing coolant.

All the movements taking place underlined just what a dangerous environment a Traction Maintenance Depot could be, hence the periodic patrol by the BTC police. One petulant plain-clothed individual was positively euphoric when booking unauthorised incursion on the depot, his colleague showing signs of disbelief on occasions. On a Sunday late turn, with my trusty Shift Clerk, Dick Humber, holding the fort, I would wander through the depot, the only sounds interrupting the eerie silence coming from the blow-down valves of the Class 47s and the fluttering of the pigeons. Decked out in my check suit, having left the dustcoat back in the office, and aware that 'PC Plod' was in the vicinity, I made my way down No. 4 road when a voice bellowed 'Oi!' Not turning round, I continued with a spring in my step round a Class 47 into No. 3 road, the footsteps behind me quickening. 'Oi you!' echoed round the vast interior. Still I walked unperturbed whilst my pursuer was now running. After a third and final bellow I stopped, turned around, looked him firmly in the eye and told him my name was not 'Oi'. With a disconsolate look on his furrowed brow, he panted: 'Oh it's you.'

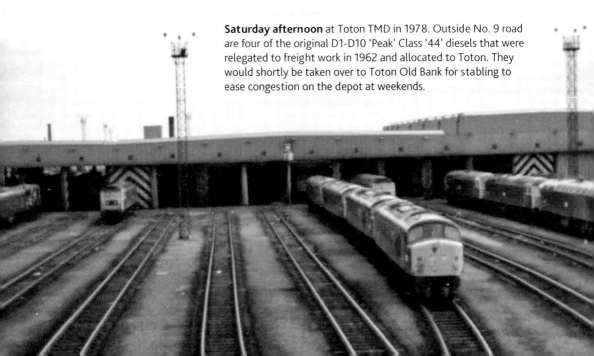

Saturday afternoon at Toton TMD in 1978. Outside No. 9 road are four of the original D1-D10 'Peak' Class '44' diesels that were relegated to freight work in 1962 and allocated to Toton. They would shortly be taken over to Toton Old Bank for stabling to ease congestion on the depot at weekends.

A Type '4' Class '47' heads towards Toton Traction Maintenance Depot. The stored wagons are in what is left of Toton West Yard. Behind them, the silver birch trees have eroded the East Yard.

A fascinating BR publicity shot shows the depot exterior from the south end with a 'Peak' and Brush Type '4's at the fuelling point, plus Type '4's and a Type '2' at the inspection and light maintenance side of the shed. The closed chevron door leads to the wheel-profiling bay.

Depot visits were allowed on Saturdays once a month, by permit, but enthusiasts often turned up on Sundays hoping for a tour of the depot. Some came from far afield – the drawing power of the original ten Peak Class locomotives was intense. Enthusiasts would come to the window and ask permission to go round the depot and, when given short shrift by some supervisors, would probably end up by going round anyway. On other than the designated Saturday, in which visits were allowed, Les Matthews was particularly hostile to any visitors coming to the window seeking a look round the depot, telling them in no uncertain terms to clear off. His anger probably stemmed from his time as Shedmaster at Colwick. So, when I was working late turn on a Sunday, I decided that for 50p per person a tour would be granted with either me or the crew bus driver to accompany them. The proceeds were paid to the Administration Office the following day, with a stipulation that the funds go to St Christopher's Orphanage, Derby.

Toton TMD has four through roads, the other eleven having access from the north end. The dead end roads were capable of holding two Type 4 diesels, only one of which could be accommodated in the bay – elevated platforms, that were not provided on the three lifting roads.

It was the movement of locomotives out of and into the bays that was most time consuming, as many of the diesels were dead. The problem was of selecting a 'dead' road in conjunction with the maintenance planning supervisor where there would be unlikely to be any movements from inside that particular shed road. Whilst the marshalling of locomotives for maintenance was taking place, other diesels were arriving on the depot, having rung in to the TCS from the 'ashpit' phone. From there the driver was instructed towards No. 1 fuel line if for exam/repair, and to No. 2 line if clear. In all cases the diesel number, originating point, and the drivers name, together with his time on duty, were tendered.

The Traction Arranger was responsible for the efficient, punctual and safe working of locomotives on and off the depot, this together with the movements required by the maintenance department and for the supervision of the footplate staff in the preparation and disposal of diesel locomotives. At the start of each shift the TCS would crosscheck his locomotive stop list with the shed plan held by the TA; this would also reflect the diesels on hand right for work. The Traction Arranger would then have a face-to-face board check with the Planning Supervisor in the maintenance office situated on what was referred to as the flight deck. From there, on the way to the fuel line, a physical check of the locomotives on the shed front was undertaken. A couple of hours into the shift the Planning Supervisor would give an estimate of the locomotives likely to be released during the turn, together with any big shunts that may be required. The number of 'stopped' engines varied: on one occasion there were no fewer than sixty-eight locomotives for repair/exam on the depot, in addition to those diesels available for traffic.

A day of inclement weather. On the left is a Class '44' for exam/repair; on No. 2 fuel line is another of the original 'Peak' diesels with a pair of Class '20' locomotives behind. On the extreme left is the tank road, with the avoiding line on the right. Geoff Griffiths

Toton Traction Arranger's shed plan.

	1	44008 20 178		08 014 08610 08141 08388 08929 08 330
	2	45 132		
	3	47 859 47 357		
SCOTCHED HO 192	4	45 112 45 119		45 057 45 066
STORES BAY 08 685 STRATFORD 08 957 } DEMESNED LONGSIGHT 08 915	5	45 128 47 323		47 320 47 356 47 326 47 324 47 338
	6	45 102 45 040		44 004 44 005 44 003 44 002
	7	20 161 45 070		20 186 25 133 25 294 / 25 811
	8	45 065		
	9	20 198 25 250		20 141 / 20 197 20 169 / 20 181 20 113 / 20 136
	10	47 189		
	11			
	12	44 009 20 044		SCOTCHED W/M 45 054 45 125
	13	20 045		
	14	45 001		20 009 20 001
	15	45 076		20 069 20 076 / 20 150 20 003 / 20 005
1 SLIP		20 045 / 20 088 20 182 / 20 199		20 157 / 20 174 20 185 / 20 193 20 144 / 20 148
2 SLIP			3 SLIP	36 TON CRANE DD √s
W/LATHE		08 399 014 021 741 293 230	L/TEST	DEAD BEADY 45 106 47 201 20 075
L.E. D END	s/	TOOL VAN HCR 17 56 031	SAND. D.	20 018
L.E. D END		DD √s	F. LINE 2	
TANK RD.	√s	08 757 3 FULL TANKS	F LINE 1	
WASHEN RD				8 MT TANKS

97

In 1973, a modification was carried out on fifty Class 45 locomotives when the steam heating apparatus was removed in favour of electric train heating equipment; this was completed in 1975 with a reclassification to 45/1. Nottingham was always at a premium for passenger power; normally the incoming diesel on a Sheffield-London express would re-engine the next train from St Pancras going north. When 'waiting power' – an extremely common occurrence – the priorities between the operating and maintenance departments became even more apparent. A Class 45/1 would arrive at Toton on No. 1 fuel line for an 'A' exam and brake block change. After the diesel had been serviced and the necessary paperwork was completed by the outside receptionist, it would be washed and berthed inside the depot. It then had a pre-maintenance exam before the 'A' exam and blocking was undertaken. Afterwards it would undergo a pre-traffic exam by a supervisor. Seldom, even in time of acute shortage of power, would a 45/1 be released in much under a shift. Admittedly, the loco was not always staffed immediately; it most certainly should have been under the circumstances.

It was generally accepted that train crew mess rooms were not the cleanest of places. Indeed, harking back to the old relief cabins, they were downright filthy, and the blame lay firmly on the individuals using them. This included the Traction Arranger's accommodation, a brick building housing the fuellers and the outside receptionist in one part and, next door, the TA with the enginemen

Twenty-four hours at Toton

Locomotives arriving on Toton Depot, Wednesday January 29 1975

Diesel Number	Time	From
25245/25269	00.45	Wellingborough
20149/20170	01.15	Burton
25021	01.30	Tyne
20155	01.40	Ratcliffe
20009/20040	01.40	Bestwood Park
25112	02.00	Bescot
20139/20159	03.00	Wellingborough
47315	03.10	Langley Mill
44007	03.25	Northampton
40045	03.30 (Fuel only)	Masborough
20071	04.00	Westhouses
47322	04.15	Didcot
47178	04.15	York
45128/47329	05.00	Nottingham
20175/20006	05.40	Lloyds
40052	05.40	York
44003	05.45	St Marys
47320	06.20	Westhouses
44002	06.20	Whitemoor
44008	06.20	Burton
31231	07.05	Burton
20067/20162	07.10	Westhouses
45135	07.55	Northampton
45125	07.55	Nottingham
44004	08.00	Birmingham
44005	08.25	Northampton
47321	08.30	Didcot
44007	08.30	Tinsley
20141/20090	08.35	Lloyds
20210/20212	08.45 (Fuel only)	Worksop
47366	09.10	Didcot
44003	09.50	Northampton
20013/20197	10.00	Three Spires
25091	10.35	Barrow Hill
20143	10.40	Burton
20146/20136	10.50	Lloyds
20066/20193	10.50	Wellingborough
20159/20139	11.15	Clipstone
25254	11.35	Derby
20192/20156	12.05	Wellingborough
20149/20170	12.30	Northampton
47381	12.35	Didcot
20091/20059	12.55 (Fuel only)	Worksop
47345	12.55	Nottingham
20146	13.00	Ratcliffe
20155	13.20	Humberstone Rd
08828	13.20	Ballast
47366	14.05	Didcot
25079	14.10	Tinsley
47324	14.50	Didcot
44002	15.05	Northampton
44008	15.10	Stoke
47315	15.50	Didcot
45135	15.55	Coventry
44004	16.05	Lloyds
25075	16.20	Bescot
44007	16.30	Birmingham
44006	17.35	Three Spires
44005	18.50	Corby
45076	19.15	Burton
08610	19.25	46 Trip
25091	19.25	67 Trip
44003	19.35	Wellingborough
20139/20159	19.45	Rotherwood
25067	19.50	Wellingborough
20075	20.10	Stanton Gate
20066/20193	20.20	Wellingborough
45007	20.50	Fletton
20076	21.05	Westhouses
45111	21.40	Nottingham
47354	21.45	Northfleet
25079	22.00	Tinsley
25245	22.25	Whitemoor
20155/20074	22.30	Clipstone
20170/20149	23.10	Lloyds
47320	23.15	68 Trip
46037	23.30	Betteshanger
24044	23.30 (Fuel only)	Stoke
20197/20013	23.40	Willington
20141/20146	23.50	Three Spires

Diesel locomotives arriving on Toton TMD over a 24-hour period on January 29 1975.

Diesel locomotives arriving on Toton TMD over a twenty-four hour period on 29 January 1975.

The 'Thames-Clyde Express', Glasgow to London (St Pancras), has just crossed the viaduct over the River Trent and is about to enter Red Hill Tunnel, hauled by a BR/Sulzer Type '4' diesel.

Two BR/Sulzer Class '45' diesel locomotives on the down main line pass under the Toton East and West arrival lines, en route from Derby to Toton Traction Maintenance Depot in 1986.

and situated adjacent to the fuel lines. The interior of the TA's office (cabin would be a more fitting description) was absolutely abysmal, a stone floor littered with cigarette ends and tea stains, the walls yellowed by the smoke of anything up to ten enginemen occupying the room at any one time, which induced a feeling of nausea on entering the room out of the fresh air. It was not, I deemed, a fitting place for a supervisor to abide; indeed, the chargeman in the West yard had his own office and was not subjected to having to be housed along with the shunting staff.

For my part, the other Traction Arrangers were all ex-footplate staff so obviously they were not as vehemently opposed to the conditions as I was. Nevertheless, one of the deputies, himself a driver (it was the practice to use selected drivers to cover the TA's post), also abhorred the state his colleagues had left the cabin in. In a letter to Mr Pattison I outlined the disgraceful and out of date working conditions in the fuel line cabin. This was followed up by a further letter a couple of months later which was signed by three other TAs and two of the deputies. The office accommodation was on the agenda of an LDC 'A' meeting held on 26 February 1975, the chairman of the staff side being none other than A.W. (Bill) Jacques, who was aware of our grievances, but chose to do little to put matters right. The negative response prompted me to write to the local Nottingham Branch of the Transport Salaried Staffs' Association who must then have questioned Bill Jacques as to what was going on. I realised then that there would be action of some kind as a resolution on office accommodation was passed at the 1974 Annual TSSA Conference. The Executive Committee was instructed by Conference to tackle the problem as a matter of extreme urgency. The TSSA Senior Assistant General Secretary, Mr Tom Jenkins, added, 'We will be watching this matter very closely indeed, but the message from the managements concerned was clear – they will be prepared to look into any complaint about inferior standards of offices.'

When Bill Jacques found out that I was the perpetrator in going over his head in writing to the TSSA he was furious. We hadn't seen eye to eye on a number of issues, including having to cover his shift on a Saturday night whilst he was on special duties; the relationship was strained to say the least. Nevertheless I had achieved the following: a reasonable desk, improvements to the seating arrangements, linoleum covering for the floor, installation of an extractor fan, and a coat of paint for the walls. Not everyone, however, was so reticent about the continual special duties, least of all Fred West. He was the Traction Arranger on the shift with Bill Jacques and so stepped up vice him on higher grade duty; consequently his earnings were far in excess of the other TAs. Jacquey, the staff representative, had worked a fast one three years earlier at an LDC 'A' (Supervisors) meeting, inserting a clause in the working arrangements whereby: *The 14.00 hours Saturday, Running Foreman, would be required to cover a temporary vacancy for TCS/TA at 22.00, the resultant Running Foreman's vacancy being allocated to a Deputy Foreman.* All very nice and cosy.

Transport Salaried Staffs' Association

WALKDEN HOUSE · MELTON STREET · LONDON NW1 2EJ

General Secretary
D. A. MACKENZIE

Assistant General Secretaries
T. H. JENKINS
C. A. LYONS

Your Ref. A.1910

Our Ref. 45700

Telephone:
01-387 2101

6th May 1975.

Dear Mr. Scott,

OFFICE ACCOMMODATION : MR. R.H. FOWKES,
TRACTION ARRANGER, DIESEL MAINTENANCE
DEPOT, TOTON

    With reference to your letter of 22nd March 1975, I have now
received a reply from the Divisional Staff Office indicating that the
chairman of L.D.C. 'A' has recently submitted a request that the
existing facilities be improved by the following arrangements:-

    1.   Provision of a reasonable desk.

    2.   Improvements to the seating arrangements.

    3.   Lino. covering for the floor.

    4.   Installation of an extractor fan.

    In Mr. Kitching's view this request is not unreasonable and he is
making strong endeavours to provide the additional facilities including
the provision of a small mess room table which it is hoped will
alleviate the majority of the complaints.

    The Divisional Staff Officer has said that one of the main requests
of the supervisors, i.e. for separate accommodation, can only be
achieved by extending the present building and this aspect has been
declined on the grounds that the cost cannot be justified by either
economies or significant increases in efficiency.

    I should be obliged if you would advise the members concerned and
if there is undue delay in providing the recently requested additional
facilities, perhaps you will let me know.

                    Yours fraternally,

                    H.W. CHEN
                    L.M. DIV. SECRETARY
                    per:

229. NOTTINGHAM

Letter confirming improvements in traction arranger's office accommodation.

Weekend staffing in the
train crew office, engineered
by A.W. Jacques.

MINUTES OF MEETING OF TOTON L.D.C. 'A'
(SUPERVISORS AND CONTROLLERS) HELD ON 20.12.72.

Present:

Management	Staff
R. Pattison, Chairman	A.W. Jacques, Chairman
J.R. Langford	A.H. Green
P.A. Woods, Secretary	

Minute 5   Week End Staffing Arrangements - Toton T.C.O.

In connection with the revised arrangements to be introduced on 25.12.72
following the consultation meeting on the above subject held on 1.12.72. the
following points were agreed:-

1.   Rest Day Rosters

Rest Day Rosters shown as Appendix 'A' to this minute should be
implemented.

2.   Rest Day Relief - TCS/TA and Running Foremen

No specific duties would be allocated on the additional spare days and
the staff concerned would be utilised to best advantage.

3.   22.00 SO TCS/TA Turn of Duty

The 14.00 hours Saturday Running Foreman would be required to cover a
temporary vacancy for TCS/TA at 22.00 the resultant Running Foreman's
vacancy being allocated to a Deputy Foreman.

4.   Spare Sunday Turns arising through Sickness Leave etc.

Any vacancies on Sunday turns would be filled in the following order of
priority:-

4.1.   06.00 and 22.00 TCS/TA

4.1.1.   TCS/TA not rostered for duty.

4.1.2.   Running Foreman from vacant shift.

4.1.3.   Running Foreman not rostered for duty.

4.1.4.   Running Foreman R.D.R.

4.2.   14.00 TCS/TA

4.2.1.   Running Foreman not rostered for duty.

4.2.2.   Running Foreman R.D.R.

4.2.3.   TCS/TA not rostered for duty.

4.3.   22.00 Running Foreman

4.3.1.   Running Foreman not rostered for duty.

4.3.2.   Running Foreman R.D.R.(if available).

4.3.3.   Deputy Running Foreman.

5.   Additional Sunday Turns

Where it is necessary to supplement rostered Sunday turns due to
increased traffic requirements an additional Supervisor will be booked
on duty at appropriate times providing 10 or more trains are ordered
between 06.00 hours and 14.00 hours in addition to the normal ballast
programme of 6 trains. The figure of an additional 10 trains will be

reviewed in the light of experience gained.

The agreements contained in these minutes do not in any way constitute a
legally enforceable agreement between the parties.

Signed

Management	Staff
R. Pattison.	A.W. Jacques
.... Chairman	....
P. Woods	A.H. Green
.... Secretary	....

102

I objected to this. When I was on the rest-day-relief, it frequently fell to me to have to cover the 22.00 turn. Representation had been made to John Langford, Assistant Area Manager (Traincrews), over the anomaly – I might just as well have contacted Marks & Spencer for all the good that did – stating, that if and when special duties were required, they should be encompassed on a Monday to Friday basis. This obviously didn't bother Bill Jacques, who, after working his double Sunday shift, would come back on the Monday late turn for a few hours and then be on the day turn the rest of the week, receiving all his night rate enhancements.

The TCS was responsible for the provision of train crews to meet the requirements of the traffic department, and hour-by-hour allocation of traction in conjunction with the Power Controller at Nottingham. Class 20 diesels were not assigned to Whitemoor, Rotherwood or Tinsley services as they would have been impounded by the Eastern Region. The provision of the D1-D10 Peaks would ensure their return on an out-and-back diagram as other depots did not have the requisite traction knowledge. A ploy often used by the controllers in the case of foreign crews working into Toton from the north was when refusing to load back, instruct them, 'loco(s) to shed, make your way home!' This invariably had the desired effect.

Never one to resist the opportunity to poke fun at the expense of my ex-Control Office colleagues reminds me of a conversation with the Power Controller, Arthur (Fesser) Foden. I was not always at my best when having doubled up from the Saturday night shift to the late turn Sunday, but not necessarily any the worse for the lunchtime domino school at the Navigation Inn at Breaston, a situation which would not be tolerated today and quite rightly so. A couple of minutes past two o'clock the telephone rang and the conversation went thus:

'Hello!'
'*Nottingham Power here, who's that?*'
'Toton 3209'
'*Who's that?*'
'TCS!'
'*Yes, but who's that speaking?*'
'Bond... James Bond!'
'*Right Jim, will you send 45137 to Nottingham for the 15.00 to St Pancras?*'
For the remainder of the shift I was Jim!

The first of the original 'Peak Class' locomotives, No. 44003 (D3) *Skiddaw*, was withdrawn in the summer of 1976, followed three months later by the doyen of the class, No. 44001 (D1) *Scafell Pike*. Also in the same year the Romanian-built Class 56 diesels appeared on the scene. They would displace the Class 45 and some of the Class 47 locos on various air-braked services before being ousted themselves to the Eastern Region some years later by the Class 58 diesels. Then came the Class 60s and later still the Class 66 & 67 locomotives.

Romanian built in September 1977, 56028, named *West Burton Power Station,* is seen in September 1988. It was withdrawn in November 1993 and broken up at Crewe Works in September 1998.

Built in Valencia, Spain, by Alstom, thirty of these Type '5' locomotives at 3,200hp were deemed as replacements for the Class 47 on high-speed mail and passenger trains. At rest in Dock 4, Plymouth station, is No. 67010, in multiple with another member of the class.

'**Long Tom Bridge**' provided a good vantage point at the south end of Toton sidings. In the background on the East and West arrival lines are the chalker's cabin and the down Hump Room. Class '58' No. 58039 *Rugeley Power Station* ambles by with a train of coal for Didcot Power Station.

Another product from the Brush Works at Loughborough, Type '5' Class 60 No. 60097 passes through Derby station with a train of 100t petroleum tanks. Initially named *Pillar* and later *APB Port of Grimsby & Immingham*.

General Motors 3,300hp No. 66185 at Derby heading west with a lone steel-carrying wagon.

The DAA Railtour Society/Diesel and Electric Group ran 'The Peaks Express' in October 1977 from St Pancras to Manchester Piccadilly, using a different Class 44 locomotive on each of the three legs of the tour. 44007 ran light diesel from Toton to London and worked to Toton Centre from where 44008 took over to Manchester and return. 44009 had the honour of the final leg from Toton to London returning LD.

Although only in the post a few months, I wrote at length to Ray Pattison outlining my thoughts on the working arrangements that existed between the Traincrew Supervisor and Traction Arranger. My immediate reaction was that train crews ringing on the depot would be better communicating with the TA instead of the TCS. Later I learned that this proposal was highlighted in a report undertaken in 1973 by the Productivity Section at Furlong House. In the mid-1970s, there was a skeleton maintenance shift on duty at 00.05 Sunday, specifically to clear diesel locomotives that required 'A' exams (one up from a fuel and water), a practice, which ceased a few years later. On the Sunday night turn the TCS would allocate the locomotives to trains in the order in which they stood on the depot, taken off the TA's shed plan. Usually this was done amicably; only when foreign locomotives were on hand was there any deviation to this, unless of course there happened to be an obstreperous individual in the Control Office who wanted to play the numbers game. This didn't happen very often, and when it did he was given short shrift by the TCS/TA. There were very few engines arriving on the depot on the Sunday night turn as the freight yards were closed until Monday morning. It wasn't unusual, however, to receive a cavalcade of often up to five locomotives coupled arriving for exam/repairs from Derby, Nottingham or even Leicester. The Class 47s that were prone to losing their coolant over the weekend would have to be dragged over to the fuel line for the necessary additive. When a driver booked on duty for a turn in which he worked an engine off the depot to one of the respective yards, his diagram would show him either to prepare his own loco, or that it was already prepared, this by one of the fuel line sets; these were often referred to as P&D (prepare & disposal) sets. The preparation time for a main line locomotive was twenty minutes, whilst two English Electric Class 20 diesels in multiple were allowed thirty minutes. The locomotives could operate single-manned if coupled bonnet to bonnet, otherwise, if working singly or coupled cab to bonnet, a secondman was required. At 00.05 (Monday) there were a further five P&D sets of enginemen, three being the turns that prepared the locos, the other two on fuel line duties. Each of the prep sets were given nine or ten locos to get ready. Some, with the exception of the Class 47s, would require sand, as did the Class 08 shunt diesels that would then be taken to the respective yards by the prep sets. Any faults found on the locomotives were reported to the Planning Supervisor who would make the necessary arrangements for the driver's request to be actioned. As far as the three prep sets were concerned it was a 'job and finish' situation. I did find it unbelievable, not to say

BRITISH RAILWAYS BOARD
LONDON MIDLAND REGION.

To: General Manager, Crewe.
     Regional Controller.
     Ref: P12/6/803
           P15/407/DNG
           015/407/HC
           P16/S/703

     Divisional Manager,
     Room 125, Euston House.
     Ref. OPR.

     D.C.C., Room 8,
     Euston House.

     Operating Inspector,
     Cricklewood.

     Area Manager:
       Buxton
       Guide Bridge
       Toton
       Leicester
       St. Pancras
       Sheffield.

     Passenger Stock Inspector,
     Cricklewood.

     Divisional C. & W.,
     Room 122, Carlow Street.

     Div., Chief Running Inspector,
     Room 125, Euston House.

From: Divisional Manager,
       London L.M.R.

Ref: PX1/DAA/0110/77

Extn: 063-4009

Date: 19th September, 1977.

A.M.E.:
  Willesden
  Cricklewood.

Station Inspector:
  Bedford Midland
  Kettering
  Loughborough
  Dinting

Divisional Manager:
  Manchester
  Nottingham

Traffic Asst:
  Luton
  Cricklewood

'THE PEAKS EXPRESS'

THE D.A.A. RAILTOUR SOCIETY/DIESEL AND ELECTRIC GROUP CHARTER TRAIN ST. PANCRAS,
ETC. TO MANCHESTER PICCADILLY AND BACK.   SATURDAY, 1st OCTOBER, 1977.

	OUTWARD	REP. NO. 1Z96	RETURN	
	09.00.dep.	ST. PANCRAS	arr. 21.20	
	09.40 "	LUTON	" 20.43	
	10.09 "	BEDFORD MIDLAND	" 20.19	
	10.36 "	KETTERING	" 19.52	
	—	LEICESTER	" 19.19	
	11.23 "	LOUGHBOROUGH	" 19.03	dep. 19.05
arr. 11L38	11L48 "	TOTON	" 18L35	" 18L47
" *13.21	13.36 "	PENISTONE	—	—
—	—	BAMFORD	*" 17.32	" 17.42
" 14.04	14.06 "	DINTING	—	—
" 14.26		MANCHESTER PICCY.		" 16.40

  * Photo stop   L Loco Changes at Toton

The first of the original ten 'Peak' Class (D1-D10), 44003, *Skiddaw,* was withdrawn in July 1976, followed three months later by the doyen of the class, 44001 *Scafell Pike*, both being scrapped at Derby Works. The DAA Railtour Society/Diesel and Electric Group organised 'The Peaks Express' Charter Train from St Pancras to Manchester Piccadilly and back, using a different Class '44' locomotive on each of the three legs of the tour.

THE D.A.A. RAILTOUR SOCIETY/DIESEL AND ELECTRIC GROUP CHARTER TRAIN ST. PANCRAS,
ETC. TO MANCHESTER PICCADILLY AND BACK.   SATURDAY, 1st OCTOBER, 1977.

	OUTWARD		REP. NO. 1Z96	RETURN		
	09.00 dep.	.	ST. PANCRAS	arr. 21.20		
	09.40 "		LUTON	" 20.43		
	10.09 "		BEDFORD MIDLAND	" 20.19		
	10.36 "		KETTERING	" 19.52		
	-		LEICESTER	" 19.19		
	11.23 "		LOUGHBOROUGH	" 19.03	dep. 19.05	
arr. 11L38	11L48 "		TOTON	" 18L35	" 18L47	
" *13.21	13.36 "		PENISTONE	-	-	
-	-		BAMFORD	*" 17.32	" 17.42	
" 14.04	14.06 "		DINTING			
" 14.26			MANCHESTER PICCY.		" 16.40	

* Photo stop   L Loco Changes at Toton

- 2 -

No. 1939 G.
Continued..

SATURDAY, 1 OCTOBER (Continued...)
0Z96 LD to work

Toton DD	dep 05//20	Wigston North Jn.	(06 08)	Flitwick	(07X55)
	GL	Kibworth	(06 25)		SL
Ratcliffe Jn.	(05X35)	Market Harborough	(06 40)	Luton	(07 46)
	ML	Desborough North	(06 47)	St. Albans	(07 58)
Loughborough	(05 42)	Kettering	(06 57)	Elstree	(08 08)
Syston South Jn.	(05 49)	Wellingborough	(07 05)	Hendon	(08 16)
Leicester	arr 05L57	Sharnbrook	(07 15)	Finchley Road	(08 25)
	dep 05L58	Bedford North	(07 22)	St. Pancras	arr 08//31
To work 1Z96					

0Z00 LD after working

St. Pancras	dep 21//45	Bedford North	(23 06)	Wigston North Jn.		(00 10)
Finchley Road	(21 51)	Sharnbrook	(23 16)	Leicester	arr	00L16
	LL	Wellingborough	(23 29)		dep	00L17
Hendon	(21 56)	Kettering	(23 38)	Syston South Jn.		(00 24)
St. Albans	(22 16)	Desborough North	(23 45)	Loughborough		(00 30)
Luton	(22 32)	Market Harborough	(23 50)	Trent Jn.		(00 42)
Flitwick	(22 52)	Kibworth	(23 59)	Trent		(00 43)
				Toton DD	arr	00//53

After working 1Z96.

For Locomotive Programmes see Special Workings.

CRICKLEWOOD - See Special Drivers & Guards Programmes.
TOTON - See Special Drivers Programmes.
LEICESTER - See Special Drivers Programmes.

TUESDAY 4 OCTOBER

• **St Pancras** to Toton: 44007
• Toton to Manchester Piccadilly and return to Toton: 44008
• Toton to St Pancras: 44009

The train will be marshalled as shown below:-

   TSO TSO TSO TSO CK BSK TSO TSO TSO TSO = 10 vehicles Circuit 662
                                                          ex Cricklewood C/S.

   (See special note below)

Will Area Managers concerned please arrange for a blackboard notice to be
exhibited directing passengers to the appropriate platform. Will they also
note that passengers will be in possession of Charter Control tickets (one-piece)
specially printed in the name of the Society, and I shall be pleased if they
arrange for the passengers to be passed at their stations accordingly:-

D.O.S. Euston.

Please ensure that the stock forming this train is in good, clean condition and
is fully watered.

D.M.E. Euston.

Please ensure that the train is fully tested ▮▮▮▮▮▮▮▮▮▮▮▮▮▮▮
▮▮▮▮▮▮▮▮▮▮▮▮▮▮ for any ▮▮▮▮ defects.

Class 44 Locomotives

A different Class 44 Locomotive will be used on each of the three legs of the
tour, i.e.:-

        1.   St. Pancras to Toton
        2.   Toton to Manchester Piccadilly and return to Toton
        3.   Toton to St. Pancras.

I would be grateful if the D.M.O. Manchester would arrange for the train to be
fully serviced for the return journey.

THE CO-OPERATION OF ALL CONCERNED IS REQUESTED TO ENSURE EFFICIENT WORKING
THROUGHOUT.

SPECIAL NOTE

THIS TRAIN HAS BEEN FULLY BOOKED, ALL 578 SEATS HAVE BEEN SOLD BY THE PROMOTOR
AND EVERY EFFORT MUST BE MADE TO MAINTAIN THE PRESENT FORMATION AND STOCK.

A.R.O'Donoghue
for Divisional Manager

'The Peaks Express' timings and LD movements.

Special diesel locomotive programmes for 'The Peaks Express'.

L33445

A delightfully nostalgic scene from August 1969, to rekindle thousands of childhood memories, taken off 'Long Tom Bridge' at the south end of Toton sidings. Class '44' 'genuine Peak' D8 *Penyghent* heads south from Toton with a rake of iron-ore tipplers bound for Wellingborough. What else were schooldays for? And what were the chances of framing the nameplate so perfectly a second time? 44008 was utilised along with stable mates 44007 and 44009 on 'The Peaks Express' Railtour in October 1977.

SATURDAY 1 OCTOBER
EXTRACT OF WESTERN REGION
LAIRA
            No.46B
    CLASS 46

As programmed to:-

Derby	14 25	14 41	5P58
Park Sdgs.	14 46	16 24	5Z42
Red Bank CS	18 35	-	LD
Derby HS	-		
	FUEL		

Works 46B

SATURDAY 1 OCTOBER
HQ POWER CONTROL PROVIDE
     CLASS 44 (Unprogrammed Locomotive)
      (1ST LOCOMOTIVE) (NO.44007) ✗

Toton DD HS	05 20	LD
St. Pancras	08 31	09 00	1Z96
(Charter to Manchester P)		
Toton Centre	11 38	-	LD
Toton DD HS	11 48	

SATURDAY 1 OCTOBER
HQ POWER CONTROL PROVIDE
     CLASS 44 (Unprogrammed Locomotive)
      (2nd LOCOMOTIVE) (NO.44008) ✗

Toton DD HS	11 28	LD
Toton Centre	11 48	1Z96
(Charter from St. Pancras)		
Manchester P.	14 26	
RELEASED		
Manchester P		LD
Longsight HS		LD
Manchester P	16 40	1Z96
(Return Charter to St. Pancras)		
Toton Centre	18 35	LD
Toton DD HS	18 45	

SATURDAY 1 OCTOBER
HQ POWER CONTROL TO PROVIDE
     CLASS 44 (Unprogrammed Locomotive)
     (3rd Locomotive) (No.44009) ✗

Toton DD HS	18 27	LD
Toton Centre	18 47	1Z96
(Return Charter from ManchesterP)		
St. Pancras	21 20	
RELEASED 21 38		
St. Pancras	21 45	LD
Toton DD HS	00 53	

SATURDAY 1 OCTOBER
EXTRACT OF ER PROGRAMMES
GATESHEAD
          No.36
    CLASS 46

Paignton		17 45	5M35
Oxley CS	23 34		LD
Bath Rd. Depot			

SATURDAY 1 OCTOBER
EXTRACT OF WR PROGRAMMES
CANTON
          No.18C
    CLASS 47

Ealing Broadway	-	1Z22
Birmingham N. St.	11 35	-	LD
Old Oak Common		

SATURDAY 1 OCTOBER
EXTRACT OF WR PROGRAMMES
LAIRA
          No.47
    CLASS 46

Bristol	01 55	1Z68
(From Truro)		
Newcastle	07 30	-	LD
Bath Rd. Depot	-		

English Electric Class '20' 20073/? passing through Long Eaton with a train of merry-go-round hopper wagons.

Brand spanking new No. D1617, built September 1964 at Crewe Locomotive Works, rests at Trent Station North Junction. The diesel locomotive was renumbered over the years – 47036, 47562, 47672 and 47760. The second Down passenger line and the sidings have been removed.

indefensible, that the Traincrew Supervisors en-bloc, were quite prepared to sit there unperturbed, as drivers and guards booked on duty, only to be told by the shift clerk that the job was running – but waiting power!

The driver would then come to the window a little later. 'Anything about yet Dick?' he would ask, and the clerk turning to the TCS received the usual shake of the head. It beggared belief that no attempt was made to locate any traction within the confines of Toton yards that could be re-manned, instead of waiting for the locomotive(s) to come onto the depot for fuel, when many of the locomotives had only done a short trip and didn't need fuel anyway.

When I was in the chair – vice the TCS – liaison with the Trent Power signal box and Yard Supervisors became a regular occurrence when the power position was tight. Whereas punctuality with maximum loadings had been the important issues in the yards, overseen by the Area Freight Assistants, there was no such urgency in the 'loco'; apathy reigned supreme. During my last couple of years at Toton, I was Traction Arranger working alongside Harry Smith. One morning, driver Tom McRobbie, a real bundle of Scottish joy, booked on duty for a Severn Tunnel job; Dick Humber the shift clerk gave him his locomotive No. 44008. Some minutes later the driver, who had been waiting a while for an engine, came back to the window to report that the panel lights on the driver's desk weren't illuminated. The usual practice then was to ring the Planning Supervisor with a driver's request for attention. Not this time. Harry told McRobbie, 'Never mind Tom it'll soon be daylight,' at which the driver was not amused. The odd Toton driver was noted for going on the tear: 'screaming' Dick Jeffries was one driver who was well known for putting his guard across the brakevan, whilst on the other hand, Dennis Thornton never knew when to go home. If he wasn't hanging the pot out on the road, then he would spend hours in the mess-room after signing off duty, playing cards or on the one arm bandit. My father-in-law, a guard at Toton, was known to have the odd day off sick when booked with either of those drivers, his bruises bearing testimony to the former driver. Back in the fuel line cabin it was always interesting listening to the banter between drivers. Some had opted for positions on the fuel line whilst others were green card men who, owing to their medical condition, could not undertake main line driving duties. It was certainly a job for active personnel, climbing on and off diesels both inside and outside the shed. Those who wanted more civilised turns of duty, but didn't want the constant alighting and climbing onto locomotives, sought refuge on the yard shunt engines. At one of the twelve-weekly link changes, or it may have been at the six monthly timetable alteration, Jacquey was out as usual with LDC 'B'. I got wind of a Stoke turn being moved from one link to another which would have entailed all twelve drivers having to learn the road, whereas it could have been placed in another link where seven drivers had already signed for Stoke. This was all too easy of course, and it wasn't being done for equalisation of earnings either – a deliberate ploy by the staff reps. My mistake was to voice my opinion in the

Built 1959 at Derby Works as D8 *Penyghent* and re-numbered 44008 under TOPS, the diesel spent time at Camden, working on the West Coast line out of Euston, before being relegated to freight work in 1962 and allocated to Toton with the other nine members of the class.

fuel line cabin adding, 'I'll go and see the old man about this.' One thing I did learn: that it doesn't do to expound your views to such an audience. Word had soon reached LDC 'B', with whom I was never flavour of the month anyway, and within the hour Harry Smith rang; Mr Pattison wanted to see me in his office. I was always apprehensive when summoned to the inner sanctum – probably how it should be – the signs of a good boss.

The one thing I had found out about Mr Pattison was that it was no use whatsoever generalising over an issue; you would sit there, across his desk until he had extracted every detail, no good at all inferring. Ray reminded me that it was unethical to air my comments in front of the staff. He was right, an off the cuff remark, but the reference to him as the 'old man' should not be construed as being disrespectful, which I believe he accepted. We then

Photograph taken on a weekend in the early 1970s, judging by the number of Class '08' diesel shunting locomotives on the Wheel-Lathe Road.

had a discussion over what prompted the meeting. I explained to him the ludicrousness of shuffling the links around for no apparent reason – LDC 'B' would challenge this of course, citing equalisation of earnings – and with the high cost of road learning he should veto the proposal. I then threw in for good measure the continuing special duties of a semi-permanent nature that were rife in the train crew office, of which he appeared unaware. The lax method of working in the train crew office was in need of a radical overhaul. That view was expounded some months before to Jim Pass, the Area Freight Assistant. He made no more to do than at morning prayers telling Ray Pattison that, 'one of his supervisors was unhappy over the working arrangements in the train crew office.' After discussing other aspects, a wry smile brought an end to the coming together.

It was plainly obvious a little later that the boss had discussed the aforementioned with interested parties regarding matters appertaining in the train crew office and the special duties in particular. With the distinct impression that I had rocked the boat somewhat, for a while the special duties were not quite as prevalent as they had been previously. Needless to say Jacquey, and I were not eyeball-to-eyeball if he saw me in the Navigation Inn at Breaston. It was a sure thing after this that he wouldn't be buying me a pint.

Owing to a temporary shortage of Yard Supervisors, I was approached to cover the position on the Up Hump (CUS), which I readily agreed to. Knowing from my previous position as Yard Supervisor that it was the usual practice for block loads to be run onto the Old Bank, one particular day the Area Manager unusually put in an appearance on the Up side. He questioned my decision of having a block train of Three Spires (Coventry) traffic over the hump and into the East yard instead of directly onto the Old Bank. What he didn't appreciate was that, although there was a train of Three Spires already on the Old Bank, the other traffic was required in the East yard for the following morning service. Round about this time Ray Pattison had been working on a project to close the Down side (with the exception of the North yard), with the cessation of hump shunting. This rationalisation plan, compounded by the drop in wagon-load traffic, the introduction of North Sea gas resulting in the closure of coal-burning gasworks, and merry-go-round operation between the collieries and power stations, many of which bypassed marshalling yards, would all serve to bring about the closure of Toton marshalling yards some years later. The initial Down side scheme did not find favour with, funnily enough, LDC 'B'; and in conversation one day with the Area Manager – I was in his office for whatever reason – he said, 'Do you know Rod, you wouldn't credit the trivial objections which they have come up with. I've spent a considerable amount of time on the scheme and now it's back to the drawing board. Owing to their intransigence to the first draft, they will probably wish that they had accepted it, as the second one will go far deeper.' Read into that what you will.

Hump shunting ceased on the Down side in 1978. Odd trains for a while still ran in via Toton East, mainly empty merry-go-round trains from Northfleet and other block-trains, which drew over the hump and into the North yard. All other trains were dealt with on the Up side with the exception of MGR empties from Didcot Power Station that was backed off in the North yard. All tracks were then lifted in the Meadow and Stowage sidings except for a couple used by the p/way department. The North yard remained largely intact although all roads later were dead-ended. On the Up side, the East yard and Chilwell have long since gone; there remain a few roads in the West yard for storing wagons whilst the Old Bank is still much as it was. The closure of

48   THE RAILWAY GAZETTE   November 16, 1951

Modernised Marshalling Yard at Toton—1

Arrival lines as seen from hump, showing arriving train on No. 5, and in centre, hump engine run-round road

View from hump of approach to sorting sidings, with brake van slip and train engine release line to right

Owing to a temporary shortage of yard supervisors, I was asked to cover the position on the Up Hump (CUS). Used with the permission of the Editor of *Railway Gazette International*.

115

A Mainline-Livery Class '58' diesel locomotive at the head of a train of merry-go-round hoppers for a CEGB power station. A new train crew signing on point is in front of the diesel depot.

the BSC plant at Corby alone accounted for a considerable loss of wagonload traffic at Toton; over 400 wagons for Stewarts & Lloyds could be despatched each day with a similar number of empties returning.

I was standing on the foot crossing near the fuel line one afternoon when Allan Casey was on his way home. He pulled up in his car outside the cabin, wound down the passenger side window and exclaimed, 'What the so and so do you want to go to Plymouth for?' Apparently the Area Manager there, Ken Hall, had contacted Allan (they had worked together some years earlier at Rowsley) to ask about me. I had applied for the post of Movements Supervisor at Laira Traction & Rolling Stock Depot and concluded that it was Allan's recommendation that eventually landed me the job, although when I asked him at the time whether he had recommended me, he wouldn't divulge. It had been a lifetime ambition to move to the West of England, anywhere west of Newton Abbot being a bonus. A previous interview held at Plymouth some years earlier for a similar position at Truro had come to nothing. Firstly BR/Sulzer Type '4' No. 45055, which had re-engined the *Cornishman* at Plymouth, promptly expired at Devonport. This thwarted my trip into Cornwall to have a look around. Secondly, knowing very little about electric token signalling did not altogether endear me to the interviewing panel. The latest interview, however, had been a good one. A couple of weeks later, not having heard anything (it was then the procedure for the applicant to be advised even if not successful), I obtained the telephone number of the Traffic Assistant at Laira. His name I didn't know, and at that juncture he hadn't heard who had been appointed. Over the ensuing weeks, with ringing Laira periodically, a rapport developed between the TA and I, and

The footpath from Long Eaton to Toton shed ran close to No.18 road in the Meadow and No.19 engine arrival line. The permanent-way department is now established in the Meadow, whilst in the North Yard, all sidings are dead ended. Toton training compound is behind the lighting pylon.

during conversation we exchanged methods of working at the two depots. In conversation with him a few days later he told me Mr Hall had been to the depot and he had asked him if an appointment had yet been made; the delay in making this apparently was by one of the supervisors locally being on leave. Although Ken Hall did not tell the Traffic Assistant who the successful applicant was, when asked if it was someone from away, he agreed that it was. His closing words to me were, 'Don't you tell 'nyone.' And I didn't, not even my wife.

Delight, apprehension, various thoughts crossed my mind whilst awaiting official confirmation. How would my children react? Alan, then eleven, Janet nine and Kevin two, would they have the same opportunity on leaving school finding employment in the south-west as they would have done locally, or in neighbouring Derby or Nottingham?

It must have been a week or so later that George Henson from the admin office came into the traincrew office. He asked me how I would fancy a move to Plymouth, and was rather taken aback when I told him that I knew this well over a week ago. He then gave me the letter of confirmation before the end of my shift, which I handed to Maureen when arriving home, with a rider: better luck next time. Some years ago with Peter Griffin we had a few jars with Colin Harrison. He recalled his days at Toton as train preparer when unable to set about his task until the shunters had formed up the train – all the more frustrating when the actual class of locomotive could not be determined. The panel operators on both the Up and Down hump rooms would clock watch with short of an hour to go, spinning out the time closing down roads instead of humping another train.

117

Vacancy W.231 List 15 Movements Supervisor
Grade 'C' Plymouth Operations Area (Located Laira)

I am pleased to inform you that you have been selected to fill the above vacancy at your existing salary and arrangements have been made for you to transfer on Monday 21st August, 1978.

On that day you should report to the Area Manager's Office, Platform 2 Plymouth, after travelling by the first available service.

Free ticket to enable you to travel to Plymouth will be made available on application to the Admin. Office.

I note you are on Annual Leave week commencing Monday August 14th and shall be pleased, therefore, if you will advise me before that time what arrangements you wish to make for payment of your Salary for W/E 19.8.78 (payable Thursday 24.8.78).

In conclusion I would like to take this opportunity of thanking you for the contribution you have made at Toton and wish you every success for the future.

H. Copeland

for Area Manager.

Copies : F. Johnson
          J. Copeman
          G. Firth
          T.C.S.
          J. Langford

Colin then went on to be a panel operator on the Down Hump and on its closure went across to the Up side. Always well turned out, I often used to ask him when on the late turn if he was calling at the Chequers Inn at Breaston, the village where he lived, but he always declined the invitation, not wanting the regulars to see him in uniform no doubt. Colin, a British Legion stalwart, did, however, have a change of clothing when working on the Up side; this enabled him to call off the late turn for a pint. He did incidentally commit the cardinal sin of moving house from Breaston to Draycott, a mile away.

Interestingly enough in the mid-1980s, No. 20 road in the North yard was home to no less than twenty-two withdrawn BR/Sulzer Type '4' diesel locomotives interspersed with three BR/Sulzer Type '2' condemned diesels. Anchored down in order of stabling from the Hump end were: 45010, 25080, 46023, 45002, 45004, 45001, 45048, 45026, 45064, 45059, 45065, 45020, 45036, 45005, 45063, 25032/209, 45069, 45074, 45131, 45123, 45101, 45077, 45102 and 45006. Over on the New Bank, No. 11 road had been given over to stabling condemned Brush Class 31 diesel locomotives.

A line of condemned locomotives; twenty-one class 45s, three class 25s and 46023 in Toton North Yard.

Not only was Toton a last haven for withdrawn diesel locomotives, there were many other locations, such as Tinsley and Swindon, which were host to many of Laira's allocation of Class 46s, and the March graveyard had its fair share of Class 45s.

Six months before leaving Toton, we had moved house from a three-bedroom semi to a detached property at Sawley just under 2 miles away. In the local Bulls Head I was repeatedly told that you don't move from Breaston to Sawley – sentiments which I echoed to Colin Harrison when he moved to Draycott. One of the planning supervisors in the maintenance department often used to tell me that it wasn't appropriate for a grade 'C' supervisor to come to work on a pushbike. Had I not moved to the west of England I would have stayed at Toton, for not long after leaving, the posts of TCS and TA were combined. That was no great surprise: fewer locomotives were coming onto the depot, with many types being withdrawn.

The complement of drivers, secondmen and guards was reduced commensurate with the loss of work owing to altered traffic flows. The cessation of hump shunting on the Down side and later on the Up side also added to the decline of Toton as a major interchange. Nothing lasts forever.

Despite lacking any footplate experience the transition from Controller and Yard Supervisor to Traction Arranger - Running Foreman – had been accomplished, and was accepted by the enginemen in general. Few if any were obstructive, although a couple of well known hammers of management needed to be treated with caution. I listened attentively to the tales from the regular fuel line drivers in the cabin – Bill Currie, Herbert Taylor, 'Buck' Walker and John Mellott – who regaled the audience of their goings-on years earlier in the steam days, interspersed with interruptions from the more junior drivers. Discussion and light hearted arguments were both commonplace and interesting.

A practice which had then ceased was for a driver and a secondman to be booked on duty every four hours on Christmas Day for the purpose of running up the engines in the event of frosty weather. Also at that time of year, and a custom now relaxed, was for the Carriage and Wagon Shops to be cleared of wagons, to enable locomotives to be stabled under cover until the New Year.

It was always an interesting experience when returning back to Breaston and Long Eaton from Plymouth, staying at mothers, and later mother-in-laws, listening to the now long-since retired colleagues, and their reminiscences of yesteryear. Once a railwayman, always a railwayman, a member of a most exclusive club.

So after the first twenty-one years working on the London Midland Region it was all about to change with my transfer to the Western Region – GWR – 'Go When Ready!'

During my time on the LMR I had progressed from Junior Porter (Control Reporter) highlighting the fun as a young lad, working with a variety of signalmen, to Telegraph Clerk at Trent, Controller at Leicester and Nottingham, and Supervisory positions at Toton that boasted both the largest marshalling yard and Traction Maintenance Depot in Western Europe.

In addition to the condemned diesels on the Down side in No. 20 road in the North Yard, No. 11 road on the New Bank was given over to stabling withdrawn 'Brush' Class '31' locomotives.

Six condemned Class '45' diesel locomotives at March Depot, Nos. 45013, 45126, 45122, 45148, 45114 and 45146, in company with English Electric 20153, wait the call to the scrap yard in 1987.

Hump shunting ceased on the Down side in 1978. This view, some six years later, is looking from the control tower towards the Hump Room and the east and west arrival lines. On the left is the engine slip road and the draw line from the two reception lines, where a train of empty merry-go-round hoppers is visible arriving on the low-level from the west.

In this later picture, all of the track work and retarders have been recovered; even the Hump Room building is now eradicated. On the extreme left is 'Long Tom Bridge', with Ratcliffe-on-Soar Power Station in the distance.

Life at Laira

On 21 August 1978, I travelled down to Plymouth on the *Cornishman*, arriving shortly before two o'clock that afternoon for a meeting with Area Manager Ken Hall, a short stocky man whose greying hair was tempered with a conspicuous blue rinse. During the relatively short interview, my new role of Movements Supervisor general-purpose relief at Laira Depot was explained to me. Unlike on the LMR, whereby a post with the same title was primarily involved with signalling, this one at Laira would relieve supervisors who were responsible for the formation of trains and carriage cleaning. It also provided relief to the Traffic Assistant – a Traincrew Supervisor with additional responsibilities.

Alongside Ken Hall was a staff clerk from the admin office; between them they decided which supervisors I would be attached to during my training. Henry Hooper and Bob Mitchell, a former Southern Region stationmaster and ex-guard respectively were to be my mentors. It should be borne in mind, and was emphasised, that there would be resistance to infiltration from other Regions. With formalities completed I asked if there was a Control Office at Plymouth, and when our meeting concluded the Area Manager escorted me to the tower block, said 'second floor', and left me to make my own way up. I deduced from then that he had little time for this department. The Control was a satellite of the Bristol office, with its two controllers, one covering the section in Cornwall, the other eastwards towards Taunton, whilst a third controller on the day turn made up the complement. Finding accommodation was the next priority. I had previously had B&B at a guest house round the corner from the station when attending an earlier interview at Plymouth. That establishment was no longer available and the Staymor, a few yards further on North Road East, would become my second home for some seven months. Meals there were taken in the basement. Each morning the proprietor would have been round with an aerosol spray in an attempt to mask the mustiness emanating from the dampness of the dining room. The hotel apart, lodging was to prove no fun at all despite getting home some weekends. After acquiring a footplate pass the remainder of the first week was spent riding around the area to Penzance, and on the Looe and Gunnislake branch lines.

Laira Traction & Rolling Stock Depot in June 1979. The carriage siding on the left is on the site of the old Laira marshalling yard. A DMU emerges from the civil engineers siding (P.A.D), formerly the motive power depot. With the HST depot under construction (opened in 1981), there is a variety of traction on view, including Class '08', '47' and '50' diesel locos and a DMU. At the time, Laira had an allocation of BR/Sulzer Type 4 Class '46' locomotives. These differed from the Class 45s as they were fitted with a Brush generator and traction motors instead of Crompton Parkinson equipment. The Class '46s', of which four can be seen here, were shared between Laira before being concentrated at Gateshead.

Laira T&RSD is 2 miles east of Plymouth station, situated close to the estuary of the River Plym, within a triangle bounded by the main line from London/Bristol to Plymouth and Cornwall, and the connecting lines between Laira Junction and Lipson Junction to Mount Gould and on into Friary yard.

The London and South Western Railway ran from Exeter across Dartmoor into Friary station until its closure in 1958. Occupying space formerly used as a marshalling yard, Laira was the first diesel maintenance depot to be built for the Western Region and was officially opened in 1961 at a cost of £880,000. Compare this with the £7,000,000 price tag of the High Speed Train Maintenance and Servicing Shed that came on stream twenty years later.

Steam power had been ousted from the West Country some years earlier, being replaced by diesel-hydraulics, 'Warship' Class 42/52s, which on my arrival had also been withdrawn. At the time Laira and Gateshead depots shared the allocation of the BR/Sulzer Class 46s.

NEW CARRIAGE DEPOT TO BE BUILT AT LAIRA

Planning consent has now been given by Plymouth City Corporation for the construction of a £4½m three-road carriage maintenance and servicing depot at Laira, Plymouth.

The new depot, which is planned alongside the diesel locomotive maintenance shop on the site of the present locomotive servicing shed, will be used to service and maintain coaches at present dealt with at several open air locations.

In addition to loco-hauled stock the new depot will handle complete high speed trains consisting of two power cars and seven Mark III coaches, for the pits will stretch the length of each of three roads in the 240 metre long depot.

built. "It will seem like paradise," said Jack. "At present we're working in the open where you can be very cold. We will have a better depot with better working conditions and, we hope, better pay."

"We need a new depot," emphasised supervisor Harold Ferris. "The work now is difficult. When we get snow or ice, the sleepers are slippery and dangerous. Roll on that new depot I say!"

Work on the project is planned to start in autumn this year with completion due in late 1981.

Depot maintenance engineer Ian Cusworth points out the site of the proposed new three road carriage maintenance and servicing depot at Laira, Plymouth.

New facilities

Fuelling facilities will be provided inside the depot together with piped lubricating oil and coolant supplies, compressed air lines and shore electrical supplies. Overhead lifting and jacking facilities will also be installed.

Layout of the existing stabling sidings, restricted in length and number, will be remodelled to provide a nest of ten full length sidings with the through line to and from Friary freight depot diverted to pass by the northside of the depot. A new carriage washing plant and toilet flushing apron will also be provided.

HST servicing

"Some servicing and maintenance will be carried out on the 14 high speed trains for the West Country service," said depot maintenance engineer Ian Cusworth. "And if the HSTs for the South West/North East/North West routes are built the bulk of their maintenance would be carried out here as well."

Fitter Jack Finnigan, a staff representative, will be very pleased to see the new depot

HIGH SPEED MAINTENANCE

When high speed trains start running on the Paddington — West of England service, most of the maintenance work will be carried out at St Philip's Marsh, Bristol and Old Oak Common near Paddington.

This means additional work for St Philip's Marsh and there is no doubt in Bristol divisional maintenance engineer Harry Hamer's mind that "A fourth covered road would make life a lot easier."

The depot at Penzance will be used to undertake day-to-day servicing, some repairs and two-day examinations while Plymouth Laira (when completed) will also do some servicing and maintenance.

If HSTs are authorised for the South West — North East/North West route most maintenance work will be carried out at the proposed depot at Plymouth Laira with the Eastern Region sharing the work. There would

also be some maintenance carried out on the units at St Philip's Marsh.

In addition, Cardiff Canton and Swansea Landore depots — already carrying out overnight fuelling and some servicing of existing high speed units — will have an increasing part to play as the Inter-City 125 network expands.

NEW STATION COMPETITION

Station competitions have been a feature on Western Region for many years. In order to give added emphasis in maintaining standards the Region is to introduce an annual customer care competition which will cover such things as safety,

cleanliness, staff appearance and availability of information.

The emphasis, as the title suggests, is on the standard of service given to the customer and the impression gained of the appearance and adequacy of station

facilities.

Stations will be grouped by size and all staff will be involved in the competition.

Valuable prizes of Stardust mini-weekend holidays will be awarded to staff at the winning stations.

Ian Cusworth was the depot engineer when I moved to Laira from Toton in 1978.

A Type '4' diesel-hydraulic 'Warship' locomotive enters the platform at Waterloo with an express from the West Country in the summer of 1964.

Built at Swindon and Crewe between 1962 and 1964, the seventy-four Class '52' diesel-hydraulic locomotives were withdrawn between 1973 and 1977. Photographed here in late 1964 is an unidentified 'Western' with a fast freight on the Up relief line in Berkshire.

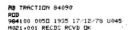

```
AB TRACTION 84090
ROD
984100 005D 1935 17/12/78 U045
M021,001 RECDS RCVD OK

K984100 001D 1935 17/12/78 U046 DN M021 BY ROD
    LOCO    LOCTN  DEPTIM  OPRSTA REASOS RESTWK LOCBKE TRNBKE
    08394  84090 12152105   N                      H      V
    08488  84090 12121745   N                      A      V
    08576  84090 10271725   N      612              A      V
    09895  85734 12150800   N                      A      X
    08937  84090 11231700   N                      A      X
    08945  84090 12131200   N                      F      X
    08954  84090 09072030   N                      F      X
    25048  85111 12170730   N                      A      X
    25052  83400 12171330   N                      T      V
    25057  83400 12171330   N                      A      X
    25058  84090 12060800   M      170              H      X
    LOCO    LOCTN  DEPTIM  OPRSTA REASOS RESTWK LOCBKE TRNBKE
    25080  85222 12161500   N                      T      V
    25155  85721 12161000   N             NM       A      X
    25206  84090 12150553   X      500              A      X
    25207  67356 12171650   N                      H      X
    25223  83421 00000000   N             NH       A      X
    25225  84090 12152225   T      AWS    NA       V      V
    37142  85222 12160506   N                      A      X
    37267  85222 12161210   N                      A      X
    46001  84090 12140635   X      XAM    NH       A      X
    46002  55246 00000000   D      317              A      X
    46003  57401 09220906   R      FRE              A      X
    LOCO    LOCTN  DEPTIM  OPRSTA REASOS RESTWK LOCBKE TRNBKE
    46004  85101 12171615   N             NH       H      X
    46005  57401 12191030   R      TWD              H      X
    46006  81700 12170725   N                      A      X
    46007  61100 12171725   N                      A      X
    46008  81700 12140930   X      XAM    M4       A      X
    46009  17150 12171100   N                      H      X
    46010  84411 12162000   N                      A      X
    46011  82099 12171114   N                      A      X
    46012  84090 12150710   X      500    MR       H      X
    46013  84090 12161400   N             N4       A      X
    46014  57411 12160755   A      410              A      X
    LOCO    LOCTN  DEPTIM  OPRSTA REASOS RESTWK LOCBKE TRNBKE
    46015  57401 11201550   W      600              H      X
    46016  78520 10232350   X      614              A      X
    46017  84090 12130815   X      XAM              A      X
    46018  82099 12161129   N                      A      X
    46019  67115 12081200   F      FRE    NH       A      X
    46020  82099 12161129   N                      A      X
    46021  78520 00000000   N                      H      X
    46022  13551 12171035   N             NH       A      X
    46023  82099 00000000   X      OTD              H      X
    46024  57401 03061800   R      FOR              H      X
    46025  76090 12160800   N                      H      X
    LOCO    LOCTN  DEPTIM  OPRSTA REASOS RESTWK LOCBKE TRNBKE
    46026  84090 12081835   M      XAM              A      X
    46027  66320 12170430   N                      A      X
    46028  84090 12162343   N             MR       A      X
    47024  73000 12171515   N                      A      X
    47026  84090 12150900   X      XAM    MR       H      X
    47027  07267 12140830   X      112    NH       A      X
    47028  84090 12121445   X      XAM              A      X
    47031  12714 12161752   N                      A      X
    47032  42121 11250500   W      REC              A      X
    47035  82099 12161325   N                      A      X
    47136  59239 12171730   N             MR       A      X
    LOCO    LOCTN  DEPTIM  OPRSTA REASOS RESTWK LOCBKE TRNBKE
```

```
    LOCO    LOCTN  DEPTIM  OPRSTA REASOS RESTWK LOCBKE TRNBKE
    47137  54311 12171815   N                      A      X
    47477  42159 12171738   N                      A      X
    47478  79304 12171325   N                      A      X
    47479  16412 12171750   N                      A      X
    47484  85734 12171735   N                      A      X
    47495  42121 11051100   W      GEN              A      X
    47496  84090 12151000   T      OTD    M4       A      X
    47497  52230 12171530   N                      A      X
    47498  84139 12171321   N                      A      X
    47499  84090 11291005   M      XAM              H      X
    47507  42121 10040930   W      410              A      X
    LOCO    LOCTN  DEPTIM  OPRSTA REASOS RESTWK LOCBKE TRNBKE
    50001  84139 12171530   N                      H      X
    50002  84090 12070425   X      XAM              A      X
    50003  73000 12171735   N                      A      X
    50004  84090 12171740   N                      A      X
    50005  84139 12171825   N                      A      X
    50006  23419 05210205   W      410              A      X
    50007  84090 12171425   N                      A      X
    50008  84139 12171930   N                      H      X
    50009  23419 11151620   W      110              A      X
    50010  73000 12171345   N                      A      X
    50011  23419 03211000   W      410              H      X
    LOCO    LOCTN  DEPTIM  OPRSTA REASOS RESTWK LOCBKE TRNBKE
    50012  84090 10050300   M      410              A      X
    50013  84139 12171630   N                      A      X
    50014  84090 12170040   X      100              A      X
    50015  85734 12171410   N                      A      X
    50016  85301 12171630   N             MR       A      X
    50017  76357 12171025   N                      A      X
    50018  84090 12171325   N                      A      X
    50019  84090 12171750   N                      A      X
    50020  73000 12171430   N                      A      X
    50021  84090 12152216   X      DLZ              A      X
    50022  76357 12171625   N                      A      X
    LOCO    LOCTN  DEPTIM  OPRSTA REASOS RESTWK TRN
    50023  73000 12171715   N                      A      X
    50024  23419 06091335   W      INT              A      X
    50025  93626 12161905   N                      H      X
    50026  81700 12170730   N                      A      X
    50027  84090 12160205   X      450              A      X
    50028  23419 06290645   W      INT              H      X
    50029  84139 12171825   N             NH       A      X
    50030  83400 12171112   F      LOP              A      X
    50031  73000 12171716   N                      A      X
    50032  84139 12171430   N                      A      X
    50033  84090 12160330   X      XAM    FW       A      X
    LOCO    LOCTN  DEPTIM  OPRSTA REASOS RESTWK LOCBKE TRNBKE
    50034  84090 12051140   M      410              A      X
    50035  85734 12162126   N                      A      X
    50036  83421 12171526   N                      A      X
    50037  23419 08220609   W      INT              A      X
    50038  85734 00000000   N                      A      X
    50045  84090 11142310   M      151              A      X
    50046  76357 12171640   N                      A      X
    50047  73000 12171915   N                      A      X
    50048  73220 12162105   N                      A      X
    50049  73000 12171800   N                      A      X
    50050  84090 12171735   N                      H      X
END
```

Complete list of diesel locomotives allocated to Laira T&RSD in December 1978.

Diesel Locomotives allocated to Laira on the dates shown were as follows:

	Class 08	Class 25	Class 37	Class 46	Class 47	Class 50
17/12/78	7	10	2	28	19	44
14/02/82	14	X	5	X	22	40

In the spring of 1982 Laira also had an allocation of 18 High Speed Train sets and 16 Diesel Multiple Units.

Shortly before eight o'clock on the following Sunday morning, I reported at Laira Depot. The Traffic Assistant (TA) and the Outside Movements Supervisor (OMS) shared the same office. I knocked and walked in, introduced myself, 'Morning, I'm Rod Fowkes, learning the Movements Supervisor's post,' hand outstretched, and met Bill Nance for the first time; he was the early turn TA. There followed a stony silence, an almost icy atmosphere, then

Bill managed to mumble something, and promptly went out of his way to exchange pleasantries with a driver who was just signing on duty. If that reception was anything to go by it was made perfectly clear that any irruption from other Regions was less than welcome here. Bob Mitchell then arrived on duty and appeared more affable, and over the next few weeks Bill Nance did become a little more receptive. I was looking forward to meeting Harry Ough; he was the person on the other end of the telephone when I used to ring up the depot from Toton to ascertain who had been appointed to the position I now occupied. Despite being a diabetic, Harry, an ex-footplateman, had a pleasant disposition and was always very helpful, totally different from Bill Nance who had also been a driver. Henry, the other regular TA who I would train with, was from the Southern Region and proud of the fact, whilst the rest day reliefman to the Traffic Assistant was an ex-controller.

Laira TMD is within the embrace of a triangle whereby both locomotives and rolling stock could be turned, and in the case of coaching stock the formation could also be reversed. Prior to the building of the HST depot in 1981, the running line to Friary goods yard ran through the carriage sidings, and the depot at that time received its fuel from the nearby Cattedown wharf by rail tankers.

In addition to providing full train formations, several 2/3-coach diner portions were diagrammed to attach

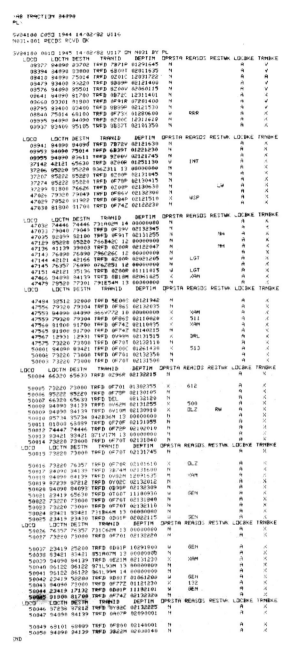

Complete list of diesel locomotives allocated to Laira T&RSD in February 1982.

in Plymouth station (still referred to by many as North Road) to the flagship InterCity services in the West Country, the *Golden Hind*, the *Cornish Riviera* and the *Cornishman*. A long distance loco-hauled cross-country service, the

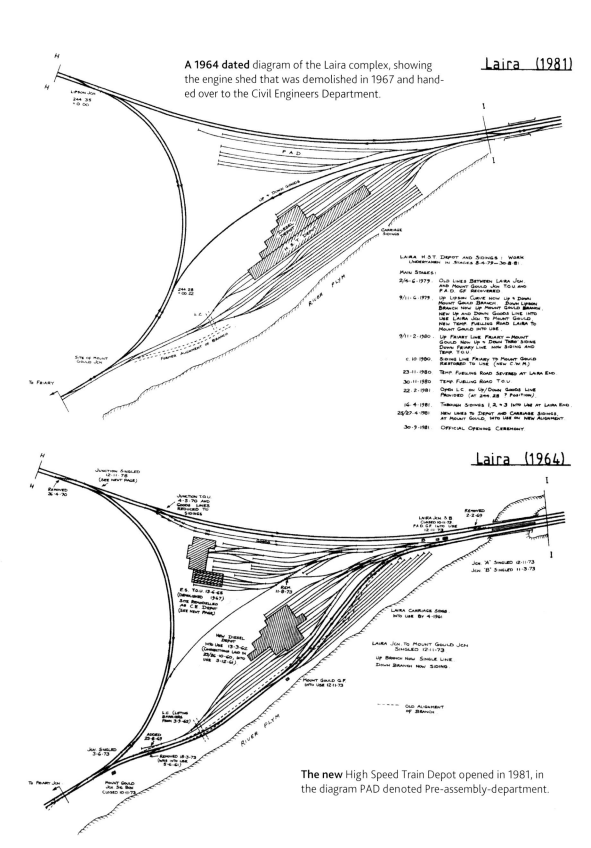

A 1964 dated diagram of the Laira complex, showing the engine shed that was demolished in 1967 and handed over to the Civil Engineers Department.

Laira (1981)

LAIRA H.S.T. DEPOT AND SIDINGS : WORK UNDERTAKEN IN STAGES 8·4·79—30·8·81

MAIN STAGES :

2/4·6·1979. OLD LINES BETWEEN LAIRA JCN. AND MOUNT GOULD JCN T.O.U. AND P.A.D. G.F. RECOVERED

9/11·6·1979. UP LIPSON CURVE NOW UP & DOWN MOUNT GOULD BRANCH. DOWN LIPSON BRANCH NOW UP MOUNT GOULD BRANCH. NEW UP AND DOWN GOODS LINE INTO USE LAIRA JCN. TO MOUNT GOULD. NEW TEMP. FUELLING ROAD LAIRA TO MOUNT GOULD INTO USE.

9/11·2·1980. UP FRIARY LINE FRIARY — MOUNT GOULD NOW UP & DOWN THRO' SIDING. DOWN FRIARY LINE NOW SIDING AND TEMP. T.O.U.

c. 10·1980. SIDING LINE FRIARY TO MOUNT GOULD RESTORED TO USE (NEW C.W.R.)

23·11·1980. TEMP. FUELLING ROAD SEVERED AT LAIRA END.

30·11·1980. TEMP. FUELLING ROAD T.O.U.

22·2·1981. OPEN L.C. ON UP/DOWN GOODS LINE PROVIDED (AT 244·28 ? POSITION).

16·4·1981. THROUGH SIDINGS 1, 2 & 3 INTO USE AT LAIRA END.

25/27·4·1981. NEW LINES TO DEPOT AND CARRIAGE SIDINGS, AT MOUNT GOULD, INTO USE ON NEW ALIGNMENT.

30·9·1981. OFFICIAL OPENING CEREMONY.

Laira (1964)

The new High Speed Train Depot opened in 1981, in the diagram PAD denoted Pre-assembly-department.

Guards Train Loading Report for the 09.50 (Friday) Edinburgh to Plymouth before the additional coach was attached.

Additional coach now conveyed on the 09.50 (Friday) Edinburgh to Plymouth.

07.36 Plymouth to Edinburgh and the 09.50 return train, was initially formed of air-braked Mark II abc dual-heated stock until sufficient air-conditioned Mark II def vehicles became available.

Formed of BG BSO 4TSO RBR FO FK 3TSO, the train afforded seating for 500 standard and 84 first class passengers. The accommodation on the Anglo-Scottish service wasn't sufficient on Fridays or Sundays, certainly south-west bound, when the guard's train loading report regularly showed the train full and standing over considerable distances. A further perennial problem, compounded by the sheer number of passengers, was the state of the toilets: many were regularly blocked, having run out of water hours earlier, which wasn't appropriate for the image of InterCity travel. I made various representations to the local manager and also to the NE/SW Investigator at Derby who was at the time none other than Jack Henshaw, late of QSS at Toton. Locally there was little interest, although Ken Hall did speak to the Bristol Divisional Office about the overcrowding, whilst Jack, the fuddy-duddy that he was, promised to take it on board with the other thousand and one things that required his attention. The overcrowding continued year round, and my persistence eventually paid off in that Tony, the passenger rolling stock clerk in the Divisional Manager's Office at Bristol, finally succumbed to my badgering of increasing the load by an extra TSO from Plymouth on Thursday, remaining in circuit Friday, returning to Scotland on

Saturday and being detached at Laira on the Sunday night. The arrangement continued until the service went over to HST working in 1982. The topping up of the toilet tanks en route was also done at York and Bristol as and when time permitted.

After completing my training, and taking charge of the OMS position, it was then time to learn the Traffic Assistant's duties, which were akin to those of Traincrew Supervisor at Toton, excepting that the complex with its single line between Laira Junction and Mount Gould Junction required a biennial rules examination that was undertaken by John Forrester at Bristol. A clerical officer, Ron Snell, undertook the rostering of enginemen, guards, shunters, carriage cleaners, workobus drivers and supervisors. Although a Bristol Control Office function, the Traffic Assistants' jealously regarded the allocating of power as their integral duty. The Traction Controller was responsible for the depots at Penzance, Exeter, Bristol Bath Road, Westbury and Gloucester – St Blazey being largely self-contained – and would furnish the numbers of all locomotives on trains to Plymouth and into Cornwall as well as ECS moves from Exeter off the Waterloo line into Laira. Regional Headquarters Paddington also advised the diesels arriving on the depot, which were due 'A' exams. Locomotive diagrams for Western Region depots, together with extracts from those on the LMR and ER — namely Crewe, Toton, Tinsley, Holbeck and Gateshead, whose locos worked into the south-west — were formulated into a simplifier.

Balances were usually maintained, with the exception of the early morning departures, which had diesels that had been released off maintenance on the previous late turn. One particular tight balance was the Holbeck Class 45 off the *Cornishman*, due on the depot around 14.15 and off again at 15.48 to work the 16.18 Plymouth to Birmingham. No problem here if it required just fuel and water, but an 'A' exam and/ or brake block change was extremely tight as the maintenance shift changeover was 14.30. Derek Land, a Senior Shift Maintenance Supervisor

	INWARDS – MONDAY – SATURDAY			1979/80	
	0027 Exeter R/Side	MSX		0001 St.Bz-Longport	WO
	0130 LD Exeter-St.B	MSX HST		0515 Pz-Paddn	
	1816 Sittingbourne	MO		0624 Pz - Paddn	
	0030 Paddington			0747 Pz - Lpool	
	0005 Paddington			0834 Pz-Paddn	
	2343 Paddington Pcls	MX		0922 Pz-Paddn	SX
	0450 N.Abbot ECS	SO		Plymouth	SO
	0010 Severn T.Jcn	MX		1023 Pz - Leeds	
	1728 Ince & E & Assist	TO		1100 Pz-Plymouth ECS	FO
	2327 Fawley & Assist	MWO HST		1121 Pz - Paddn	
	0300 Bristol(2120 Bham)	MX		1220 Pz - Paddn	
	0650 Exeter R/Side	MO		1245 Pz - Crewe Pcls	SX
	0710 Exeter			1356 Pz - Bgham	
	2049 Bradford	MX		1510 Truro-Ince & E	MO
	0635 Bristol	HST		1500 Pz - Paddn	
	0345 Severn T Jcn	MX		1510 Pz - Paddn Pcls	SX
	0802 Bristol			1609 Pz - Paddn	
HST	0710 Paddington			1620 Pz-Clapham Milk	SO
	0756 Cardiff			1642 St.Erth-Wood Lane Milk	SX
	0830 Paddington			1810 St.Bz-Longport	SX
	0916 Gloster (0815 Bham)			1835 St.Bz-Friary	SX
	0935 Paddington			1806 Pz-Sheffield	SX
H.S.T.	1030 Paddington			Bristol	SO
	0735 Leeds (0656 Bford SO)			2015 B'gullow-S'Bourne	ThO
H.S.T.	1140 Paddington			1927 Pz-Paddn	SX
	1218 Gloster (0920 Lpool)			2050 St.Bz - T'Mills	SX
	1215 Bham (1023 Manchr)			2120 St.B-Carlisle	SX
	1330 Paddington			2135 Pz - Paddn	
	1045 Scombe	ThSX			
	0424 Stoke-on-Trent				
	1530 Paddington				
	1617 Gloster (1322 Lpool)				
	1545 Bristol Pcls	MSX			
	1630 Paddington	SX			
	0950 Edinburgh				
H.S.T.	1740 Paddington				
	1818 Gloster (1439 Leeds)				
	0805 Stoke-on-Trent	WO			
	1830 Paddington (1829 FO)				
	1833 Paddington	FO			
	1930 Paddington				
	2120 Bristol (1848 Paddn FO)				
	2030 Paddington	SO			

Traffic assistant's incoming list. The traction controller at Bristol would furnish the locomotive numbers of all incoming services to Plymouth and into Cornwall. HSTs had been introduced on selected workings.

On occasions, poor availability of Class '50' locomotives necessitated the usage of Brush Class '47s' that had a lower fuel capacity, although later, some were fitted with extra fuel tanks, giving them an extended range. Traction control would monitor the fuel position commensurate with the mileage of the diagram. Pictured here skirting the sea wall at Dawlish is an unidentified '47' with an eastbound express.

told me he staffed the diesel with all available personnel, this being an overriding attitude down in the south-west (compare this with the previous details of working at Toton).

As a general rule, when allocating diesels to diagrams Class 47s would suffice if a Class 50 was not available; the Control would then monitor the fuel position. At the behest of the maintenance department, some diesels released off exam/repair would work the first trip into Cornwall. If any problems came to light, the loco could be taken off at Plymouth on its return. Those released

One of the ubiquitous BR/Sulzer Class '45s', which could be found working in most geographical locations, the exceptions being the Southern Region and north Scotland.

50042 *Triumph* worked its last train in October 1990 and was withdrawn the same month due to it being surplus to requirements, becoming the twenty-third Class 50 to be withdrawn after over twenty-two years of active service. Here, passing Lipson Junction with the 15.05 Plymouth-Manchester, the locomotive was eventually purchased by the Bodmin & Wenford Diesel Group.

Emerged from Derby Works in 1961 as D20, withdrawn in 1987 from Tinsley, and carried the unofficial name *Wyvern*. Stored at March Depot before being cut up at M.C. Metals, Springburn, Glasgow, in February 1994. Photographed arriving at Laira Depot.

off major exams – D and E – usually had a light trial run to Totnes before being attached to the 08.23 from Plymouth to Penzance with a QCI riding. For sheer devilment, and much to the annoyance of my relief, Henry Hooper, the ex-Southern stationmaster, I often booked a Class 45 on the 03.00 (02.50 MO) parcels to Penzance. Perhaps what may well have been an unprecedented occurrence was the overnight stabling of no less than three Toton-based Class 45s at Penzance on 3 January 1982 – 45103, 45107 and 45111. Apart from the Brush electrical equipment, the Class 46 of which Laira had an allocation was in all other respects mechanically similar to the Class 45, and one of these locomotives was diagrammed to work the Saturday Newquay-Manchester forward from Plymouth. If a Class 46 was unavailable, then a Class 47 would be substituted, but not a 45 owing to traction knowledge as the train was booked to run via Craven Arms.

The procedure for trains arriving at Laira carriage sidings was that they were propelled through the wash plant into the sidings; the train engine was then released to the depot. The carriage and wagon staff would then examine the coaches and carry out brake block changes in the sidings if required. For the departures, the yard pilot would draw the coaches out of the siding towards Friary and the train engine would then be attached; it was also possible to reverse the formations out via Laira Junction. There were two shunters on each shift. On the night turn they would normally walk past the office on the way into the shed to see what moves, if any, the maintenance supervisor required. It was patently obvious to me from the outset that there were not two shunters on duty much after midnight, any night. So, what do you do about it? A practice that had gone on since time immemorial, do you call a halt to it and make yourself highly unpopular, knowing full well that the following week normal working would apply? Did it matter anyway? The work was getting done by the one man instead of the two which were required, safety being compromised by the plunger in the cupboard wedged with a piece of wood, which allowed the yard pilot back into the sidings, when the other shunter, instead of on duty, was at home in bed. When mentioned to one of the other outside movement's supervisors he looked at me in total disbelief, wondering no doubt which planet this fellow had dropped in from. The irregular working arrangements would cease with the opening of the new HST depot, although the procedures for clocking on and off would continue to be abused by some.

In looking for property, I was dependent on estate agents taking me around; then, the majority of houses up for sale did not have 'for sale' boards outside. As my car was back with my family in Sawley, I asked the Traincrew Manager if one of the many vehicles kept at the depot could be put at my disposal, a request that was firmly declined despite my agreeing to keep the fuel topped up. It was one of the reasons for changing most of my early turns for the late shift, as when finishing at 14.00 I had the rest of the day to myself; the novelty of walking down to Plymouth Hoe quickly abated. However, one

HMS *Ark Royal*, fresh from fly-on-the-wall series *Sailor*, was decommissioned at Devonport Dockyard in 1978, and moored in the Hamoaze until September 1980, before being towed to Cairnryan.

evening on the Hoe and looking over towards Devonport, the giant aircraft carrier *Eagle* was moored in the River Tamar where it had been for some considerable time. I set off walking in the general direction in order to obtain a better view. It was certainly a long trek and I ended up well beyond the vessel almost at the Torpoint Ferry. Not long after, *Eagle* was towed out of the Hamoaze to a Scottish breaker's yard at Cairnryan. Two months later, in December 1978, another aircraft carrier, *Ark Royal* arrived in Plymouth for the last time for decommissioning. *Ark Royal*, a celebrity from the BBC TV fly-on-the-wall series *Sailor*, would also be moored in the Hamoaze until September 1980, before being towed to the same breaker's yard at Cairnryan.

On one occasion when on duty on the Sunday night turn, I travelled down on the 16.10 Derby-Plymouth, a loco-hauled set which stabled at Laira until the following Friday before working the 12.30 to Manchester, primarily for matelots going home on leave for the weekend and relieving pressure on the *Cornishman*. Returning to my digs just after seven o'clock on the Monday morning, and just about to put the key into the lock, the door opened and the landlord appeared, full of apologies, lamenting on having let my room. After being up for almost twenty-four hours and none too pleased, I ambled down to the Hoe and curled up under one of the shelters for an hour or two. When on the late turn, a normal daily ritual would consist of, after breakfast, walking down North Hill visiting the many estate agents with a cursory visit to Debenhams and Dingles department stores, then to the market for some onions to go with the cheese and rolls for packing up. This was rounded off with stew and dumplings at the jacket potato shop.

During the period I was lodging I often travelled home on the *Cornishman* 10.23 Penzance-Bradford, which left Plymouth at 12.40 after attaching a diner portion and a fresh loco. Having spoken to the Bath Road driver, I rode with him on the 'Peak', initially as far as Bristol Temple Meads. The Saltley driver then told me I could 'stay put' and I continued to Birmingham New Street.

Beyond Westerleigh Junction to the top of the Lickey Incline, the power handle was wide open except for the slowing over Standish Junction, Gloucester avoiding line and through Cheltenham station. Those Saltley lads certainly waltzed the twelve coaches along at high speeds, the smell of the fuel percolating through the engine room door. During a conversation with the driver, the subject of Toton came up, and he remembered Bill Jacques, who had moved from Saltley or Rugby some twenty years earlier.

By and large the Laira drivers spoke well of the 'Peak' diesels, some preferring them to a Class 47. One spoke volumes of ascending the South Devon banks, Dainton and Rattery, with the Down *Cornishman* made up to fourteen coaches on a summer Saturday. On my arrival the Class 46s were being gradually moved out of the south-west, some were withdrawn and despatched to Swindon Works, while the remainder were concentrated at Gateshead depot and monopolised the Midland Main Line.

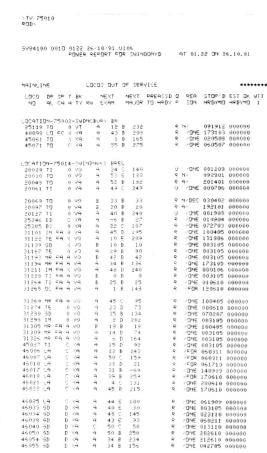

Eight of Laira's allocation of Class '46s' and seven from Gateshead were amongst other condemned locomotives languishing at Swindon in 1981.

Easing slowly over the 'Speedway' crossing on the way to the depot for servicing before taking up its next duty, the 10.23am Penzance to Bradford (12.40pm ex-Plymouth) the *Cornishman* is 'Peak' 45144 *Royal Signals* after working out the coaching stock off the 06.35 Bristol to Plymouth, to the flushing apron.

Monopolising the Midland Main Line until the introduction of HSTs in 1982; the Class 45s, in addition to CrossCountry work, then became regular performers on the Trans Pennine route, working services from Liverpool Lime Street and North Wales to Scarborough and Newcastle. Withdrawn in 1988, 'Peak' 45124 is at rest at St Pancras.

Later, the Class 45s, held sway over the north-east/south-west axis for some years, would also be seen in fewer numbers after the introduction of HSTs over the CrossCountry route. The 45/1 Peaks, still allocated to Toton, then found work across the Trans-Pennine route on services from Liverpool and North Wales to Scarborough and Newcastle. Cycling the locomotives back to the parent depot for exam and repairs could be a problem, and Longsight and Allerton depots assisted in providing facilities when problems arose.

It is with some regret that I unintentionally brought about the premature banishment of the Peak diesels, west of Bristol. It all came about by a chance remark to one R.J. (Bob) Poynter, Regional Operations Manager on the Western Region. He had arrived at Nottingham just before I left for Toton, and he certainly stamped his authority on the GWR. Very often, when riding in the cab he would speak to the Deputy Chief Controller at Swindon and demand an explanation when sighting adverse signals. He commanded respect, and when his presence was imminent there was usually a sense of urgency about the place, management staff in particular having a spring in their step. An unexpected visit to Laira T&RSD in the summer of 1985 by the Area Manager 'Jim Collins' accompanied by Bob Poynter was a case in point. They had come to look over the coaching stock being cleaned for the lunchtime Exeter-Waterloo service. As we returned to my office we passed BR/Sulzer Type '4' No. 45109, forlorn looking, on the stop blocks of the oil road. It was then a comment turned out to be an act of crass stupidity was directed to RJP. Bob listened intently as I told him that 45109, allocated to Toton had been languishing at Laira for almost three weeks 'waiting material'. It had previously had had an 'A' exam at Leeds (Neville Hill depot) on the Friday prior to working empty stock to York, a relief train to Plymouth and empty coaching stock to Laira. When the loco was being serviced it was found to have a number of wafer thin brake blocks, others missing and some brake hangers hard on the wheels.

Receiving an update on the condition of the locomotive from the Maintenance Supervisor, RJP spoke to the Traction Maintenance Controller at Swindon and asked why the loco had not been hauled back to Toton. Obviously he was far from satisfied with the reply, as his clenched fist hit the desk with a crashing blow. Bob exclaimed 'I'll stop these diesels coming down the south-west!' He was as good as his word. A directive was issued to the Traction Controllers that was rigidly adhered to, that Class 45 locos were not to work west of Bristol unless on an out-and-home basis with a Bath Road driver. The LMR, however, continued to send 'Peaks' down from Birmingham, and on occasions trains were overtime at Bristol Temple Meads, changing (and sometimes waiting for) a replacement locomotive to work the train forward. The Laira drivers noticed the absence of the 'Peaks', and some reflected what excellent performers they had been over the South Devon Banks. I reminded them, of course, that they had also been worked extremely hard over the Midland Main Line into and out of St Pancras for over twenty years. Now, alas, through a cursory ill-timed remark to a high-ranking official, an era had come to an end.

The winter months spent in lodgings was not becoming any more palatable. By chance, calling into an estate agent's office one morning brought about a visit to a village some 6 miles from Plymouth to view a property. Heavy snow restricted the road into Wembury to single track in places, and the strong easterly winds had caused severe drifting. I well remember walking into the four-bedroom semi-detached house and into the lounge where it was that cold that one's breath issued to atmosphere, despite the fact that the property was occupied. Possibly in desperation, I told the estate agent to draw up the necessary papers for the purchase of the property. I had agreed to buy a house that my wife hadn't even seen. We had already sold the house in Sawley and the family were staying with Maureen's parents. They had all previously stayed in a flat near the Hoe for a couple of days on a flying visit and the only other property that might have been of interest was at Plympton near the foot of the Hemerdon incline. After a further delay with the previous occupants relinquishing the property, Maureen and the flock moved down from the East Midlands in March 1979. The necessary arrangements for schooling had been made, and whilst Janet went off to the local primary like a little trooper the day after arriving, Alan, on the other hand, was extremely reticent and took a while to settle into his new school. An unusual situation indeed, whereby a purchase of a property was initiated by man alone; the large garden and near the sea should please them, and it did.

Don Banbury, the Outside Movements Supervisor who was on the shift with Harry Ough, and the rest-day reliefman, Ken (Doc) Ley, had been interviewed for the post that I now occupied, both being receptive in a cool sort of way, although Ken made it abundantly clear that he was most disgruntled not to have been appointed. Each weekday morning the tiresome task of the outside supervisor was to give the passenger rolling stock section at Bristol details of all the rolling stock on hand, whether spare or under maintenance, and the vehicle numbers of all services leaving Laira – tedious to say the least! The liaison between the operating and maintenance departments at Laira Depot had over the years been problematic; a distinct 'them and us' syndrome had been rife over a long period, not helped perhaps by the fact that the Area Manager was located at Plymouth station although a Traincrew Manager was housed at Laira. Up until the mid-to-late 1970s the train crews at the depot responded to the Area Maintenance Engineer, and both enginemen and guards held Harry Hamer in high esteem, as incidentally did the troops on the shop floor. By the time I arrived at the depot Harry had moved on to headquarters. The Area Maintenance Engineer was Ian Cusworth, a likeable graduate who also lived in Wembury. Ian went on to headquarters himself some years later and became Director, Fleet, at Swindon for the privatised Great Western Trains Company. He wasn't considered a dynamic AME, and when the opportunity presented itself on more than one occasion to sort out the maintenance supervisors, the issues were fudged and apathy remained supreme.

Whereas the Traction Arranger at Toton instructed the shed drivers on the stabling of locomotives and the associated moves into and out of the depot, at Laira it was different. The Senior Shift Maintenance Supervisor would arrange his moves with the shed drivers (turners); they would then stable the outgoing locomotives on an appropriate road. When the Traffic Assistant did his allocations for the following shift (he had already been

All ready and waiting to go, a Class '45', two Class '47s' and four Class '50s' are on view. No. 50027 *Lion*, front right with 'large logo' livery, compare this photograph of 50027 to that on page 150.

given a list of incoming diesels by the Traction Controller), a sheet was prepared for the Servicing Supervisor and the shed turners, and there was at the time a separate servicing shed. Normally locomotives released off repair/exam would be allocated before the incoming ones, assuming that it was the correct type of traction. The servicing shed was later demolished to make way for the HST depot; from then on the Movements Supervisor would play a bigger part in instructing the shed turners of movements required. As reflected earlier, maintenance depots and their staff do not have the same urgency as we operators; there were differing priorities. There is always an exception to this, and at Laira it was in the form of Derek Land, a Senior Shift Maintenance Supervisor. He worked in parallel with Harry Ough, who was seldom seen struggling for power. Often extremely critical, Derek would show his displeasure if there was any deviation from his requirements. When I was covering the Movements Supervisor, he often berated me for insisting that the 00.30 Exeter-Laira DMU went through the wash-plant before being berthed for servicing. Many was the occasion when out in the yard Derek would appear, his inimitable bulging eyes a trademark of his irritation, declaring, 'Don't forget, the railcars can go into service without being washed, but not without being maintained.' He was right of course, and although he'd made his point, the shed would not have the units until they had been washed, because often there was insufficient time to put them through the wash-plant after servicing. This was not the case, however, with the other outside men, who felt positively ill at ease. Consequently the units ran direct into the shed without being washed or tanked and some would enter service in that condition. There was a distinct difference in attitude between the footplatemen at Laira to those at Toton. Drivers at the LMR depot would be looking to be signing off duty after six and a half hours, while those on the fuel line would be looking for an even earlier finish. It was, therefore, surprising to hear the Traffic Assistant instruct a driver who had been on duty seven hours to get so-and-so diesel ready (twenty minutes) and 'put your ticket in', it being universally accepted as par for the course at Laira. By and large the enginemen responded well to problems encountered out on the road, as did the supervisors, but then you would expect them to. Whether it was a diesel failure or a locomotive in difficulty on one of the South Devon Banks, which was prevalent during poor rail conditions and in the leaf fall season, the response was immediate.

There was a degree of frustration by both drivers and guards at Laira relating to the content of some train crew diagrams. Many involved travelling to and from Plymouth station by service car; the fifteen-minute journey in each direction was often restrictive, especially in the days of the eight-hour diagram prior to flexible rostering.

The activity content of some turns was abysmal, often spending a couple of hours at Bristol Temple Meads waiting their back working, and at Exeter a great deal longer. A classic example of this concerned a Sunday working, the

14.40 Plymouth-Paddington, which the Laira crew worked as far as Exeter. An Exeter crew relieved them and worked to Paddington and back, and the same Laira crew who had been at Exeter for over four hours again relieved them. Determined to redress this, I did some calculations and the diagrams were later re-issued for the Laira enginemen to work the 14.40 ex-Plymouth as far as Westbury. As the guards didn't sign the road over the Berks and Hants they would still be relieved at Exeter. The re-issued diagrams were more productive in alleviating the waiting time at Exeter for the Laira enginemen; it also reduced the mileage payment for the Exeter crew.

The heavy stone working programme in the Westbury area accounted for two daily light engine moves from Laira at 05.00 and 14.10. The odd thing about the two diagrams was that they both constituted mileage turns, which were paid even if the turn was cancelled. It was a ludicrous situation, made even more so by the fact that the return leg never ran anyway. Writing to Ken Hall, I pointed out the need to amend the content of the two diagrams, which read 'return LD or as required.' What was needed was the LD being deleted and altered to read 'return as ordered' (RAO); the diagrams were later re-issued with a considerable saving in mileage payments.

Unbalanced locomotives were generally sent to Westbury, Brush Class 47s being the obvious choice although Class 46s would suffice, but not the Class 45s owing to traction knowledge restricting their use to the various destinations. Once, when relieved by Bill Nance, he turned over the night outgoing sheet to find that two locos had gone 05.00 to Westbury. He retorted: 'You don't want to give power away like that; we want to build some up for the weekend.' It was a Tuesday!

London was always short of power, as was Bath Road come to that. Frequently, Bob Morris, the Traction Controller at Bristol, would tell me that he hadn't got a wheel at Bath Road. So, if enginemen and a diesel were available it would be despatched; equally, at the start of each turn enquiries would be made to ascertain if there were any crippled diesel locomotives to fetch from any location.

When RHQ Paddington came on to give the 'A' exams, the conversation centred on the availability of locos. If they required additional traction they would put the request through Bristol. Two Class 50s were put in multiple for the 05.47 to Paddington long before advice was received from Bristol. One morning, owing to overnight tamping work on the line at Ivybridge, there was no path available for the 05.00 light engine to Westbury. Bill Harris was the driver and always wanted to 'get done'. Speaking to the Control, I suggested the loco for Westbury be attached to the 05.47 as far as Taunton; this they agreed. The 05.47 to Paddington already had two 50s in multiple and, with the additional Class 47 on, the Guard told me the following day that it was the fastest ascent of Hemerdon Bank that he had ever known!

Whilst travelling back to Plymouth one day on the *Cornishman*, I joined Bill up front at Bristol. As soon as the 'right away' was given, the power handle of

Built 1965 at Crewe Works as D1966, later renumbered to 47266 before 47629, and then operated as 47828 and named *Joe Strummer*. Pictured at Laira after working in from the LMR in the 1970s, when as 47266 it was an ideal candidate for Westbury.

the '45' was opened almost fully before being eased back. We were over the points under the overbridge, when suddenly the power handle was slammed shut. 'Bloody hell,' he cried. 'I'd forgotten about that on the rear.' 'That' was a dynamometer car for detachment at Plymouth with the diner portion. Bill would only sit down a couple of times before reaching Plymouth. He was an extremely fit individual whose pastime was diving, and it came as quite a shock to all at the depot when he died from a heart attack.

The catering vehicles out of the CrossCountry and the domestic loco-hauled coaching stock were sent to Newton Abbot for the periodic cleaning of the kitchens. When the HST depot opened in 1981 the carriage sidings at Newton Abbot closed, and the maintenance and cleaning of the coaching stock off the Waterloo-Exeter route was undertaken at Laira. That initially realised four sets of coaches off the 15.15, 17.10, 18.10 and 19.10 ex-Waterloo, three sets coming down ECS from Exeter, the other varying from running as a passenger train to Newton Abbot or Plymouth. As a result of the Newton Abbot rationalisation the shunters and carriage cleaners were also transferred to Laira, the former reflecting on the fact that seldom were trains short-formed as was the case when the work was relocated. The standard of carriage cleaning on the Southern Region was quite lamentable; whether undertaken at Clapham or Eastleigh the Mark II abc vehicles, often away from the parent depot for three days, returned in need of a good clean. The appearance at Laira of the odd Eastleigh-based coaching stock on a Saturday working from Brighton emphasised the lack of cleaning both internally and externally, supposedly to have been undertaken on the Southern Region. Before the flush-apron and wash-plant were rebuilt in connection with the introduction of HST working, the watering of the toilets was done in the carriage sidings by Fred Rawnsley. A menial task maybe, but he certainly made an excellent job of polishing the grab rails and the door handles which in later years would be painted over. What would not be tolerated today, of course, would be the dropping of the contents of blocked toilets onto the ballast and sleepers in the sidings.

The Control Office in Plymouth had now closed, two of the controllers became supervisors on the station, and a further two came out to Laira as shift clerks, with a third following a short time later. The post of shift clerk was introduced to enable the Traffic Assistant to oversee the carriage cleaning; that obviously went down like a lead balloon with Bill Nance and Henry Hooper. The thinking behind it, no doubt, was the fact that the Movements Supervisor was now more pre-occupied with actual movements and the associated shunting, which ensued after the opening of the HST depot.

Visiting Laira one day in his capacity of Passenger Officer in the Divisional Manager's Office at Bristol was A.W. (Tony) Smith; he had appointed me to my first position on British Railways some twenty-five years earlier. Tony was often referred to as running the Bristol Private Railway, often ignoring the higher echelons at RHQ Paddington, who were oblivious to the various happenings in the south-west.

During the summer holiday season, the Cardiff (Canton)-based four-coach vacuum sets working into Cornwall were totally inadequate. Strengthening was undertaken at Plymouth on the 08.23 and 10.20 to Penzance (07.02 Exeter and 07.50 Bristol). With spare vacuum stock at a premium, Tony Smith authorised the use of the Etches Park rake of coaches that worked the 16.10 from Derby on a Sunday and which laid over at Laira until the following Friday. The underlying problem was not attaching the vehicles in Plymouth, but of taking them off on the return Up working from Cornwall. It was particularly time consuming, with the station allowance often being exceeded, detaching front off the 18.08 Penzance-Sheffield 'Mail', which conveyed a mixture of passenger coaches and parcel vans, and then attaching further parcel vans on the rear at Plymouth. The two additional strengthening vehicles were then held in the station for the following day. The arrangement applied on a Monday to Thursday; there were no vehicles available to do any strengthening on a Friday. Indeed, it was touch and go at the time as to whether we would get the vehicles back together in time to form the 12.30 to Manchester. Tony was very well aware of what was required in Devon and Cornwall and went out of his way to improve the accommodation on overcrowded services, probably knowing full well that RHQ might well have placed an embargo on proceedings, or by the time they got around to looking at the request, it would have been too late anyway. When the DMO at Bristol closed he would, however, pay the penalty for the years of doing his own thing and ignoring the higher authority at Paddington. Tony Smith, an experienced and dedicated railwayman retired to the Isle of Arran. Over the years he penned many interesting and informative articles, supplementing his photographs to various railway periodicals, including a series for *Trains Illustrated* in 1961 entitled, *The problems of train regulation – a study of operation at Trent* by Warren Smith. He also put his collection of photographs at my disposal for my book *Last Days of Steam on the LMS & BR*.

Customer Care was very lax in the early 1980s. Some years earlier, as a matter of course, steam heating pipes were removed from coaching stock for the summer period – maybe it was warmer then. One aspect that concerned me intensely was the lack of heating on the overnight summer seasonal trains. Overnight travel is uncomfortable at the best of times, even more so when there is no heat on the train. Nights can be particularly cold in June and September and distinctly chilly in July and August, and even more uncomfortable when raining. All very well for the Traction Controllers in their cosy offices, who were responsible for allocating the locomotives, some of which were freight diesels during the week, being pressed into service at the weekends to supplement the main line fleet. The most common problem was when freight locos without any heating apparatus were working the overnight services, and also with a diesel which was capable of providing heating, but unable to do so because the driver was single-manned, which was often the case. Many were the times when on duty on a Friday night that I perused the incoming sheet for signs of the aforementioned and then set about making unscheduled engine changes in Plymouth station on trains with unsuitable traction.

Although this action was not in my remit, my colleagues along with the Traction Controllers, alas, did not share the same values. All that was required was a little thought, a pencil and a rubber – all too easy. Treat the customers right and they will come again; they may well have second thoughts though if the journey is undertaken with coats and the like draped across them. On one particular foul summer's night, a train from the north-west was coming down into Cornwall with a freight loco and obviously no heat. I spoke with Bob Morris and sent a diesel up to Exeter to change locos at that point, at least providing heat for an hour longer than if the unscheduled change had been done at Plymouth. Although those events were suitably logged, very little, and more often than not, nothing was done to alleviate the situation for the following week(s). The happenings of the early hours of the previous Saturday appeared to matter little on the following Monday morning conference. It seemed that no one on the Western Region had enough clout to instruct the Midland to refrain from putting no-heat locomotives on overnight services, although as a result of my continual haranguing, a memo was received in the Control Office in regard to the overnight trains. At last something was seen to have been done.

Drivers and guards at Laira Depot in the 1980s worked no further east than Bristol, although drivers did work to Westbury. Earlier, when the HSTs were being introduced in Devon and Cornwall, LDC 'B' (local departmental

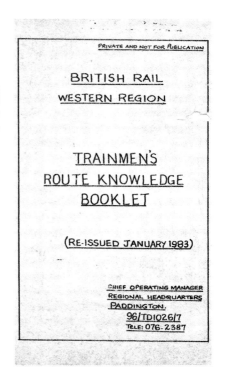

PAGE 27

DEPOT - LAIRA

SECTION 1

	FROM	TO	VIA	DVRS	GDS
1	PLYMOUTH	BRISTOL	Weston-s-Mare (Inc. Av Line). (Not Malgo V.)	✓	✓
2	PLYMOUTH	PENZANCE	-	✓	✓
3	PAR	NEWQUAY	-	✓	✓
4	NEWTON ABBOT	PAIGNTON	-	✓	✓
5	PLYMOUTH	GUNNISLAKE	-	✓	✓
6	LAIRA	MARSH MILLS	-	✓	✓
7	LAIRA	PLYMOUTH FRIARY	-	✓	✓
8	LAIRA	SUTTON HBR	-	✓	✓
9	LAIRA	PLYMSTOCK	-	✓	✓
10	LAIRA	CATTEWATER	-	✓	✓
11	LAIRA	BULL POINT	-	✓	✓
12	LAIRA	DEVONPORT DK YD	-	✓	✓
13	TAUNTON	WESTBURY	-	✓	-

SECTION 2

	FROM	TO	VIA	DVRS	GDS
1	LISKEARD	LOOE	-	✓	-

Routes over which Laira drivers and guards worked.   **Trainmen's Route** Knowledge Booklet.

committee-footplate) were making more rumbling noises regarding the diagrams. There was talk that no training of HSTs would be undertaken unless Laira enginemen worked further afield, London being their goal, as it was in the steam days. That, however, would not be realised until around ten years later. Although Penzance drivers worked through to Exeter, in those days their diagrams were productive, achieving six hours driving out of eight. LDC 'B' sought an assurance from management that Exeter drivers would not be allocated work into Cornwall and this was conceded.

Every now and then, there appears on the scene someone who is abhorred by the majority of staff. One such character that followed Ken Hall as Area Manager was Charles Nichols: self-opinionated, bigoted, and as ignorant as he was tall, all six foot seven of him. He certainly didn't endear himself to the LDC staff representatives, in particular the guards who gave him a parting shot by coming out on strike on one of the busiest Saturdays of the year. He actually swore at me one day!

The bitter ASLEF dispute of 1982 left many drivers bewildered at the BRB decision to issue dismissal notices and some were having a rethink over their actions. The strike began on 4 July and ended on 19 July when the ASLEF executive agreed to accept flexible rostering under protest. During the dispute, only one driver belonging to the NUR turned up for work at Laira. Now, if there was one thing more than any other that the British Railways Board liked, it was to be seen running a train on a strike day, irrespective of whether there were any passengers on it – a token gesture aimed at undermining the unions' solidarity.

Harry Ough was in the chair on the night shift running into the strike day and I was his outside man; the shift clerk was Gerald Heard, an ex-controller from the closed Plymouth office.

Driver Larry Birkenhead was booking on duty around 06.00 on the strike day and there was no word left as to what, if anything, to do when the driver signed on duty; even the Bristol Control Office were reticent about whether to run a train or not. I suggested to Harry that he give the Area Manager, Charles Nichols, a ring to seek his guidance. With clouds of smoke being emitted from his pipe he retorted, 'Not likely, you give him a ring, I wouldn't bother, he should know the situation.' As Gerry rightly remarked, 'Charlie should make the decision, given the position.' At a quarter to eleven I rang the Area Manager, and after what seemed an eternity he finally answered and was most irate, refused to offer direction, and promptly put the phone down. 'You shouldn't have disturbed him, he might have been otherwise engaged,' said Gerry. For a man in his position who courted the media, Nichol's attitude was reprehensible. Many would be pleased to see the back of him.

I unwittingly upset LDC 'C' (Guards) by allowing into passenger service a prototype railcar. The DMU on the Gunnislake branch had failed and there was no other unit available. Even Derek Land couldn't pull one out of the hat on this occasion. Provision of buses in lieu generated difficulty owing to the nature of the line and the location of the stations in the Tamar Valley. When road transport was resorted to, and it was always problematical during the school run, one bus would be required from Gunnislake calling at Calstock and running direct to Plymouth whilst another would start from the other side of the river at Bere Alston serving Bere Ferrers – all very well if transport could be obtained. That particular day, the prototype 140 unit was on the

British Railways Board
Sir Peter Parker MVO
Chairman

June 1982

Dear Member of Staff.

YOU, YOUR FAMILY AND YOUR JOB

It is now one minute to midnight. Unless commonsense from ordinary railwaymen takes over, the railways are now due to start the most disastrous strike in their history.

Nobody regrets this head-on clash with responsible union leaders more than I do. But on this occasion, they are wrong, and I am writing again to urge you to ask your union leadership to think again.

Wars are easy to start. Very difficult to end.

So for your sake, the sake of your family and the future of the railway system, help me stop the strike before it starts.

I want you to know these things:

* **If there is a strike, there will be no pay increase.**
* We will not withdraw our productivity conditions.
* I do not believe for a minute the Government will intervene to find the cash we haven't got.
* If the strike does go on, **thousands** of railway jobs, perhaps yours, will disappear forever. That is fact.
* Our business will be crippled. Passenger services will be cut back. I believe we could lose the contract for Post Office letter mail.
* Speedlink and Freightliner traffic will be lost. It will mean less rolling stock and, therefore, fewer maintenance jobs in Regions and in BR Engineering Ltd.
* With less business there will be a substantial reduction in white collar jobs.

Think about it—is it really worth the risk?

I am asking you to follow your own interests. I am asking you not to strike.

If you decide not to strike, the Board will not accept loss of trade union membership as a cause for dismissal.

If the strike goes ahead, this will happen immediately:
For the first week, all staff who report for work will be paid, even if they are unable to do their normal jobs. You must make an effort to get to work, even if no trains are running, and if you don't succeed, you will not be paid.
If the strike lasts beyond one week, the Board will have to decide, after assessing the response to trade union calls for strike action, whether it can continue to pay ANY staff.

We will continue to try to find common cause with your leaders—but I think it is going to be up to the commonsense and intervention of you and other workers this time if we are going to avoid disaster.

Please think very seriously before supporting a strike call. Make no mistake. If there is a strike you may well not have a job to come back to.

Yours sincerely

Peter Parker

Euston Square, PO Box 100, London NW1 2DZ Telephone 01-262 3232 Telex 24678

Letter from the Chairman of British Rail, Sir Peter Parker.

June 1982

Dear Member of Staff,

YOUR JOB AND YOUR FUTURE AT RISK

I am taking the unusual step of writing direct to you and to everyone employed by British Railways Board, because the industry in which we all work is facing the most dangerous crisis in its history.

We are going to lose about £165m in 1982, even after the government and local authorities have paid us over £800m. The latest estimate of the cost of the 17 days of ASLEF strikes is £80m. We can't afford to borrow the money we need to renew and repair the railway, and this is limiting the service we give the customers who are our bread and butter.

We are in deep trouble. You could say we're broke. This time the threat to jobs will affect you all. I want you to think seriously before you are drawn into industrial action and into a fight which nobody can win.

The real fight now is not between ourselves or with government. It's for survival. Last January and February many of our customers found they could do without our services.

This is the background against which the Board, on 28 May, made the following offer: **to increase rates of pay by 5% from 6 September, provided that negotiations on all the six items in the 1981 productivity agreement have been completed by 30 July 1982. If agreement on the productivity items is not reached by 30 July 1982, the pay offer will be withdrawn.**

No one who has examined our proposals for flexible rostering objectively has been able to fault them. Lord McCarthy and the Railway Staff National Tribunal supported our plans. They also proposed safeguards—safeguards which the Board, as a responsible employer, has already accepted in drawing up flexible rosters for guards. In addition to a 39 hour week, guards on flexible rostering will now receive a flat rate payment of 50p per rostered turn worked.

We cannot delay any longer moving to flexible rosters for drivers, nor can we delay on the other outstanding issues still to be resolved—covering train manning agreements, including the new electric trains for the Bedford/St. Pancras services.

If you have already co-operated in productivity measures affecting your particular job, the delay on your 1982 pay increase must seem unfair. But without the co-operation of everybody, we cannot afford to give the recognition due to you for your efforts.

Perhaps you feel that you have been through a crisis like this before—and it will all be all right in the end. But we can expect no help, whatever government is in power, unless we accept that we must change the way we do things. All around us, in other industries, some with long and honourable traditions of service like ours, people are facing up to the need for change and getting rid of restrictive practices. We will get no sympathy if we continue to resist change until it is forced on us, more painfully.

So what happens if your union calls you out on strike, or orders some form of industrial action which wrecks the railway? The answer, I am afraid, is no pay increase, no job to come back to for many, no prospect of investment in electrification.

What can you do to help yourself in this crisis? You can speak up; let those who represent you and negotiate on your behalf know that you want this industry to survive. If we fight the competition instead of each other, we can still save many of the jobs that are already at risk.

Yours sincerely,

Peter Parker

Implications regarding the strike, the chairman's letter to footplate staff.

Introduced in 1980, with the exception of the cabs, much of the bodywork was constructed by using the bus components of Leyland National. The Class 140 was the forerunner of the Pacer DMU.

New lightweight diesel train

British Rail has produced a prototype lightweight diesel train, which is to be tested on a number of routes. This brochure explains why the new train - the Class 140 - has been built.

British Rail has a large but ageing fleet of diesel multiple unit passenger trains which are used mainly on local and commuter services in many parts of the country. Most of the trains were built during the period 1957 to 1960 and so have an average age of more than 20 years.

Many of the trains have been refurbished to improve passenger comfort, but this is essentially a short term policy, adopted because of the shortage of capital and restriction upon investment which have delayed the building of new trains. It will be necessary in the long term to have a new generation of diesel trains for the local services, and British Rail has now produced prototypes of two classes of local train to replace the existing stock.

Owing to a DMU failure, and with no other unit available, Laira LDC 'C' (Guards) was non-too enamoured when I put the prototype 140 unit into traffic at short notice on the Gunnislake branch.

The Class 210
Two prototypes of a new class of diesel multiple unit train - the Class 210 - will enter service in 1981. One set has four cars and the other three. They have been designed to replace existing local trains on routes with heavy traffic flows. In design the Class 210 trains have many features in common with the latest electric multiple unit trains. Although diesel engined, they have electric transmission of power to the wheels, and a standard of passenger comfort and performance comparable to their electric counterpart.

It would, however, be uneconomical to use the Class 210 in replacement of all the existing diesel train fleet, and so a prototype lightweight train has been produced to serve less heavily trafficked lines. This is the Class 140.

The Class 140
The most obvious difference between the new lightweight Class 140 prototype and conventional multiple unit trains is that each of the two passenger cars has only four wheels, instead of the orthodox arrangement of eight wheels in two four-wheeled bogies. The design of the Class 140 derives from an experimental four-wheeled 'railbus' produced by British Rail's Research and Development Division in collaboration with Leyland Vehicles Limited. The Leyland Experimental Vehicle (LEV) consists basically of two Leyland National bus bodies joined back to back and mounted on an underframe carrying the engine, transmission and running gear. This pioneer railcar has proved very successful during field trials in this country and it has also run successfully in the U.S.A.

Each car of the Class 140 unit has its own underfloor engine driving one of the axles through a four speed gearbox. The vehicle bodies have been built by Leyland Vehicles Limited, and the complete cars turned out by British Rail Engineering Limited at their Derby Works. The pair of cars provide a total seating accommodation for 102 passengers. There is adequate standing room for about 100 passengers as well, and the corridor connection between the cars allows ready access to the single toilet compartment.

The doors are power operated and of the swing/plug type, their operating mechanism being designed to provide a safe and positive lock when they are closed. They are under the overall control of the train crew, but within this arrangement they may be individually opened or closed by passengers by means of push buttons placed each side of the doorways, both inside and outside the vehicles. This system has been designed for the greater convenience of the passengers, and it will help to conserve warmth during station stops in cold weather.

Flexicoil springs with hydraulic damping result in excellent ride quality at up to 75 mph. A pressure heating and ventilation system is fitted. The seats are of the kind used in the latest suburban trains, with spring seat cushions and covers which can be readily removed for cleaning. The interior trim fully meets British Rail's stringent specifications for fire safety; fire extinguishers are carried in the passenger saloons and automatic fire extinguishing equipment protects the engines.

The Class 140 has an unladen weight of 38 tons - less than 70 per cent of the weight of a conventional two-car train - and this should help to make it significantly cheaper to run than the existing type of stock while providing a high quality of service for the passengers.

Trial Operation
The prototype Class 140 unit will be tested on specially selected routes to help British Rail to assess the fitness of this design for its purpose.

It is hoped that the trials will show that a production build of vehicles based on the Class 140 prototype will be appropriate for many services, including those in and around the major conurbations, where traffic is insufficient to justify replacement by Class 210 units. If a decision were reached to build vehicles specifically for rural branch lines they would not necessarily be to quite the same specification.

depot for static driver training. It had been cleared for route availability on the line, so I approached the Traction Inspector and he agreed to utilise it on the Gunnislake branch. The problem was that some of the guards had not been trained on the 140 unit, the operation of the doors being the main concern. I asked guard Ron Vale if he would work the unit if a Guards Inspector could be found to accompany him as tutor on the doors. Ron agreed and off they went, maintaining a service without resorting to unavailable road transport. LDC 'C' soon got wind of this and a deputation went to see the Area Manager. I considered that the decision to use the 140 unit was correct, they however thought otherwise and there was even a veiled suggestion in the ranks of a threat of strike action.

The straw that broke the camel's back came a week or two later when one Saturday the guard who was to work the lunchtime service to Gunnislake was taken off to work the breakdown vans to Newton Abbot in connection with a derailment there, and the early turn guard on the branch would not work an extra trip, so the service to Gunnislake was uncovered.

Each Saturday, there was a management presence on duty at Plymouth station; on that particular day it was the turn of Harold Joyner, an odd sort of fellow, who for his sins was the Signalman's Inspector. How he managed to persuade the driver to go is not clear, but Harold quite foolishly worked the DMU to Gunnislake and back in lieu of the guard. Still simmering from the previous episode of the 140 unit being pressed into service, the Guards LDC were up in arms at this latest incident.

A meeting was convened at the Laira Staff Association Club with some members demanding strike action; all efforts by Area Manager Charles Nichols to placate them failed. Some even wanted disciplinary action taken against Harold Joyner, and I was not the flavour of the month with a few of them either. A couple of hard-liners had swung the vote for a one-day strike, and thousands of passengers were inconvenienced as a result of their actions. Many services to the West Country were terminated well short of their destinations, some thirty-seven trains being affected on 21 July 1984, and it even made the national BBC television news. It was said afterwards that had it been any other Area Manager other than Nichols then they would have called off their action at the eleventh hour, albeit after letting management stew for a while.

Harry Ough was an ex-footplate man who always showed a degree of purpose, in stark contrast to the lethargic bunch of incompatibles in the Toton train crew office. One of the 'old school', he always referred to the signalman as 'officer' and to Derek Land as 'my mechanical foreman', and when relieving him he would refer to a spare ETH Class 47 as a 'big 47'. He had an amicable couple of years with Gerald Heard, displaced from the Control Office and accommodated as his shift clerk. Harry had a sense of humour: one day we were coming out of the Plymco superstore and as he was just about to come through the door, he looked skywards; it was as black as thunder

'Dear Old' Harry Ough would refer to a spare ETH Class '47' as a 'big 47'. A Crewe-built Type '4' diesel in Inter-City livery, No. 47606 *Odin*, awaits its next duty at Laira. This was the first of the class to be named.

and he turned to Maureen and said, 'Has your mother come down?' Harry had been off work some weeks with a frozen shoulder during which time I covered for him, and later in 1984 when he retired I moved into the permanent position of Traffic Assistant, working alongside Derek Land, the Senior Shift Maintenance Supervisor! Unlike his two colleagues, Derek – I gave him the pseudonym of 'number one', an appellation he held even after he retired – would stroll up to the office at the start of each turn. He always relieved early and his appearance usually coincided with the Traffic Assistants changing over. He was the nearest to being an operator that a maintenance man could be. This was reflected in him releasing a locomotive, not altogether in prime condition, when the power position was extremely tight in order to maintain the service. The diesel would then be allocated to a less important train with a QCI riding. His estimate of locomotives for release during the shift usually proved correct; this was particularly helpful when allocating power for the following shift. Derek Land led from the front and overall we achieved a great deal together.

The forerunner of Pathfinder Tours was F&W Railtours, run by Gloucester-based Peter Watts. Very often, when a trip started early from Plymouth, two or three nonentities would present themselves at the depot around midnight. Although not welcomed on the other two shifts, together with the Senior Shift Maintenance Supervisor, Derek Land, we afforded them a supply of soap, paper towels and black bags. In return, most of the rubbish from the tour would be bagged up, thereby assisting the cleaning staff.

The type of traction was as specified but if the allocated one was not to their preference – for example, not the right livery or used previously, then I would offer them a choice, bearing in mind the fact that dedicated Class 50 locomotives were nominated for the Exeter-Waterloo services.

THE
VALIANT THUNDERER

Saturday 23rd November, 1991

In November 1991, 37142 piloted 50015 *Valiant* and 50008 *Thunderer* with Pathfinder's 00.30 Manchester Piccadilly to Newquay 'Valiant Thunderer' Railtour. The '37' was attached at Newton Abbot as 50015 had a defective speedometer. A presentation in aid of Guide Dogs for the Blind is about to take place in Plymouth station, after which Class '50' No. 50033 will be attached on the rear.

Gloucester-based Peter Watts operated F & W Railtours, the forerunner of Pathfinder Tours, and although the type of traction was specified, if the allocated one was not of their preference I would offer them a choice – within reason – commensurate with the dedicated Class '50' diesels being the preserve of the Exeter to Waterloo services.

149

Miles and Chains	Location		Schedule	Actual		Miles and Chains	Location		Schedule	Actual
0.00	MANCHESTER PICCADILLY	PU	0030			27.52	Hawkeridge Jct.		0539	
5.70	STOCKPORT	PU	0039 0041			28.17	Westbury		0541	
8.11	Cheadle Hulme		0045			29.51	Fairwood Jct.		0543	
12.06	Wilmslow		0048½			32.73	Clink Road Jct.		0547	
26.21	Sandbach		0059½			34.75	Blatchbridge Jct.		0549	
			(2)			39.05	East Somerset Jct.		0553	
30.71	CREWE	PU	0109 0111			47.64	Castle Cary		0602	
38.77	Madeley Jct.		0121½			70.24	Cogload Jct.		0624	
49.79	Norton Jct.		0131			75.27	Taunton		0628	
55.28	STAFFORD	PU	0136 0138			89.41	Tiverton Loop		0645	
			(3)			104.67	Cowley Bridge Jct.		0659	
69.05	Bushbury Jct.		0155			106.07	Exeter St.Davids	CC	0701 0703	
70.59	WOLVERHAMPTON	PU	0158 0200			116.49	Dawlish Warren		0715	
72.43	Portobello Jct.		0204½			126.21	Newton Abbot		0725	
			(2)			134.37 / 0.00	PAIGNTON	Break/Rev	0739 1030	
76.60	Bescot Stadium		0208			8.16 / 0.00	NEWTON ABBOT	RR	1045 1100	
81.17	Perry Barr North Jct.		0214			-	Dainton Tunnel		1107	
83.39	Aston		0217			8.57	Totnes		1113	
86.15	BIRMINGHAM NEW STREET	PU	0222 0224			21.13	Ivybridge		1130	
89.46	Selly Oak		0231½						(2)	
91.60	Kings Norton		0234			25.04	Hemerdon		1136	
96.68	Barnt Green		0240			30.29	Lipson Jct.		1143	
102.44	Stoke Works Jct.		0244			31.69	PLYMOUTH	AAE	1145 1210	
113.61	Abbotswood Jct.		0252			34.61	St.Budeaux Jct.		1216	
131.59	CHELTENHAM SPA	PU	0306 0308			36.07	Saltash		1219	
138.09	Gloucester Yard Jct.		0315			41.05	St.Germans		1225	
144.19	Standish Jct.		0320			49.47	Liskeard		1235	
165.57	Westerleigh Jct.		0338			54.62	Largin Signal Box		1242	
170.27	BRISTOL PARKWAY	PU	0344 0346			62.15	Lostwithiel		1250	
174.46	Stapleton Road		0351			66.50	Par		1255	
176.09 / 0.00	BRISTOL TEMPLE MEADS	Rev/LC/PU	0355 0455			67.00	St.Blazey	T	1257 1301	
0.60	North Somerset Jct.		0457			72.24	Goonbarrow Junction	X/T	1314 1318	
11.35	Bath Spa		0512			87.13 / 0.00	NEWQUAY	PS/Rev	1350 1420	
13.51	Bathampton Jct.		0516							
22.45	Bradford Jct.		0530							

Miles and Chains	Location		Schedule	Actual		Miles and Chains	Location		Schedule	Actual
14.49	Goonbarrow Junction	X/T	1453 1457			44.30	CHELTENHAM SPA	SD	2013 2015	
20.13	St.Blazey	T	1510 1514			62.28	Abbotswood Jct.		2031	
20.43	Par		1517			73.45	Stoke Works Jct.		2040	
24.78	Lostwithiel		1522						(4)	
32.31	Largin Signal Box		1530			79.21	Barnt Green		2051	
37.56	Liskeard		1536						(3)	
46.08	St.Germans		1545			84.29	Kings Norton		2058½	
			(3)			86.43	Selly Oak		2101	
51.06	Saltash		1554			89.74	BIRMINGHAM NEW STREET	SD	2108 2110	
52.32	St.Budeaux Jct.		1558			92.50	Aston		2115½	
55.24	PLYMOUTH	RL	1603 1643			94.72	Perry Barr North Jct.		2118½	
56.64	Lipson Jct.		1646			99.29	Bescot Stadium		2124½	
62.09	Hemerdon		1653						(2)	
66.00	Ivybridge		1658			103.46	Portobello Jct.		2131	
78.36	Totnes		1711			105.30	WOLVERHAMPTON	SD	2136 2137	
-	Dainton Tunnel		1717			107.04	Bushbury Jct.		2140½	
87.13	Newton Abbot		1722			120.61	STAFFORD	*/SD	2153 2206	
96.65	Dawlish Warren		1733			126.10	Norton Bridge		2212½	
107.27	Exeter St.Davids		1744			136.59	Madeley Jct.		2221½	
108.47	Cowley Bridge Jct.		1745						(3)	
123.73	Tiverton Loop		1759			145.18	CREWE	SD	2232 2234	
138.07	Taunton		1816			149.68	Sandbach		2241½	
143.10	Cogload Jct.		1821			164.03	Wilmslow		2254½	
149.52	Bridgwater		1828			167.78	Cheadle Hulme		2257½	
155.74	Highbridge		1834			170.19	STOCKPORT	SD	2301½ 2303	
163.15	Uphill Jct.		1841			176.09	MANCHESTER PICCADILLY	SD	2312	
166.08	Worle Jct.		1844							
170.71	Yatton		1849							
182.73 / 0.00	BRISTOL TEMPLE MEADS	LC/SD	1903 1923							
1.43	Stapleton Road		1926							
5.62	BRISTOL PARKWAY	SD	1932 1934							
10.32	Westerleigh Jct.		1940							
31.70	Standish Jct.		1957							
			(3)							
38.00	Gloucester Yard Jct.		2005							

CODES USED:-

PU	Passenger Pick Up Point	T	Single Line Token Exchange
Rev	Train Reversal Point	X	Pass Train on Single Line
LC	Locomotive Change	PS	Photographic Stop
CC	Crew Changeover ONLY	RL	Rear Loco's to Front
RR	Loco's Run Round Train	SD	Passenger Set Down Point
AAE	Attach Assist Loco at Rear	*	Pathing Requirement Stop

STOCK FORMATION

A	B	C	D	E	F	G	H	J	K	L	M	
TSO	TSO	TSO	TSO	TSO	BFK	BFK	TSO	TSO	TSO	TSO	TSO	= load 12 AB/EH

Timings for 'The Valiant Thunderer', the 00.30 Manchester-Newquay and return.

1Z37 00:30 CHARTER MANCHESTER PICC TO PAIGNTON

ADD'L   SAT 23/11/91

STATION	ARRIVE	DEPART	STATION	ARRIVE	DEPART
BARNT GREEN		02/40	BATHAMPTON JN		05/16
BROMSGROVE		02/43	BRADFORD JN		05/30
STOKE WORKS JN		02/44	HAWKERIDGE JN		05/39
ABBOTSWOOD JN		02/52	WESTBURY		05/41
CHELTENHAM SPA	03:06	03:08	FAIRWOOD JN		05/43
BARNWOOD JN		03:08	CLINK RD JN		05/47
GLOUCESTER YD JN		03/14	BLATCHBRIDGE JN		05/49
STANDISH JN		03/15	EAST SOMERSET JN		05/53
CHARFIELD JN		03/20	CASTLE CARY		06/02
WESTERLEIGH JN		03/30	COGLOAD JN		
BRISTOL PARKWAY		03/38	TAUNTON		06/28
FILTON JUNCTION	B	03/44 03/46	NORTON FITZWARREN		
STAPLETON RD		03/48	TIVERTON LOOP		06/45
DR DAYS JN		03/51	COWLEY BRIDGE JN		06/59
BRISTOL TM		03/52	EXETER ST DAVIDS	07:01	C 07:03
BRISTOL EAST JN	03:55	L 04:55	DAWLISH WARREN		07/15
NORTH SOMERSET JN		04/56	NEWTON ABBOT		07/25
BATH SPA		05/12	PAIGNTON		07/39

PATHFINDER "VALIANT THUNDERER" RAILTOUR. B - 6C14 TO FOLLOW
NOTE: MAX SPEED 60 MPH FROM BRISTOL TM (50008/015 FROM BRISTOL)
LOAD. 12 AB/EH

5Z37 07:45 ECS PAIGNTON TO GOODRINGTON CHS

ADD'L   SAT 23/11/91

STATION	ARRIVE	DEPART	STATION	ARRIVE	DEPART
PAIGNTON		07:45	PAIGNTON		
GOODRINGTON CHS	W 07:50	RR 10:15		10:20	

ECS OFF 0030 EX MANCHESTER , ECS TO FORM 1030 CHARTER TO NEWQUAY.
W - STOCK TO BE WATERED.
LOAD. 12 AB/EH

1Z37 10:30 CHARTER PAIGNTON TO NEWQUAY

ADD'L   SAT 23/11/91

STATION	ARRIVE	DEPART	STATION	ARRIVE	DEPART
PAIGNTON		10:30	ST GERMANS		12/25
NEWTON ABBOT	10:45 RR	11:00	LISKEARD		12/35
DAINTON TUNNEL		11/07	LARGIN SB V EAST		12/31
TOTNES		11/03	LOSTWITHIEL		12/42
IVYBRIDGE		11/30	PAR		12/50
HEMERDON		11/36	ST BLAZEY		12/55
LIPSON JN	[2]	11/43	GOONBARROW JN	12:57 t	13:01
PLYMOUTH	B 11:45	L 12:10	NEWQUAY	13:14 Xt	13:18
ST BUDEAUX JN		12/16		13:50	
SALTASH		12/19			

PATHFINDER "VALIANT THUNDERER" RAILTOUR. B - ATTACH ASSIST LOCO REAR.
HAULED BY CLASS 50'S 50008"THUNDERER" & 50015"VALIANT" NOTE: MAX SPEED 60MPH.
LOAD. 12 AB/EH

INTERCITY

Great Western
British Railways Board
Intercity House
Plymouth
PL4 6AB
Telephone 0752 662888

FROM: **David Thomas**
Station Manager

TO: Len Wooldridge
Rod Fowkes
Duty Manager Plymouth
David Bridges
Public Affairs Manager Swindon

Your ref

Our ref DLT/jldb
EXT: 079-2360
Date 5 November 1991

SATURDAY 23 NOVEMBER 1991

Laira (Rod Fowkes and Geoff Hudson) are organising a presentation in aid of GUIDE DOGS FOR THE BLIND on the above date. They want to do this when the Class 37 Railtour (timings attached) arrives. Presentation to take place on Platform 4. Press etc to be in attendance. Duty on-call retail manager (should be Len Wooldridge) to be in attendance.

Necessary platform alterations:

1Z37		Platform 4	1145-1210
1Z37		Platform 8	1603-1643
1C36	1235 Paddington-Plymouth	Platform 7	1540-16#20*
2C74	1600 Plymouth-Liskeard	Platform 4	

*Rod Fowkes to arrange for 1C36 stock to leave for Laira at 16#20 instead of 17#20.

Nick Gibbons to arrange. Apols 8/n.

(signature)

DAVID THOMAS

Enc

Revised platform arrangements in Plymouth station in connection with Pathfinder Tours 'The Valiant Thunderer'.

Special Traffic Notice in connection with 'The Valiant Thunderer' with 50008/50015. A Class '37' diesel was attached on the front from Newton Abbot to Plymouth, owing to a speedometer fault on 50015, and 50033 was attached on the rear from Plymouth into Cornwall.

50033 hauled 'The Valiant Thunderer' from Newquay with 50008/50015 on the rear. On arrival at Plymouth 50033 stood aside then went to Laira, whilst 50008/50015 worked the train forward as far as Bristol Temple Meads.

```
              NEWQUAY TO PAR                                    SAT 23/11/91
 DD'L
    STATION            ARRIVE    DEPART  STATION          ARRIVE      DEPART

 NEWQUAY                          12+40  ST BLAZEY         13:31   t  13:32
 GOONBARROW JN        13:12 Xt    13:18  PAR               13+34

 2B48 13.25 EX NEWQUAY RUNNING ECS BACK TO PAR ,CONSEQUENTIAL OF 1Z37.
 13.25 WILL BE REPLACED BY A BUS SERVICE.  UNIT TO FORM 1440 PAR - NEWQUAY
 LOAD. 00 DMU
```

```
 1Z37 14:20 RETURN CHARTER NEWQUAY TO MANCHESTER PICC            SAT 23/11/91
 ADD'L
    STATION            ARRIVE    DEPART  STATION          ARRIVE      DEPART

 NEWQUAY                          14:20  SILK MILL LC              18/14
 GOONBARROW JN        14:53 Xt    14:57  TAUNTON WEST JN
 ST BLAZEY           15:10 t      15:14  TAUNTON                   18/16
 PAR                              15/17  TAUNTON EAST JN
 LOSTWITHIEL                      15/22  COGLOAD JN                18/21
 LARGIN SB                        15/30  BRIDGWATER                18/28
 ST PINNOCK V EAST                15/31  HIGHBRIDGE                18/34
 LISKEARD                         15/36  UPHILL JN                 18/41
 ST GERMANS                       15/45  WORLE JN                  18/44
 SALTASH          [3]             15/54  YATTON                    18/49
 ST BUDEAUX JN                    15/58  BRISTOL WEST JN           19/02
 PLYMOUTH         (c)  16:03 L    16:43  BRISTOL TM          19:03 L  19:23
 LIPSON JN                        16/46  DR DAYS JN                19/25
 HEMERDON                         16/53  STAPLETON RD              19/26
 IVYBRIDGE                        16/58  FILTON JN                 19/30
 TOTNES                           17/11  BRISTOL PARKWAY     19:32    19:34
 DAINTON TUNNEL                   17/17  WESTERLEIGH JN            19/40
 NEWTON ABBOT WEST                       CHARFIELD                 19/48
 NEWTON ABBOT                     17/22  STANDISH JN               19/57
 NEWTON ABBOT EAST                       GLOUCKSTER YD JN    [3]   20/05
 DAWLISH WARREN                   17/33  BARNWOOD JN               20/06
 EXETER CITY BASIN                       CHELTENHAM SPA      (2) 20:13    20:15
 EXETER ST DAVIDS                 17/44  ABBOTSWOOD JN             20/31
 EXETER RIVERSIDE NY              17/44  STOKE WORKS JN            20/40
 COWLEY BRIDGE JN                 17/45  BROMSGROVE                20/42
 TIVERTON LOOP                    17/59  BARNT GREEN         [4]   20/51
 NORTON FITZWARREN

 MAX SPEED 60 MPH NEWQUAY TO BRISTOL TM.
 PATHFINDER "VALIANT THUNDERER" RAILTOUR (50008/015 LAST RUN BEFORE WITHDRAWAL)
 LOAD. 12 AB/EH
 (c) TRAIN LOCO STAND ASIDE, 50005/50015 RUN ROUND (REAR TO FRONT) RE-ATTACH TRAIN LOCO.

 FORWARD CLASS 50. 2×50. 12 AB/EH.
```

```
 SPECIAL             ON
 REGIONAL OF         S MANAGER
 SWINDON        23 OCT 1991
```

One of the dedicated Class '50's to work the Exeter to Waterloo services, No. 50027 in Network South-East livery, minus its nameplate, *Lion* stands outside No. 3 road at Laira T&RSD. Withdrawn in 1991 and bought privately, it is now a resident on the Mid Hants Railway.

Driver Jack Knapman on 37269 to Bristol en route to Cardiff Canton, together with 50028 *Tiger* on the 07.40am Penzance to Liverpool, passing Laira Junction in this undated shot, which relates to the incident mentioned in the text.

One infiltrator, Peter Rolstone, worked for Mothers Pride and acted as a steward on the railtour. He would organise a degree of hand cleaning of the diesel locomotive in conjunction with Derek Land. Some staff would perceive this as a hindrance and be dismissive over such trivia. For a time the railtours were referred to in the Weekly Train Notice as 'Crankex', a reference I considered insulting, but which was no doubt treated light-heartedly by some jumped-up timing clerk. My observation was passed on to the Traincrew Manager to make representations to RHQ Swindon, and some time later the term was dropped in favour of 'Charter', which was more meaningful. After all organisers paid a lot of money to run the railtours.

Although Laira had an allocation of English Electric Type 3 Class 37 locomotives, they were housed and operated from St Blazey, only coming to Laira for repair or 'B' exams and above. Only three drivers at Laira knew Class '37' traction, two of those for preparation and disposal only. The other driver, Jack Knapman, booked on duty one morning 09.00 spare. On the depot was 37269, which was required at Cardiff Canton. Pathing of diesels running light wasn't a problem as far as Newton Abbot, but from there to Exeter, with trains off the Torbay line and under semaphore signalling, it was a case of taking a chance with other services. With this in mind I told Jack to take the 37 into Plymouth station and go attached to the 07.40 Penzance-Liverpool as far as Bristol Temple Meads. This train usually arrived from Cornwall a minute or two early, where it was booked to change diesels and attach a TSO and RMB.

Except when in multiple, two locomotives on the main line were manned by a driver and a secondman on the leading diesel, with a 'rider' on the other. The rider must be a man in the line of promotion and conversant to

153

operate the handbrake on the loco if necessary. It need not be a driver, indeed secondmen were often used. At Toton the secondman performing this duty was paid commensurate with his grade. Not at Laira though, secondmen or relief drivers always put in a drivers ticket when performing such duties. I considered this incorrect and endorsed the relevant ticket as such. There was no argument, of course, as long as the individual was conversant with operating the handbrake which was all that was required. It was not a popular decision, even though there were only a few pounds involved, but I stuck by what I believed to be correct. Flexible rostering and the relaxation of the manning agreement would later solve the problem.

When moving to Laira, I was most surprised at the ages of the secondmen, some being in their late fifties, on occasions acting as secondman to a driver who was years younger. Old traditions die hard. Ron Snell the roster clerk, when compiling the daily alteration sheet for the enginemen, would still show p/f (passed fireman) before the name of the man being upgraded.

A surprise, also, was finding that there was no canteen at Laira, unlike Toton where I had been used to either plain toast or eggs on toast for breakfast when on the early turn and a roast dinner at lunchtime. Meals, which were very reasonable at Toton, were subsidised from the proceeds of the one arm bandit. A machine which I steered clear of – so many didn't, couldn't and wouldn't, it was an addiction to quite a few; some would go straight upstairs from the pay office to the canteen to try their luck.

Strange as it may seem, even after the opening of the new HST depot in 1981, Laira was seldom off the block each evening. A new toilet-flushing apron had been installed, where all trains were tanked and the toilets serviced. Loco-hauled trains were then hauled through the wash-plant by a Class 08 shunt loco; whilst in the case of a HST it was just a matter of changing ends and driving through the wash-plant after the tanking was completed, then running either into the depot or the sidings. Many drivers, most irate at

Three HSTs in InterCity livery, plus a set of trailer cars and two loco-hauled coaching sets in Laira carriage sidings.

A line up of domestic and cross country High Speed Trains in the newly completed carriage sidings at Laira T&RSD.

Just one rake of loco-hauled coaching stock alongside six HSTs at Laira T&RSD.

standing out waiting a path to the flush-apron, were particularly vociferous when signing off duty, some even abandoning their trains on the running line. Others would remark that on occasions it took longer from leaving Plymouth station to putting a HST to bed at Laira, a distance of just over 2 miles, than it took to run from Bristol to Plymouth.

Relations between the operating and the maintenance departments at Laira varied from shift to shift; although generally good, there was certainly a closer rapport than was evident at Toton. As reflected earlier, a Class 45 requiring an 'A' exam and brake blocking at the LMR depot could take the whole shift, (even when short of power there was little deviation to that), whereas at Laira just under two hours would suffice. Locomotives due a 'B' exam and above were programmed on a weekly basis. On the day due, if there were too many diesels stopped, the locomotive for exam would be allocated on an out and back diagram, to be stopped on return or when convenient. Conversely, if a locomotive arrived on the depot almost due a 'B' exam or above and the power position was fluid, then I would offer it to the maintenance supervisor. Two of the Senior Shift Supervisors would kick to touch, with, 'Oh, leave it for Frank in the morning.' Frank Bellamy being the Chief Maintenance Supervisor. No such hesitation with Derek Land though: he'd have the diesel on the cleaning pit, underframe cleaned on the night shift and berthed for the early turn, the exam being well under way by the time Bellamy arrived.

That was what effective supervision was all about, as distinct from operating a twenty-four hour railway on the day turn. Over the years, certainly since I went to Laira in 1978, the management were perceived by the staff as being negative. The maintenance staff was supposed to have one twenty-minute meal break and a ten-minute tea break per shift. However, it was the practice for the staff to take two thirty-minute breaks. Successive managers threatened to resolve that anomaly but failed to do so, much to the consternation of some of the maintenance supervisors. Those though were not without their critics; one shift in particular had more than its fair share of onerous individuals.

There was talk that Ian Cusworth planned to redeploy his supervisors to alleviate the problem; instead, he took out a Senior Shift Supervisor! His replacement was a likeable fellow who unfortunately couldn't handle the bunch of incompatibles, before he in turn was replaced.

The lack of authoritative management over the years by successive Depot Engineers only served to increase the degree of apathy on the shop floor. The plain fact was that management were seen not to be managing and losing credibility. Had it not been for the constant chivvying by the operating department, the performance of services emanating from Laira would have been less than satisfactory.

Each location has its fair share of skivers who are well known. Fred Bratby, foreman's assistant in the train crew office at Toton, had a top ten. When the GPO telephone rang, Fred would identify the caller more often than not, even before answering the phone. 'That's *so-and-so*, ringing in sick', and he was usually correct. One day, a driver had rung in reporting sick; there did appear some dubiety about this and his home was later contacted. His father answered the telephone and when asked about his son, who was himself getting on in years replied, 'oh! Ken has gone to Skegness for a few days.' Some train crew, when on the late turn and rest day Saturday, would ring in, or get someone on their behalf to report them sick for the Friday. They wouldn't be rostered on duty on the Sunday so it made a nice long weekend, even more so when a double rest day intervened. What was taboo at Toton, unlike Laira, was the reporting sick and right for work in the same telephone call. That was clearly right, how could anyone say that they were sick today but right for work tomorrow? There was nothing wrong, of course, by intimating that they might possibly resume the following day or whenever. I saw the need for this arrangement to apply at Laira and although some of the staff representatives objected, it was adopted.

There was a feeling of frustration that management were slow to act with persistent individuals. Sickness, genuine but more often than not engineered, was allowed to go unchecked. Gerry Heard often used to remark that it was high time David Langton, the Traincrew Manager, had so and so in and read the riot act to them. Interestingly enough, Bernard Brown, the chief staff clerk in Plymouth, came to the depot one day to interview some of the carriage cleaners regarding their sickness and absenteeism.

Armed with a batch of papers, he was coming down the passage as I was leaving the office. 'Hello Rodney, we've come to sort the buggers out,' he said. 'Very good Bernard,' I replied, 'You're eighteen months too late,' and with that continued down into the shed. When I returned to the office some time later, Gerry casually said, 'You've upset Bernie. What did you say to him? He came in here with a face like thunder,' adding, 'That bloody Fowkesy.'

It was not a deliberate attempt on my part to be obstructive; indeed, the staff office had enough ammunition to have acted positively considerably earlier. The meeting, however, had little or no effect on those seen.

I remember being on a supervisory training course at Crewe, when one of the guest speakers was a Traincrew Manager from East Anglia. His perception of sickness/absenteeism was to deviate from the recognised disciplinary procedure and instead expend the condition of letters 1, 2 & 3, whereby letter 1 was basically a warning, letter 2 being the final warning and letter 3 - on yer bike. Swift and effective! He even reflected on visiting a hospital and issuing the patient with his final letter 3. Later, poor performance was monitored with periods of thirteen weeks, and then further durations were introduced which would augur well for the defaulters.

The eagerly awaited Class 142 Pacer units were, according to higher management, to be the salvation for the branch lines in Devon and Cornwall; such optimism, however, was short lived. The lightweight diesel multiple units with Leyland National bus bodies mounted on BR-designed bogies was progressively introduced to replace the older conventional DMUs. Nicknamed Skippers, the Class 142 units were after a while withdrawn from the west of England because of mechanical problems and excessive flange wear due to track curvature on some of the area's routes. A total of thirteen two-car units were removed from the St Ives, Looe and Gunnislake branches for more suitable lines in the north-west and the north-east. Welcome back to the First Generation units.

As mentioned earlier, the Traffic Assistant undertook the allocation of power, which, however, didn't change significantly when the Divisional Manager's Office at Bristol closed. RHQ at Paddington then assumed responsibility and later that office was relocated to Swindon. From then on, with the assistance of POIS (Passenger Operations Information System), a follow on from TOPS, the allocations would be input into the system that would be reflected in the Power Report (TV) for the area concerned. I found the allocating of power now being done at the appropriate level difficult to adjust to, so much in fact, that relations with the Traction Controller became

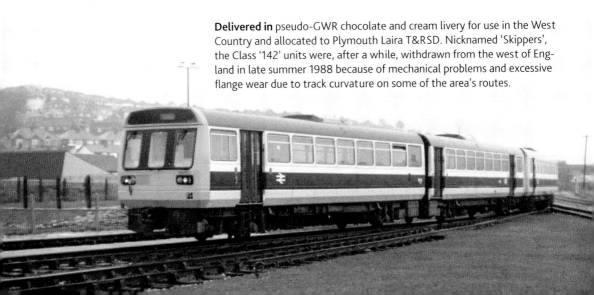

Delivered in pseudo-GWR chocolate and cream livery for use in the West Country and allocated to Plymouth Laira T&RSD. Nicknamed 'Skippers', the Class '142' units were, after a while, withdrawn from the west of England in late summer 1988 because of mechanical problems and excessive flange wear due to track curvature on some of the area's routes.

The BR 'First Generation' DMUs were built between 1956 and 1963 and were more adaptable to working on the branch lines in Devon and Cornwall.

somewhat strained to say the least. It had got to such a pitch that the Chief Controller at Swindon told the Traincrew Manager at Laira that a meeting would have to be convened to resolve the differences between the Traction Controller and myself. It was ironical really: the Controller was doing his job of allocating the power, and I was jealously trying to hang on to an outmoded method of working. With fewer locomotives now to deal with, it was no longer worth the hassle.

On a summer Saturday, telephone calls were often received at the depot purporting to come from various individuals describing themselves as a 'secondman' at Birmingham New Street and the like. The question was always the same: 'Could you tell me what the diesel is working the such and such train?' Invariably Bill Nance would give them his stereotype reply of 50051. Some, without thinking, would say thankyou.

In September 1987, the line between Plymouth and Penzance including the branches became de-controlled, that is to say Swindon RHQ would exercise control of the line only as far as Plymouth. At the time I was the supervisor's staff representative, and managed to secure a Grade 'E' for the additional responsibility. The Traffic Assistants generally relished the challenge; two ex-controllers had now found their way to Laira as a result of the retirements of Bill Nance and dear old Harry Ough. Henry, now to some extent, was the odd man out once again, in that he had no Control Office experience. Nonetheless, the signalmen in Cornwall were generally very good at furnishing information, the ex-controllers having dealt with them regularly a few years earlier, whereby Henry and myself had a day or so out on the area visiting them.

The 7-mile single-line stretch between Burngullow and Probus – reinstated in 2004 to double track at considerable expense – was controlled by the signalman at Par. Regulating over this portion of line was that Up trains in general had priority over those going into west Cornwall.

Duty Manager Plymouth

The spring of 1988 heralded a significant change for the Laira-based train crews. Guards were the first to be transferred to Plymouth station, signing on and off there, followed a year or so later by the footplate staff. The Traffic Assistants, then re-designated Duty Managers, were relocated with the guards, whilst the shift clerks remained at the depot and would transfer later with the drivers, secondmen and trainmen. In the interim, the Movements Supervisor at Laira oversaw the booking on and off of the drivers and would also coordinate the allocation of power with Swindon Control Office.

Being relegated to the position of shift clerk from Controller must have been frustrating, however Gerry – and to a lesser extent Mike Smith on the relief – had been given a free hand at Laira making decisions in my absence, something that Henry would never allow his shift clerk David Causley, another ex-Controller, to do. Gerry was a keen gardener; he liked a bet, played euchre and had a problem with the wind. He lived in a bungalow, the previous occupier being an ex-Plymouth Argyle football manager. His jovial approach endeared him to train crews; as such, rarely did he have a refusal whereby they would not come off their rostered turn for whatever reason. He hadn't had a holiday for many years, didn't own a car and was extremely careful with his money. One afternoon, Paul Rowe was my shift clerk – Gerry was rest day – and a job cropped up at short notice requiring the movement of HST vehicles from Laira to Bristol St Philips Marsh depot. We had looked at all the options and couldn't find a driver, and then I saw one last possibility: Reg Collings. He had just worked a DMU down to Liskeard, was travelling back to Plymouth and his next job was not for around three hours. Paul exclaimed, 'You've got as much chance of that driver going as you have seeing Heardy coming out of Lunn-Poly!'

Around this time, the Area Manager, Jim Collins, had moved on and his successor was an ex-Royal Naval submarine commander, Andy Johnson. Derek Land reliably informed me that he captained the only non-nuclear submarine to take part in the Falklands war. Ably supported by Martin Wright, David Langton and Ken Ley, Andy soon had the respect of the staff and despite references between seafaring and running a railway, the transition was quickly fulfilled. On one occasion, when the sea wall was breached at Dawlish, in my office were Andy and David. Not wishing to be without a management presence during disruption, David was to be in attendance on the Sunday morning. To say this directive was not well received was an understatement.

A combination of a high tide and an east/south-easterly gale brought the usual problems between Dawlish and Teignmouth, with the Cross Country 'Voyagers' often being terminated at Exeter St Davids and Newton Abbot, whilst the HSTs could traverse the section of line until it was closed owing to the high seas.

This stretch of the main line in Devon is always susceptible to the ravages of the weather. Network Rail requires ongoing maintenance of the sea wall on the line at Dawlish.

He was the regular organist at the parish church in South Brent and would leave Plymouth a couple of years later. Before relinquishing his parochial duties upon his transfer to the north-west, together with Maureen and Janet we went to his final service at South Brent Church. After the congregation had departed, David settled down to give his rendering of *Widor's Toccata* from the Organ Symphony No. 5 opus 42. Morley Crago, a retired guard's inspector, still smiles when I recall David hobbling down the road from Arnolds Point to Laira Depot. It was raining. He wasn't hurt; just a hole in the sole of his shoe. Life in the station was certainly different from being at the depot; the degree of involvement on the platform differed from shift to shift. I had a nightly ritual of going through the Newcastle train on arrival in the hope of acquiring a *Derby Evening Telegraph* newspaper as I had done over the years at Laira. The Duty Manager was also instructed to make frequent visits, particularly on the night shift to the panel-signal box; read into that what you will.

One night, the 1A03 22.15 Penzance-Paddington sleeper service suffered a horrendous delay. The driver had informed the Truro station chargeman that the Class 47 diesel was in trouble, and that a change of locomotive would be required to work forward from Plymouth. A fresh engine was summoned from Laira. Preceding the sleepers in Cornwall were two diesels coupled, one live the other dead, from Penzance to Laira. Too late to loop

The driver working the Penzance to Paddington sleeper service was having problems with his Class '47' diesel. A similar type, No. 47786 *Roy Castle OBE*, has just arrived in Plymouth with a charter train going to Cornwall.

them at Par, I told the signalman at Lostwithiel to hold them in his goods loop to follow 1A03 in case the train got into difficulty up Largin Bank. As it was, the train appeared to be proceeding normally passing the last manual signal box out of Cornwall, St Germans. Then, Plymouth panel box reported the train appeared to be at a stand. The driver, after walking some distance to a telephone, advised the signalman that the diesel had failed and that assistance was required; no real problem then, as the two light diesels were then already approaching St Germans. It was almost midnight, an absolutely foul night, high winds and pouring rain; I walked across to platform 7 to advise the passengers of the impending delay. The minutes ticked by – when a failure occurs out in the middle of nowhere and in the dead of night it is usually a slow process. Three-quarters of an hour elapsed, and still no movement with the assist locos going in. The situation might have been less complicated had not the panel signal box and the manual box at St Germans both been involved, however, the underlying feature of the incident was the breakdown of communication, firstly between the train crew themselves, and then between them and the signalmen concerned. The signalman at St Germans, quite rightly, would not allow the assist diesel into the section until he had received advice that the guard was on his way, walking back to protect his train. In those situations the clock is the enemy, remorselessly seeming to gather pace. I went over to platform 7 again to advise what passengers there were of the continued delay. A message was then received from the panel that the train was on the move – the time around 01.45 – at last; certainly the delay had been excessive, even given the circumstances prevailing at the time. The relief, however, was short lived. It transpired that the driver, no doubt through a combination of frustration and the apparent lack of action, had managed to restart the diesel and moved off, albeit without his guard, from whom nothing had been heard. After only a short distance the diesel then succumbed altogether; we were now back to square one. A contravention of the BR Rule Book had taken place and the driver had committed the cardinal sin: when agreeing that assistance is required the driver gives an assurance that his train will not be moved. During the whole of this time there had been no movement at all on the Down road into Cornwall. The replacement diesel to work the sleepers forward was manned by an Exeter driver who didn't sign the road into Cornwall. I'd spoken earlier with the standby signalman in the Panel, as to whether it was prudent to go out in the van in an attempt to locate the failed train in east Cornwall. The first train to go through over the Down road was the Exeter Riverside-St Blazey freight at about 02.30. The train was stopped and the driver advised of the circumstances pertaining on the Up line, and to keep a lookout for the guard off the sleepers. In addition to keeping the Control informed I rang the on-call manager, Ken Ley, and explained the position to him that the train had been at a stand for almost three hours and nothing had been heard of from the guard, and that assistance was in place. Ken came to the office; by this time the Down freight had arrived at St Germans signal box with the guard off the failed sleeper train on board the diesel, and so the assist loco was finally allowed into the section. 1A03 finally arrived in Plymouth at around 03.45. Ken interviewed the guard. As to his account of the proceedings, it transpired that he had been sheltering in Wiveliscombe tunnel. Ironically there was a lineside telephone at the east end of the tunnel that he should have used to contact the signal box. A Traction Inspector would interview the driver later that day. After attaching the Plymouth sleeping car with the fresh locomotive, the train left some three and a half hours late. What a debacle.

Regulations for Train Signalling cover the situation where the section is obstructed by a disabled train:

Reg. 14 (a) (ii) *'Except during fog and falling snow, it will not be necessary for the Signalman in rear of the obstruction to detain the second train until the arrival at his box of the Guard or Secondman of the disabled train, if information has been received that the obstruction is being protected in rear. On receipt of this information the Signalman in rear may allow the second train to enter the obstructed section after the Driver has been instructed to keep a lookout for the Guard or Secondman of the disabled train.'*

Reg. 14 (a) (iii) *'If there is a tunnel in the obstructed section the second train must not enter such tunnel until the Guard or Secondman of the disabled train has come back and met the train or it has been ascertained that the tunnel is clear. The Signalman must instruct the Driver of the second train accordingly.'*

As Duty Manager, having responsibility to oversee the decontrolled line through Cornwall, authorisation had to be sought from RHQ Swindon in respect to the holding of trains for connectional purposes. Depending on who the Section Controller was usually had a bearing on the decision. On occasions it was prudent to maintain the connection and advise the Control afterwards.

One train where a hold was almost always declined was the 17.35 Paddington-Penzance (the *Golden Hind*) and, as so often happened, the Pullman would precede the 09.10 Aberdeen-Plymouth from Cogload Junction (Taunton), when the latter was around ten minutes late. Frequently the *Golden Hind* would have just left the station as the train from the Granite City was arriving under restrictive signals, connection severed, the next service into Cornwall nearly two hours later, except on a Friday when a wait of an hour was necessary. I argued to no avail that by the time the *Hind* reached Plymouth it had lost its Pullman status, insofar as the number of passengers travelling into Cornwall was negligible, so a hold of say five minutes would not be unreasonable. Knowing the DCCs was an advantage; John Cheeseman, Ray Cundy and John Pincott could be relied on to condescend in granting a five-minute hold to make the connection. Not so with an individual called Main, he was totally intransigent, I loathed the guy. He had no qualm over the

Freight traffic in Cornwall, never particularly heavy in the latter years, was worked mostly by Class '37' locomotives based at St Blazey, and mainly used on the movement of China clay to Fowey and from Marsh Mills. This photograph shows 37425 at Truro working empty fuel tanks from Long Rock Depot, Penzance. It was painted especially to mark the end of loco-hauled service on the Cardiff to Rhymney line in April 2005.

fact that passengers from north of the border, already having spent over eight hours on the train, would now be subjected to a further two-hour sojourn in Plymouth, all for the sake of a paltry five minute hold on a train, which would not jeopardise connections in west Cornwall as the Falmouth branch was the only one to be affected.

Freight traffic in Cornwall, insignificant to that of years earlier, varied and, whilst never particularly heavy, was centered on the St Blazey area; predominantly China clay transported in bulk to the potteries and the Port of Dover for the continent. Fowey Docks also provided an outlet for the shipping of the commodity, which found its way to that point from Marsh Mills and the St Blazey area, being tripped via Lostwithiel. In addition to the daily services to Severn Tunnel Junction and Stoke-on-Trent, the latter often attaching a couple of wagons at Plymouth from Marsh Mills, the service to Dover operated more sporadically. A Thursday only slurry train ran from Burngullow to Sittingbourne; both that and the Polybulks to Dover required an assist diesel from Plymouth to Newton Abbot over the South Devon

Banks. A road-building scheme in west Cornwall produced a flow of cement traffic, conveyed in Presflos to Chacewater from the Blue Circle works at Plymstock. When the contract ceased the line over the River Plym to the cement works was severed; years earlier the line had continued to Turnchapel and Yealmpton.

A late Sunday afternoon freight departure from the Wirral, the relatively heavy Ince & Elton to Truro train, detached fertiliser wagons en route, including a Lapford portion at Exeter Riverside. An assist diesel would then be attached to Plymouth, where a further portion was taken off for Friary, and, locomotives changed, the assist diesel then worked into Cornwall, whilst the train engine went to Laira for servicing. Detaching rear and changing locomotives in Plymouth was time consuming. I wrote to David Langton suggesting that whilst the train was inside Riverside yard the train engine, a Class 47 should also be taken off to then become the assist engine allowing the Class 37 to become the train locomotive, thereby eliminating a double shunt on the front at Plymouth, in addition to detaching rear. This arrangement worked locally until the diagrams were amended.

One extraordinary working which ran for a while was the transportation of fish, supposedly mackerel, which was conveyed in sixteen-ton open mineral wagons from Fowey Docks to wherever it was destined for up the line to be processed into fishmeal. Not only did the stench linger long after the passage of the train, the residue dripping from the wagons left a film on the rails that had subsequent train engines losing their feet on the inclines at Largin, Hemerdon and Dainton. Autumn leaf fall also caused problems. Those things, together with poor weather, created difficult rail conditions resulting in low rail adhesion, with some trains slipping to a stand on the banks.

Largin in the woods was particularly vulnerable, and the problems were not only confined to the rising gradient, as on occasions a considerable degree of skill was required when descending the incline, many an unwary driver being caught out with the poor rail conditions and finding his DMU slipping by the Down platform at Bodmin Parkway. To alleviate this annual problem, a specially converted DMU vehicle was fitted out with a hopper that contained a gel, intermixed with sand, and fed through pipes directly onto the rails. A Trainman/Guard operated it and the driver sounding the horn on the diesel locomotive was the necessary intimation at strategic locations to commence sanding. The 'Sandite' worked between Laira, Newton Abbot and Lostwithiel from late afternoon and through the night from October to the end of November. Pathing was sometimes a problem, as was having to return to the depot for another mix, that excuse being a deliberate ploy on the part of some train crews, they being fully aware of the line occupation that would result in a lost trip. Later a Class 37 diesel was modified to sand the line concerned; this was obviously more convenient as it eliminated the need to run-round at Newton Abbot and Lostwithiel and also dispensed with the trainman.

One evening, I fulfilled an ambition when Duty Manager in Plymouth. There was no station announcer on duty after six o'clock; so, leaving Gerry to hold the fort, I stepped in to cover. Now, something which had bugged me for years had been a change in the announcing procedure, whereby at other than terminal stations the announcer would say (using Derby as an example), *'the next train to arrive at platform six is the 9.55 from Bradford, the 12.26 to Paignton calling at....'* The majority of passengers waiting on the platform to board a train are not particularly concerned from where it originated, only to where it is going and the calling points. Far better, when in the steam days the announcement went thus: *'the next train to arrive at platform six is the 12.26 to Paignton – this is the 9.55 from Bradford – calling at...'* For a couple of hours that particular evening, I was in my element, deviating from the prepared script, which wasn't to hand anyway. Even a station postman passed a favourable comment. I thought at the time 'Radio 4 here I come!'

At Plymouth there were two Travelling Post Office trains, one of which was a 22.13 to Paddington that connected out of the 19.30 Penzance-Newcastle which later would be staged only as far as Bristol with the TPO staff joining at Plymouth. The loss of the newspaper traffic to road meant losing the complimentary daily and Sunday newspapers.

During a twelve-hour Saturday night turn as Duty Manager in Plymouth, I was to endure my worst hours of worry. The driver for the 19.45 Sprinter unit to Bristol had not booked on duty at his rostered time. The shift clerk rang his home, only to be told by his wife that he had left some time earlier on his push bike. The driver, Gordon, eventually arrived at around twenty-to-eight; I said to him that he had left it a little late, and he remarked on having difficulty negotiating the Cattedown roundabout. Other than that he appeared quite normal and after booking on, off he went to the locker room to collect his gear. Some minutes later, the station chargeman on platform 7 called up on the radio to ascertain if the driver was on his way over. I went into the mess room and he was still there chatting to a couple of his mates. 'Driver', I said, 'your train over on seven should have left over five minutes ago.' He acknowledged, and said he was going straight over. After the train had departed I went back into the mess room and spoke to the drivers who Gordon had been talking to. Neither of them attached any significance to the situation except one, who then remarked that Gordon had been observed of late doing things which were a little out of character, such as throwing paper balls into the air and catching them. I began to have doubts as to whether he should have been allowed to sign on duty. Having said that, I saw no real justification for taking him off, nevertheless still felt more than a little uneasy, not enough though, to have the driver seen at Bristol by a Traction Inspector, who would not have known anything about him. His return working from Bristol was the 1C02 Paddington-Penzance sleepers. I must admit I watched the ATR (automatic train reporting) machine on the progress of 1C02 with more than a little interest – South Liberty, Cogload, Exeter East, Dawlish

Warren, Newton Abbot, Totnes and Tavistock Junction – recalling some years earlier going to see the film *The Longest Day*, which I thought was quite long and drawn out, but it was nothing compared with that night. Seldom had I been so pleased to see an individual; I met Gordon on the platform off the sleepers and asked him how he was, and he replied, 'All right.' There was certainly a very relieved Duty Manager from that moment. Naturally, I had to bring my observations to management and the following day Gordon was taken off footplate duties. His manner had changed; what was all the more upsetting was the fact that his colleagues had been aware of it and refused to do anything about it. The throwing up in the air of balls of paper was a cry for help. Sadly, Gordon died a few months later, suffering a tumour on the brain. A few years earlier, he had worked away from Laira the Class 140 prototype unit, the new lightweight diesel train which had only four wheels to each car instead of the orthodox arrangement of eight wheels in two four-wheeled bogies. It had undergone trials on the various branch lines in Cornwall, in addition to the unannounced trip on the Gunnislake branch, much to the consternation of LDC 'C'. Initially Gordon was booked to work the 140 unit as far as Bristol, but as Bath Road had no driver who knew the traction, they provided one for route knowledge; Gordon carried on to Birmingham. Saltley was also unable to supply a driver who was conversant with the Class 140 unit and he ended up working it through to Derby.

Ian Cusworth, the Area Maintenance Engineer, had left a few years earlier for pastures new at Swindon RHQ, and, after a temporary appointment, Tony Coles came to Laira from Eastleigh. If things weren't on the slide before he came, they certainly were after he arrived. When the drivers had been relocated to Plymouth station, the Area Maintenance Engineer at Laira (Coles) then saw fit to dispense with the services of the operating supervisors at the depot. Punctuality and service went to bits in a matter of weeks. I recall as the supervisors' staff representative, sitting in on a meeting when Coles declared that he no longer required the movements supervisors at Laira – despite the fact that trains were regularly standing out waiting acceptance onto the depot!

Malcolm Wishart, another outsider, from Old Oak Common, had been appointed Depot Engineer. He would spend most evenings in the station decked out in his orange anorak, ignoring all around him whilst going into each power car of terminating trains before retiring to a local guesthouse. Tony Coles' tenure didn't last long at Laira, being removed overnight and clearing his office in the small hours. He left without any farewells, which was not surprising, although a few of his supervisors saw him in a different light. His lords and masters at Swindon had him replaced in 1989, Geoff Hudson from Neville Hill, or maybe it was Bounds Green, taking over.

Early in 1990, Martin Wright called me up to his office. 'Rod,' he said, 'Geoff Hudson has been on the phone and asked me if I could assist in providing someone to put together the summer timetable in the light of what

British Railways Board

ACTING OPERATIONS MANAGER

Rod Fowkes, one of the Duty Managers at Plymouth Station, is being seconded to the depot to help resolve some of the operating problems that we have. He will be here for approximately 2 months preparing plans for the May Timetable, looking at more effective ways of operating the depot and trying to find ways of improving capacity particularly at night.

If you have any good ideas or helpful suggestions I am sure he will be only to pleased to listen. His office will be in the former first aid room next to the pay office.

G P A HUDSON
Area Fleet Manager, Plymouth

Martin Wright called me up to his office. Laira required assistance in preparing the 1990 summer timetable.

To: R H Fowkes Esq
    Duty Manager
    Plymouth

From: Area Fleet Manager
       Plymouth

Ext : 079 2290

o/r :

Date: 1 June 1990

Dear Rod

Thank you very much for your comprehensive report on your stint at Laira. There are some very interesting issues that you have raised which I would like to discuss with you. Unfortunately for the next two weeks I shall be on leave and by that time you will be back at North Road. However, once I have returned I will have a word with Martin Wright and see if we can get together for a couple of hours. In the meantime I have asked Graham to go through the points with you next week.

Without doubt your contribution and effort were a major factor in the success of launching the May timetable and it is quite clear to me that without your efforts we would have had a repeat of the shambles of the previous May timetable. I attach a copy of the letter from the General Manager expressing his thanks to all those that have contributed and may I add my personal thanks as I feel that you, more than anybody else, have contributed to the successful launch of this timetable as far as Laira is concerned.

During your stay I recognise that you have put in a considerable amount of work on our behalf and I sincerely thank you for all your hard work in pointing us in the right direction and helping us to start to resolve some of our most critical issues.

Best wishes

G P A HUDSON
Area Fleet Manager, Plymouth

Letter of thanks from Geoff Hudson for my involvement in launching the 1990 summer timetable applicable to Laira.

happened regarding the debacle of last year; would you be interested in going on secondment? 'I was of course fully aware of what did and didn't happen with the previous timetable changeover. It was an utter shambles and Laira at the time didn't have a very good reputation for delivering the services expected of it. No doubt someone at the depot had put my name forward and I agreed to go back for a possible eight weeks. I had been away from the depot for almost two years, during which time Derek Land would usually pay me a visit in Plymouth station once a week on the night turn and I would go out to the depot on the workobus, albeit not all that often.

Having my own little office on the depot I was never short of visitors. Working closely with the train planners and diagramming section at Swindon and to some extent with the CrossCountry department at Birmingham, the introduction of the 1990 summer timetable went ahead without a hitch. On my return back to Plymouth there was a suggestion that an operating management position was to be created at Laira, no doubt triggered by my involvement with the implementation of the then current timetable, and with a look over the shoulder of the previous year's breakdown. The post was duly advertised as Movements and Planning Manager. In the frame was newly titled Production Manager Derek Land, one of his colleagues, Ken Ley, and me, and there may well have been another applicant from away. Considered by some to be the favourite for the post, the interview conducted by Geoff Hudson and Graham Boot Handford went well. In the ensuing weeks Derek would ask me on most days had I heard who had been appointed; he was convinced that I knew something but didn't. He was later told during a meeting with Geoff that he hadn't got the job and that I had. This didn't seem to concern Derek too much and his attitude towards me never waned in the slightest.

A few weeks later, Ken Ley went back to Laira for another interview, on this occasion for the post of Safety Manager which was filled internally – a foregone conclusion. I always felt a degree of sympathy for Ken; he had attended the two interviews without any chance of getting either position. It had always been my opinion that when management wanted to discreetly leak something to the staff, they would tell Ken in confidence. Having said that, he, being an ex-signalman, was extremely competent in rules and regulations.

BRITISH RAIL - WESTERN REGION

TO: Mr R.H. Fowkes   FROM: Area Manager
      Duty Manager   Plymouth/Cornwall
      Plymouth
                               EXTN: 2363

                               O/R : AM/ER/PF

                               DATE: 6/12/90

Dear Rod,

Vacancy WO.130 List 37 : Movements Planning Manager, Laira, MS2.

I am pleased to inform you that you have been selected to fill
the above vacancy and will transfer to your new post on
Monday 7th January 1990.

Your appointment is subject to you signing a "Statement and Terms
of Employment of Management Staff". Two copies are enclosed, please
return one copy to me, duly signed, in due course.

May I congratulate you on your promotion and offer you my best
wishes in your new post.

Yours sincerely,

Hugh David

Area Personnel Manager

My final appointment as Movements Planning Manager at Laira T&RSD.

171

A return to Laira

Now, there was some soul searching taking place; after thirty-five years of shift working, did a regular day job have any appeal? Initially there would be a drop in salary of around £5k per annum. I sought advice from the personnel manager and, after getting the thoughts of Andy Johnson, Martin Wright and David Langton, was finally persuaded to take the position; had I refused Derek Land was waiting in the wings. Little did I realise, that in five years time I would be leaving the railway altogether. Shortly afterwards, there was a further reorganisation, this time involving the Plymouth Duty Managers who were to have their title changed to Resource Managers and lose control of the line in Cornwall to the Duty Manager at Penzance. That, I wouldn't have enjoyed.

I joined a ten-strong management team at Laira Traction and Rolling Stock Depot, three of whom I knew from my days there as Traffic Assistant. Appointed at around the same time to the post of Materials Manager was Alan Combes, an ex-airline pilot. Alan would often come and sit in my office and we would talk through matters discussed at the weekly management meeting together and other relevant topics. He had a thankless task of trying to instil some sense of urgency and consolidation into the stores department, perpetually ridiculed for its ineptness. On his way from the car park to the depot one morning, Alan was clearly having difficulty walking; suggesting that it might be thrombosis. Not long after, he was admitted to a hospital in Torquay and sadly a few months later he passed away. Given time, he would no doubt have stamped his authority on the stores organisation. As it was, his successor, christened 'Spoof', was promoted to the post from stores clerk. The stores administration was the laughing stock of the depot, continuing to frustrate management, supervisors and the rest of the workforce. Some appointments defy logic, as Derek Land aptly remarked – incompetence personified!

The position of Movements and Planning Manager was also referred to as Operations and Planning Manager. There were no staff directly responding to the post, although I undertook the responsibility for the staffing of shunters, carriage cleaners and shed drivers at the depot. The periodic appraisal of staffing

AFM Plymouth Management Team

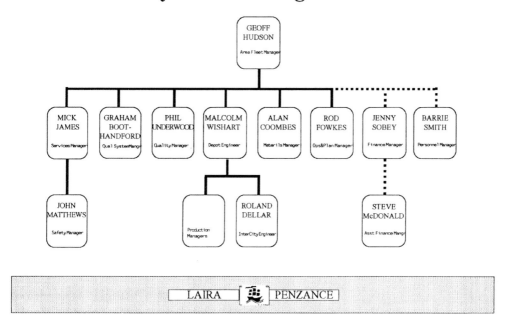

The ten-strong management team at Laira.

did not endear me to certain factions. Having said that, a manager in his quest for controlling costs has to make unpalatable decisions and stand by them.

As so often happens, a nudge is sometimes required in order to appreciate a given situation. At one of the weekly managers' meetings, where it must be said that very often little was achieved, indeed, various members of the team considered the meetings to be a complete waste of time, Phil Underwood, forever doodling, produced a flip chart depicting the costs incurred at Laira T&RSD. Rather surprisingly, the greatest expense was that of train crews, a staggering £751,000 per annum in 1991 – more than the whole of the management and supervisory staff at the depot. I immediately set about a rolling programme, taking out selected shed drivers and pilot diagrams with further turns being reduced at the subsequent annual timetable change. As to be expected, there was of course a degree of opposition from LDC 'B' and some drivers dug their heels in and worked slow for a time. Brian Clark, the Driver Manager in Plymouth was under pressure and taking a lot of flak and requested my attendance to explain the reasons to the Drivers' LDC for the number of turns being withdrawn on the depot. The elimination of the loco-hauled coaching stock on the Waterloo-Exeter route meant considerably fewer locomotive movements both onto and off the depot, hence the need to reduce some turns. On entering the meeting room in InterCity House I was greeted with, 'Here comes the cutter from Laira.' That kind of discourse would only heighten my resolve.

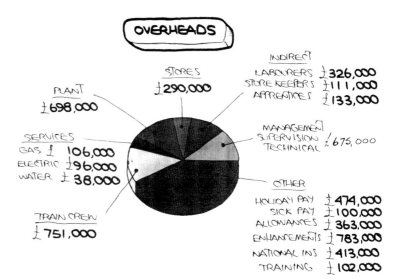

OVERHEADS

PLANT
£698,000

STORES
£290,000

INDIRECT
LABOURERS £326,000
STORE KEEPERS £111,000
APPRENTICES £133,000

MANAGEMENT
SUPERVISION £675,000
TECHNICAL

SERVICES
GAS £106,000
ELECTRIC £96,000
WATER £38,000

OTHER
HOLIDAY PAY £474,000
SICK PAY £100,000
ALLOWANCES £363,000
ENHANCEMENTS £783,000
NATIONAL INS £413,000
TRAINING £102,000

TRAIN CREW
£751,000

This chart highlighted the high costs incurred by train crews; rationalisation of drivers and secondment turns, and shunting and carriage cleaning staff, realised a saving during my tenure of £500,000.

Devonport Management Limited (DML) in HM Dockyard undertook a Fastrak programme of HST catering vehicle modification. An interesting exercise which was co-ordinated by David Wilkinson, project manager at Paddington, with project engineer Peter Kelly at Derby. It then fell to me to oversee the workings into and out of the Dockyard, liaising with the traction controller at York regarding the movement of Neville Hill-based catering vehicles down to Plymouth. John Ainsworth, a Senior Technical Officer at Laira, worked closely with DML in realising the successful venture. We were both rewarded at the close of the contract by having dinner with David Wilkinson at the Grand Hotel on Plymouth Hoe.

Scenes like this were fast disappearing; the HSTs were working the CrossCountry diagrams in addition to the Great Western services. Then, the loss of the Exeter to Waterloo loco-hauled trains meant fewer diesel locomotives visiting Laira Depot; this necessitated reducing the complement of driving turns on the depot.

Geoff Hudson decided to take the management team away for three or four days on a seminar at Langdon Court, a hotel half a mile from my home. It coincided with my fiftieth birthday, and not wishing to miss out on happenings in the evenings, I decided to stay over with the rest of the team. After dinner one evening, I returned home only to find my family had gone out. On the kitchen table was my birthday cake, which Janet had gone to great pains over by having it made by Mary Manley, whose husband Dave was a maintenance supervisor at the depot. Without a second thought, I took it back to Langdon Court to be shared with my colleagues who were unanimous in their praise of a beautifully decorated cake, complete with a vegetable theme. Needless to say, I wasn't the flavour of the month when returning home from the seminar – a very expensive cake which none of my family had the chance to sample. Prior to this team building exercise, arrangements were made for me to attend a Core Management Skills course at The Grove, Watford, over the years a good grounding for new managers.

The first Open Day at Laira Depot for six years took place in 1991. The committee was already in place when I returned there as Operations and Planning Manager and it was no surprise that I was 'roped in' on it.

The original intention was to bring back all of the preserved 'Western' Class diesel-hydraulic locomotives for the event. Unfortunately, D1041 *Western Prince* was trapped on the East Lancashire Railway, owing to the severance of its main line link at the time. Another, D1048 *Western Lady*, was the subject of protracted talks with the Bodmin & Wenford Railway. The locomotive, in a rather shabby condition, was left in Cornwall as the movement and its subsequent return could not be agreed with its owner.

Nº 2507

British Rail | Western Region

Laira Diesel Depot
Plymouth

British Rail Western Region

LAIRA OPEN DAY

SATURDAY 7 SEPT 1985

Souvenir Programme 50p

Previous open day in 1972.

Previous open day in 1985.

BRITISH RAIL WESTERN

LAIRA OPEN DAY
SUNDAY 25th APRIL, 1982

Inter City 125 trains being serviced inside the new shed. March 1982
Photo: T. N. Bowden

Souvenir Programme 30p

Programme No 3868

Previous open day in 1982.

Summary of Trains incoming for Laira Open Day

ⓓ Monday 9 September
7X54 12.05 Westbury – Laira (Arr 16.00)
D 7017 D821 D1015 D1023

ⓓ Thursday 12 September
7Z65 (Renumbered 7X65) 11.0c Totnes – Tavistock Jn (Extd Laira)
Class 20 Loc 20110

③ Thursday 12 September
6X57 13.32 Taunton Fairwtr – Laira TMD (Arr 16.00)
P7017 D1035

④ Thursday 12 September
PC05 (Renumbered 8X05) 11.38 Exeter Riv – Tavistock Jn
45133 55015
* Move to Laira under Local Arrangements *

⑤ Friday 13 September
6X55 22.15 Exeter Riv – Laira (Arr 23.33)
D1013 D1062 G1 26
C150 Loco Required for : – ①, ③, ⑤
and 6X61 11.52 Paignton – Goodrington Riverside FRI 13 SEPT.

RHQ Swindon drew up a summary of services, bringing incoming exhibits to
Laira for the open day.

LOCOMOTIVES REQUESTED FOR LAIRA OPENDAY 1991

LOCO No.	TYPE	BRAKE AIR/VAC	COMING FROM	RETURNING TO	COMMENTS
1010 (1035)	Western	Air	West Somer-set Rly	West Somerset Railway ~~Bodmin~~	To be confirmed
1013	Western	Air	Severn Vly Railway	Severn Valley Railway	See 1062
1015	Western	Air	Old Oak Common	Old Oak Comm-on depot	See 821
1023	Western	Air	Old Oak Common	NRM York	See 1015. £250 to cover staff costs and free rail tickets for staff.
1041	Western _N/A_	Air	East Lancs Railway.	East Lancs Railway. Bury.	May not be available due to severence of rail link.
1048	Western _No_	Air	Bodmin & Wenford.	Bodmin & Wenford.	Looks a real mess!!
1062	Western	Air	Severn Vly Railway	Severn Valley Railway	See 1013
7017	Hymek	Air? _Vac_	Didcot Rly centre. _West Somerset Railway_	Didcot Rail-way centre. _West Somerset Railway_	To be confirmed
7xxx _7018_	Hymek	Air? _Vac_	West Somer-set Rly	~~West Somerset Railway~~ _Bodmin_	To be confirmed
821	Warship	Vac	Old Oak Common.	North Yorks Moors Rly.	May be arranged to have temporary air brake fitted, watch this space. See 1015 & 1023.
590xx	Foster Yeoman	Air	Westbury	Westbury TMD	**Must be released to arrive back at Westbury no later than 21:00 Hrs.**
591xx	ARC	Air	Westbury	Westbury TMD	**Must be released to arrive back at Westbury no later than 21:00 Hrs.**
~~60xxx~~	~~Cl 60~~	~~Air~~	~~Cardiff~~	~~Cardiff TMD~~	~~Awaiting confirmation.~~ _Two on S.Wales_
45133	Cl 45	Air	Butterley Midland Railway.	Butterley Midland Rail-way centre.	See 55015. S.Coles to arrange.
55015	Deltic	Air	Butterley Midland Railway.	Butterley Midland Rail-way centre.	See 45133.
08xxx	Cl 08	Air	Laira TMD	Laira TMD.	Possibly repainted into Parcels "Red" livery or Network Southeast.

LOCOMOTIVES REQUESTED FOR LAIRA OPENDAY 1991

	CURRENT STATUS		ACTION REQUIRED		LOCO No.
	U.A.T.	RUNNING EXAM	U.A.T.	RUNNING EXAM	
	Not known	Not known	Not known	Not known	1010 (1035)
	Out of date	Out of date	To test	To examine	1013
	Out of date	Out of date	To test	To examine	1015
	In date	In date	N/A	N/A	1023
	In date	In date	N/A	N/A	1041
	Out of date	Out of date	To test	To examine	1048
	Out of date	Out of date	To test	To examine	1062
	Not known	Not known	Not known	Not known	7017
	Not known	Not known	Not known	Not known	7xxx
	In date	In date	N/A	N/A	821
	N/A	N/A	N/A	N/A	590xx
	N/A	N/A	N/A	N/A	591xx
	N/A	N/A	N/A	N/A	60xxx
	In date	In date	N/A	N/A	45133
	In date	In date	N/A	N/A	55015
	N/A	N/A	N/A	N/A	08xxx

Provisional list of desired exhibits for display, Laira Open Day.

DIESEL MULTIPLE UNITS REQUESTED FOR LAIRA OPENDAY 1991

UNIT NO.	CLASS	BRAKE AIR/VAC	COMING FROM	RETURNING TO	COMMENTS	CURRENT STATUS RUNNING	EXAM	ACTION REQUIRED RUNNING	EXAM
P1xx	Cl 121	Vac	Laira TMD.	Laira TMD.	Reg.Rlys & Green liveries	U.A.T.	N/A	N/A	N/A
P8xx	Cl 101	Vac	Laira TMD.	Laira TMD.	To be arranged.	N/A	N/A	N/A	N/A
50 2xx	Cl 150/2	Air	Cardiff	Cardiff TMD.	To be arranged.	N/A	N/A	N/A	N/A
53 xxx	Cl 153	Air	Cardiff	Cardiff TMD.	To be arranged.	N/A	N/A	N/A	N/A
58 xxx	Cl 158	Air	Cardiff	Cardiff TMD.	To be arranged.	N/A	N/A	N/A	N/A

LOCOMOTIVE HAULED COACHING STOCK REQUESTED FOR LAIRA OPENDAY 1991

VEHICLE NO.	CLASS	BRAKE AIR/VAC	COMING FROM	RETURNING TO	COMMENTS	CURRENT STATUS RUNNING	EXAM	ACTION REQUIRED RUNNING	EXAM
5xxx	mk2a/b	Air	Laira TMD.	Laira TMD.		N/A	N/A	N/A	N/A
106xx	mk3sle	Air	Laira TMD.	Laira TMD.		N/A	N/A	N/A	N/A
10xxx various	mk4 various	Air	East Coast Mainline.	East Coast Mainline.	G.Hudson to liase with D.Sawyer.	N/A	N/A	N/A	N/A
80xxx	TPO's	Air	Laira TMD.	Laira TMD.	One set stabled at Laira on Sundays, suggest we utilise it!	N/A	N/A	N/A	N/A
ADBxx	BDV's	Air	Laira TMD.	Laira TMD.	Will be in use for the rerailing demonstration.	N/A	N/A	N/A	N/A
8xxxx	TPO's	Air	?	?	Post Office exhibition train, to be arranged.	Not known	Not known	Not known	Not known
xxxxx	Saloon	?	?	?	To be arranged.	Not known	Not known	Not known	Not known
xxxxx	Test cars	Air	RTC	RTC Derby	RD to liase with RCE.	N/A	N/A	N/A	N/A

(handwritten annotations near 8xxxx row: "Not A. White" / "? Alan White 003 OH 4")

HIGH SPEED TRAINS REQUESTED FOR LAIRA OPENDAY 1991

UNIT NO.	CLASS	BRAKE AIR/VAC	COMING FROM	RETURNING TO	COMMENTS	CURRENT STATUS RUNNING	EXAM	ACTION REQUIRED RUNNING	EXAM
43188	Cl 43	Air	Laira TMD.	Laira TMD.		U.A.T.	N/A	N/A	N/A
43xxx	Cl 43	Air	Laira TMD.	Laira TMD.	To be named "Plymouth Laira TMD" by Dr John Prideaux.	N/A	N/A	N/A	N/A
43xxx	Cl 43	Air	Laira TMD.	Laira TMD.	To be named "Evening Herald" assuming Alan Harrison can arrange.	N/A	N/A	N/A	N/A
Set 018	HST TC	Air	Laira TMD.	Laira TMD.		N/A	N/A	N/A	N/A

LOCOMOTIVES REQUESTED FOR LAIRA OPENDAY 1991

LOCO No.	TYPE	BRAKE AIR/VAC	COMING FROM	RETURNING TO	COMMENTS
~~20xxx~~ 20xxx Bxxxx	Cl 20	Air	~~Toton TMD~~ D.V.R.	~~Toton TMD~~ D.V.R.	R.Dellar to arrange with Depot Engineer ~~Toton TMD.~~ Dart Valley Railway.
25xxx	Cl 25	Air	Dart vall-ey Rly. Paignton.	Dart valley Railway, Paignton.	To be confirmed
31xxx *(31xxx to go)*	Cl 31	Air	Crewe TMD	Crewe TMD	To be arranged *061o537 Alan Monteton eye to ...*
33xxx	Cl 33	Air	Eastleigh /Exeter.	Eastleigh /Exeter.	Hopefully in NSE livery. *plc to Mainl of EH*
37xxx	Cl 37	Air	St Blazey.	St Blazey.	
478xx	Cl 47	Air	Bristol Bath Road.	Bristol Bath Road TMD.	J.Cronin has confirmed that a Bath Road "Royal" will be made available.
47xxx *(Rt to Arrange.)*	Cl 47	Air	Crewe TMD	Crewe TMD	To be arranged, for Parcels livery loco.
50007/ 50008/ 50015/ D400.	Cl 50	Air	Laira TMD.	Laira TMD.	
~~56xxx~~	~~Cl 56~~	~~Air~~	~~CF WY TMD~~	~~CF WY TMD~~	~~To be arranged~~
58xxx	Cl 58 *None Arranges.*	Air	Toton TMD	Toton TMD.	~~To be arranged~~
86xxx	Cl 86	Air	London Midl -land Reg.	London Midl- and Region.	G.Hudson to liase with J.Blaydon.
87xxx	Cl 87	Air	London Mid -land Reg.	London Midl- and Region.	G.Hudson to liase with J.Blaydon.
89xxx ?	Cl 89	Air	Doncaster Training School- G.N.	Doncaster Training School G.N.	~~G.Hudson to liase with C.Broch.~~ Available from ...
90xxx	Cl 90	Air	London Midl -land Reg.	London Midl- and Region.	G.Hudson to liase with J.Blaydon.
91xxx *No W/A*	Cl 91	Air	East Coast Mainline.	East Coast Mainline.	G.Hudson to liase with D.Sawyer.
73xxx	Cl 73	Air	Stewarts Lane TMD.	Stewarts Lane TMD.	R.Dellar to liase with P.Bentley.

LOCOMOTIVES REQUESTED FOR LAIRA OPENDAY 1991

CURRENT STATUS		ACTION REQUIRED		LOCO No.
U.A.T.	RUNNING EXAM	U.A.T.	RUNNING EXAM	
N/A	N/A	N/A	N/A	20xxx 20xxx
Not known	Not known	Not known	Not known	25xxx
N/A	N/A	N/A	N/A	31xxx
N/A	N/A	N/A	N/A	33xxx
N/A	N/A	N/A	N/A	37xxx
N/A	N/A	N/A	N/A	478xx
N/A	N/A	N/A	N/A	47xxx
N/A	N/A	N/A	N/A	50007/ 50008/ 50015/ D400.
N/A	N/A	N/A	N/A	56xxx
N/A	N/A	N/A	N/A	58xxx
N/A	N/A	N/A	N/A	86xxx
N/A	N/A	N/A	N/A	87xxx
Not known	Not known	Not known	Not known	89xxx
N/A	N/A	N/A	N/A	90xxx
N/A	N/A	N/A	N/A	91xxx
N/A	N/A	N/A	N/A	73xxx

179

Just emerged from the paint shop at Crewe Locomotive Works in December 1963, is a brand new Class '52' diesel-hydraulic locomotive for the Western Region.

In most organisations there is usually a fully paid-up member of the awkward squad. Not so with Bill Griffiths in the freight section at Swindon and Frank Orme at Rail House, Crewe; both were most helpful in the movement of the exhibits down to the south-west. Although showing signs of displeasure at times over the whole proceedings, their normal duties still had to be undertaken; they were resolute in the quest to ensure that the requirements for the Open Day were realised. With one of the other managers on the committee, we had a meeting with Bill at Swindon to formulate a plan for the working of exhibits down to Laira. Personal contact does bring rewards, and from then on there was no problem in getting the selected diesels down. Although it was out of my remit, Bill had put me in touch with his opposite number at Crewe, Frank Orme. Frank gave the impression that using the telephone was not one of his favourite activities. He told me that he commuted from Derby each day, and during the conversation it transpired that he had recently been to Breaston, Longmoor Lane no less, just a few doors from where my mother still lived; these exchanges would guarantee the utmost cooperation. The Divisional Civil Engineer had agreed that locomotives for display could travel on Civil Link services between Toton/Bescot and Tavistock Junction. Also sanctioned was the use of his two diesel locomotives, 50008 and 50015, to fetch exhibits from the various staging points.

Sunday, 15 September was the chosen day for the event. This was clearly wrong for two very good reasons. Firstly, had it been held on a Saturday the whole area could have been more easily managed, with no movements at all off the depot. As it was, four trains had to be worked away on the Sunday morning. This hindered the progress of the DMU shuttle service running between Plymouth station and a temporary platform on the single line between Mount Gould Junction and Laira Junction. Two Railtours also had to be brought onto the depot. Health and Safety aspects had to be addressed with various sections of the complex cordoned off. Secondly, the attendance figures would have increased considerably with a more diverse Saturday service. Indeed, on the day in question anyone travelling from the Midlands and the North by ordinary service train would not have arrived in Plymouth until late afternoon. Despite my protestations, Sunday it was, and it could easily have been so different.

To promote the Open Day, I rang BBC Radio Devon and Geoff went to the Plymouth studio to be interviewed on their lunchtime programme.

On Monday, 9 September the first cavalcade left Old Oak Common for Laira:
7X51 02.55 Old Oak Common TMD - Westbury DN TC hauled by Class 47 No. 47364.
7X54 12.05 Westbury DN TC - Laira TMD hauled by Class 50 No. 50008. Conveyed D7018 (TOPS 35018), D1015 (TOPS 52015), D1023 (TOPS 52023), D821 (TOPS 42021).
Two exhibits from the Midland Railway Centre at Butterley were worked on Civil Link services.

Tuesday, 10 September.
8G15 02.45 Toton New Bank - Bescot DS hauled by Class 31 Nos. 31105/31459.
8X01 14.53 Bescot DS - Gloucester NY hauled by Class 37 No. 37158. Conveyed 45133. 55015. Connect:
7X01 07.49 Gloucester NY - Westbury DN TC hauled by Class 37 No. 37054, 11/09.
6X96 09.38 Tonbridge - Meldon Qry (15.55 Westbury DN TC - Exeter Riverside) hauled by Class 33. Nos. 33008/33208. 8X05 18.34   Exeter Riverside - Tavistock JN then trip to Laira TMD. 12/09.

Thursday, 12 September.
7Z65 11.00 Totnes - Tavistock JN then trip to Laira TMD. Class 20 20110 hauled by Class 50 No. 50015.
On the same day two privately owned locomotives on the West Somerset Line were worked down as far as Taunton, from where they were hauled to Laira.
6X57 13.32 Taunton Fairwater - Laira TMD hauled by Class 50 No. 50008. Conveyed D1035 (TOPS 52035), D7017 (TOPS 35017). Also on the same day two more privately owned locomotives, this time off the Severn Valley Railway, set off from Bescot via Gloucester and Westbury and arrived at Exeter Riverside the following day behind Class 37 No. 37372. From there D1013 (TOPS 52013) and D1062 (TOPS 52062) were hauled to Laira TMD by Class 50 No. 50046.

Confirmation that the Director of Civil Engineering was agreeable for locomotives to pass on Civil Link services Toton/Bescot/Tavistock Junction.

R DELLAR

To R FOWKES

Plymouth Laria Depot.
Area Fleet Manager.

We would be agreeable for 4 locomotives to pass on our Civil Link services Toton/Bescot/Tavistock Jcn for your Open Day.

No charges will be raised for this move.

For the Director of Civil Engineering

12th August 1991
phone 00-30699

C.2

F.T.N No 24
05.09.91

MONDAY 09 SEPTEMBER

EXCEPTIONAL LOADS

7X51 02.55 OLD OAK COMMON TMD - WESTBURY DN TC
SPECIAL HAULED BY CL 47 LOCOMOTIVE (AME OLD OAK COOMON TO ARRANGE).   CONVEYS PRIVATELY OWNED EX BR LOCOS D7018 (TOPS 35018), D1015 (TOPS 52015), D1023 (TOPS 52023), D821 (TOPS 42021). ALL DEAD ON OWN WHEELS WITH VACUUM BRAKES OPERATIVE - ALL EN ROUTE LAIRA TMD.

	Arr	Dep		Arr	Dep
Kensal Green CSP	03RR10	03RR35	Twyford	04/23	
Old Oak Common West		03/40	Reading		04/30
Acton		03/45	Newbury		05/07
Southall		03/54	Woodborough		05/22
Slough		04/06	Westbury Dn TC	05.55	

Continued.....

C.4

F.T.N No 24
05.09.91

MONDAY 09 SEPTEMBER (Continued)

EXCEPTIONAL LOADS (Continued)

NOTES
(1) ENGINES MUST NOT UNDER ANY CIRCUMSTANCES BE STARTED ON PRIVATELY OWNED LOCOMOTIVES WHILST IN TRANSIT.

(2) TO TRAVEL IN ACCORDANCE WITH THE INSTRUCTIONS SHOWN IN WORKING MANUAL FOR RAIL STAFF BR 30054, WHITE PAGES, SECTION D1/2. STAFF CONCERNED MUST BE IN POSSESSION OF BR 29973, 'ADVICE TO TRAINCREWS OF EXCEPTIONAL LOADS,' WHICH IS THE ONLY AUTHORITY FOR MOVEMENT.

MONDAY 09 SEPTEMBER (Continued)

EXCEPTIONAL LOADS (Continued)

FORWARD
7X54 12.05 WESTBURY DN TC - LAIRA TMD
SPECIAL.   HAULED BY CL 50 LOCOMOTIVE (POOL DOOA)

	Arr	Dep		Arr	Dep
Westbury Dn TC		12.05	Exeter St Davids	14/26	
Fairwood Jn	12/10		Dawlish Warren	14/43	
Clink Road Jn	12/15		Newton Abbot	14/58	
Blatchbridge Jn	12/18		Totnes	15/12	
East Somerset Jn	12/24		Ivybridge	15/34	
Cogload Jn	13/08		Hemerdon	15/42	
Taunton	13*14	13*32	Tavistock Jn	15*50	15*55
Norton Fitzwarren	13/37		Laira Jn	15/57	
Tiverton	14/02		Laira TMD	16.00	

DIMENSIONS   :   WITHIN GAUGE

RESTRICTIONS   :   EXLO. MARFOR. SHUNTEX. FABRIC 45 MPH.
                       GOBI.   NO RESTRICTION ON ROUTEING.

NOTES   (1) D7018 TO BE FORMED ON BRISTOL END OF TRAIN EX OLD OAK COMMON.

         (2) ENGINES MUST NOT UNDER ANY CIRCUMSTANCES BE STARTED ON PRIVATELY OWNED
              LOCOMOTIVES WHILST IN TRANSIT.

         (3) TO TRAVEL IN ACCORDANCE WITH THE INSTRUCTIONS SHOWN IN WORKING MANUAL
              FOR RAIL STAFF BR 30054, WHITE PAGES, SECTION D1/2. STAFF CONCERNED
              MUST BE IN POSSESSION OF BR 29973, 'ADVICE TO TRAINCREWS OF
              EXCEPTIONAL LOADS,' WHICH IS THE ONLY AUTHORITY FOR MOVEMENT.

MONDAY 09 SEPTEMBER

EXCEPTIONAL LOADS

7X52 07.57 WESTBURY DN TC - MEREHEAD QUARRY (ARR 08.34)
SPECIAL.   HAULED BY NEM(CONSTRUCTION) LOCOMOTIVE.   CONVEYS PRIVATELY OWNED EX BR
LOCO D7018 (AIR PIPED) WITH 3 AIR BRAKED WAGONS (REAR).

LOCOMOTIVE D7018 TO BE WEIGHED AT MEREHEAD QUARRY

7X53 10.15 MEREHEAD QUARRY - WESTBURY DN TC (ARR 11.05)
SPECIAL.   HAULED BY NEM(CONSTRUCTION) LOCOMOTIVE.   CONVEYS PRIVATELY OWNED EX BR
LOCO D7018 (AIR PIPED) WITH 3 AIR BRAKED WAGONS (REAR).

D7018 FORWARD TO LAIRA TMD PER 7X54.

DIMENSIONS   :   WITHIN GAUGE

RESTRICTIONS   :   EXLO. MARFOR. SHUNTEX. FABRIC 45 MPH.
                       GOBI.   NO RESTRICTION ON ROUTEING.

Continued...

THE FOLLOWING MOVEMENTS TAKE PLACE IN RESPECT OF 'OPEN DAY'
TO BE HELD AT LAIRA ON SUNDAY 15 SEPTEMBER

TUESDAY 10 SEPTEMBER

EXCEPTIONAL LOADS

8V01 (RENUMBERED 8X01) 14.53 BESCOT - GLOUCESTER NY
CONVEYS PRIVATELY OWNED EX BR LOCOMOTIVES 45133 AND 55015 BOTH DEAD ON OWN WHEELS (AIR BRAKED).

CONNECT
8A01 (RENUMBERED 8X01) 07.10 GLOUCESTER NY - WESTBURY DN TC - WEDNESDAY 11 SEPTEMBER
7C06 (RENUMBERED 7X06) 15.55 WESTBURY DN TC - EXETER RIVERSIDE - SAME DAY
8C05 (RENUMBERED 8X05) 18.34 EXETER RIVERSIDE - TAVISTOCK JN - THURSDAY 12 SEPTEMBER
FORWARD TO LAIRA TMD UNDER LOCAL ARRANGEMENTS.

DIMENSIONS   :   WITHIN GAUGE

RESTRICTIONS   :   EXLO. MARFOR. SHUNTEX. FABRIC 60 MPH.
                            GOBI.   NO RESTRICTION ON ROUTEING.

NOTES   (1)   ENGINES MUST NOT UNDER ANY CIRCUMSTANCES BE STARTED ON PRIVATELY OWNED
                 LOCOMOTIVES WHILST IN TRANSIT.

           (2)   TO TRAVEL IN ACCORDANCE WITH THE INSTRUCTIONS SHOWN IN WORKING MANUAL
                 FOR RAIL STAFF BR 30054, WHITE PAGES, SECTION D1/2.   STAFF CONCERNED
                 MUST BE IN POSSESSION OF BR 29973, 'ADVICE TO TRAINCREWS OF
                 EXCEPTIONAL LOADS,' WHICH IS THE ONLY AUTHORITY FOR MOVEMENT.

THURSDAY 12 SEPTEMBER

EXCEPTIONL LOADS

7Z65 11.00 TOTNES - TAVISTOCK JN
REFERENCE EXETER ENGINEERS NOTICE E.24, PAGE 15.

WILL RUN TO LAIRA TMD AND CONVEY PRIVATELY OWNED EX BR CLASS 20 LOCOMOTIVE, DEAD ON OWN WHEELS, WITH VACUUM BRAKES OPERATIVE.

DIMENSIONS   :   WITHIN GAUGE

RESTRICTIONS   :   EXLO. MARFOR. SHUNTEX. FABRIC 45 MPH.
                            GOBI.   NO RESTRICTION ON ROUTEING.

NOTES   (1)   ENGINES MUST NOT UNDER ANY CIRCUMSTANCES BE STARTED ON PRIVATELY OWNED
                 LOCOMOTIVES WHILST IN TRANSIT.

           (2)   TO TRAVEL IN ACCORDANCE WITH THE INSTRUCTIONS SHOWN IN WORKING MANUAL
                 FOR RAIL STAFF BR 30054, WHITE PAGES, SECTION D1/2.   STAFF CONCERNED
                 MUST BE IN POSSESSION OF BR 29973, 'ADVICE TO TRAINCREWS OF
                 EXCEPTIONAL LOADS,' WHICH IS THE ONLY AUTHORITY FOR MOVEMENT.

THE FOLLOWING MOVEMENTS TAKE PLACE IN RESPECT OF 'OPEN DAY' TO BE HELD AT LAIRA ON SUNDAY 15 SEPTEMBER

THURSDAY 12 SEPTEMBER

EXCEPTIONAL LOADS

8V01 (RENUMBRERED 8X01) 14.53 BESCOT - GLOUCESTER NY
CONVEYS PRIVATELY OWNED EX BR LOCOMOTIVES D1013 AND D1062 BOTH DEAD ON OWN WHEELS (DUAL BRAKED) EN ROUTE LAIRA TMD.

CONNECT
8A01 (RENUMBERED 8X01) 07.10 GLOUCSTER NY - WESTBURY DN TC - FRIDAY 13 SEPTEMBER
7C06 (RENUMBERED 7X06) 15.55 WESTBURY DN TC - EXETER RIVERSIDE - SAME DAY
6X55 22.15 EXETER RIVERSIDE - LAIRA TMD   - SAME DAY

DIMENSIONS   :   WITHIN GAUGE

RESTRICTIONS   :   EXLO. MARFOR. SHUNTEX. FABRIC 60 MPH.
                         GOBI.   NO RESTRICTION ON ROUTEING.

NOTES   (1)   ENGINES MUST NOT UNDER ANY CIRCUMSTANCES BE STARTED ON PRIVATELY OWNED
                 LOCOMOTIVES WHILST IN TRANSIT.

           (2)   TO TRAVEL IN ACCORDANCE WITH THE INSTRUCTIONS SHOWN IN WORKING MANUAL
                 FOR RAIL STAFF BR 30054, WHITE PAGES, SECTION D1/2. STAFF CONCERNED
                 MUST BE IN POSSESSION OF BR 29973, 'ADVICE TO TRAINCREWS OF
                 EXCEPTIONAL LOADS,' WHICH IS THE ONLY AUTHORITY FOR MOVEMENT.

THURSDAY 12 SEPTEMBER

EXCEPTIONAL LOADS

6X57 13.32 TAUNTON FAIRWATER - LAIRA TMD
SPECIAL.   HAULED BY CL 50 LOCOMOTIVE (POOL DCQA).   CONVEYS PRIVATELY OWNED EX BR LOCOMOTIVES D1035, D7017 DEAD ON OWN WHEELS (VACUUM BRAKES OPERATIVE).

	Arr	Dep		Arr	Dep
Norton Fitzwarren	13/37		Ivybridge		15/34
Tiverton	14/02		Hemerdon		15/42
Exeter St Davids	14/26		Tavistock Jn	15*50	15*55
Dawlish Warren	14/43		Laira Jn		15/57
Newton Abbot	14/58		Laira TMD	16.00	
Totnes	15/12				

DIMENSIONS   :   WITHIN GAUGE

RESTRICTIONS   :   EXLO. MARFOR. SHUNTEX. FABRIC 60 MPH.
                         GOBI.   NO RESTRICTION ON RGUTEING.

NOTES   (1)   ENGINES MUST NOT UNDER ANY CIRCUMSTANCES BE STARTED ON PRIVATELY OWNED
                 LOCOMOTIVES WHILST IN TRANSIT.

           (2)   TO TRAVEL IN ACCORDANCE WITH THE INSTRUCTIONS SHOWN IN WORKING MANUAL
                 FOR RAIL STAFF BR 30054, WHITE PAGES, SECTION D1/2. STAFF CONCERNED
                 MUST BE IN POSSESSION OF BR 29973, 'ADVICE TO TRAINCREWS OF
                 EXCEPTIONAL LOADS,' WHICH IS THE ONLY AUTHORITY FOR MOVEMENT.

THE FOLLOWING MOVEMENTS TAKE PLACE IN RESPECT OF 'OPEN DAY' TO BE HELD AT LAIRA ON SUNDAY 15 SEPTEMBER

FRIDAY 13 SEPTEMBER

EXCEPTIONAL LOADS

6X61 15.30 PAIGNTON (DVR) EXCH SDGS - EXETER RIVERSIDE
SPECIAL.   HAULED BY CL 50 LOCOMOTIVE (POOL DCQA).   CONVEYS PRIVATELY OWNED EX BR CLASS 25 LOCOMOTIVE, DEAD ON OWN WHEELS (VACUUM BRAKES OPERATIVE), EN ROUTE LAIRA.

	Arr	Dep		Arr	Dep
Paignton	15/32		Dawlish Warren		15/56
Torquay	15/37		Exeter St Davids		16/09
Torre	15/39		Exeter Riverside NY	16.12	

DIMENSIONS   :   WITHIN GAUGE

RESTRICTIONS   :   EXLO. MARFOR. SHUNTEX. FABRIC 60 MPH.
GOBI.   NO RESTRICTION ON ROUTEING.

NOTES   (1) ENGINES MUST NOT UNDER ANY CIRCUMSTANCES BE STARTED ON PRIVATELY OWNED LOCOMOTIVE WHILST IN TRANSIT.

          (2) TO TRAVEL IN ACCORDANCE WITH THE INSTRUCTIONS SHOWN IN WORKING MANUAL FOR RAIL STAFF BR 30054, WHITE PAGES, SECTION D1/2.   STAFF CONCERNED MUST BE IN POSSESSION OF BR 29973, 'ADVICE TO TRAINCREWS OF EXCEPTIONAL LOADS,' WHICH IS THE ONLY AUTHORITY FOR MOVEMENT.

FRIDAY 13 SEPTEMBER

EXCEPTIONAL LOADS

6X55 22.15 EXETER RIVERSIDE NY - LAIRA TMD
SPECIAL.   HAULED BY CL 50 LOCOMOTIVE (POOL DCQA).   CONVEYS PRIVATELY OWNED EX BR LOCOMOTIVES D1035, D7017 AND CL 20 DEAD ON OWN WHEELS (VACUUM BRAKES OPERATIVE).

	Arr	Dep		Arr	Dep
Exeter St Davids	22/18		Hemerdon		23/20
Dawlish Warren	22/29		Tavistock Jn		23/28
Newton Abbot	22/42		Laira Jn		23/30
Totnes	22/55		Laira TMD	23.33	
Ivybridge	23/16				

DIMENSIONS   :   WITHIN GAUGE

RESTRICTIONS   :   EXLO. MARFOR. SHUNTEX. FABRIC 60 MPH.
GOBI.   NO RESTRICTION ON ROUTEING.

NOTES   (1) ENGINES MUST NOT UNDER ANY CIRCUMSTANCES BE STARTED ON PRIVATELY OWNED LOCOMOTIVE WHILST IN TRANSIT.

          (2) TO TRAVEL IN ACCORDANCE WITH THE INSTRUCTIONS SHOWN IN WORKING MANUAL FOR RAIL STAFF BR 30054, WHITE PAGES, SECTION D1/2.   STAFF CONCERNED MUST BE IN POSSESSION OF BR 29973, 'ADVICE TO TRAINCREWS OF EXCEPTIONAL LOADS,' WHICH IS THE ONLY AUTHORITY FOR MOVEMENT.

DAILY SUPPLEMENTARY
FREIGHT TRAIN NOTICE

TUESDAY 10 TO FRIDAY 13 SEPTEMBER

STONE TRAFFIC

6V76 08.45 Cliffe Hill - Hayes	Runs TWFO - Cancelled THO
6M68 17.58 Hayes - Cliffe Hill	Runs TWO - Cancelled THO
6Z68 17.58 Hayes - Cliffe Hill	Runs in FSX path.

SATURDAY 14 SEPTEMBER

EXCEPTIONAL LOAD

0X67 09.15 Crewe EMD - Laira TMD (arr 15.55)
Special : Cl.31 hauls Cl.87, Cl.90 & Cl.86.
Via Hartlebury 11/14, Gloucester G.156 12C05-12C07 & Exeter St.Davids 14C34-14C36.

DIMENSIONS   : Within Gauge.

RESTRICTIONS : EXLO, MARFAR, SHUNTEX, FABRIC 60, GOBI - No restriction on route.
                  PANTOGRAPHS TO BE LOCKED IN DOWN POSITION.

NOTE   : To travel in accordance with the instructions shown in Working
                  Manual for Rail Staff BR 30054 White Pages Section D1/2. Staff
                  concerned must be in possession of BR 29973, 'Advice to Traincrew
                  of Exceptional Loads,' which is the only authority for movement.

SUNDAY 15 SEPTEMBER

EXCEPTIONAL LOAD

0X68 18.30 Laira TMD - Crewe EMD
Special : Cl.31 hauls Cl.87, Cl.90 & Cl.86.
Via Exeter St.Davids 19C53-19C55, Gloucester G.239 22C52-22C54 & Hartlebury 23/56.

DIMENSIONS   : Within Gauge.

RESTRICTIONS : EXLO, MARFAR, SHUNTEX, FABRIC 60, GOBI - No restriction on route.
                  PANTOGRAPHS TO BE LOCKED IN DOWN POSITION.

NOTE   : To travel in accordance with the instructions shown in Working
                  Manual for Rail Staff BR 30054 White Pages Section D1/2. Staff
                  concerned must be in possession of BR 29973, 'Advice to Traincrew
                  of Exceptional Loads,' which is the only authority for movement.

Fresh ballast has been put down to facilitate the underfoot conditions for the anticipated large crowd expected for the open day on 15 September 1991. Hymek D7018 has been positioned in front of D1010 *Western Campaigner* disguised as D1035 *Western Yeoman* with D1013 *Western Ranger* alongside. Bernard Mills

Ask and ye shall receive. I was particularly pleased with two of my own requests. A fax was sent to A.W. (Tony) Lovell, Contracts Manager for Railfreight Petroleum, enquiring as to the possibility of having a Class 60 diesel on display. He kindly arranged for one to work throughout on 6V62 10.34 Fawley-Tavistock Junction on the Friday and run light to the depot, worked by an Eastleigh driver throughout with the Exeter driver as a conductor. Tony also cancelled Fridays return working 6079 21.40 Tavistock Junction-Eastleigh, and ran it especially on the Sunday evening, again with an Eastleigh driver, who would require a conductor driver for route knowledge to Exeter. I considered it to have been quite a scoop.

It had been the intention to bring down a Class 25 diesel off the Paignton and Dartmouth Railway, but this became unavailable. There may have been a problem over the safety of line examination, which all privately owned locomotives must have before being allowed on BR metals, or the other stipulation of a current ultra-sonic axle test certificate, which again was mandatory for privately owned locomotives. On the Thursday prior to the event, during a conversation with Tony Mosely of the Heritage Centre, Crewe, we discussed the exhibits and that the '25' was not now an option. He immediately offered D7523 (25173) *John F. Kennedy* and arrangements were made for it to arrive with a Class 86 and 90 from Crewe. Gladly accepting this latest acquisition, I rang Frank Orme to advise him of this latest development. 'Too late to do anything about it, the notice has already been issued,' he barked, 'So if it comes, it comes.' And it did!

A.W. Lovell
14/8/91.

S.T.P
Swindon

Please arrange to publish the following in connection with the Plymouth Open Day. on 15/9/91.

6079. 21.40 Plymouth   Eastleigh   cancelled 13/9.

6V62 10.34 Fawley. Plymouth. 13/9 to be worked throughout by cl. 60 loco.   Eastleigh Dr. through to Plymouth conducted by booked Drs.

21.xx Spl. Plymouth to Eastleigh 15/9 worked throughout by Eastleigh Dr. conducted as necessary.

A.W. (Tony) Lovell provided a Class 60 locomotive for the event.

189

This is the view of Lipson sidings, the site of the old Laira (83D) steam shed. At the front of No. 5 road stands 'Warship' Class D821 *Greyhound*, which was brought over to the shed front and placed in position for the open day. A cavalcade of condemned Class '50' locomotives are seen in No. 3 road awaiting disposal to a scrap yard.

Saturday, 14 September.
Also arriving that day were two Class 59 locomotives from Westbury, one from ARC that was to be named on the Sunday, the other coming from the Foster Yeoman pool. One downside to the whole affair — beginning with the arrival of the exhibits earlier in the week and the positioning of locomotives with slide rule precision at the rehearsal overseen by Geoff — on the day itself, was the discovery that the film in my daughter's camera had not wound on!

Sunday, 15 September.
The big day dawned dry and bright; an early start to the depot to make the last minute arrangements, complete with a buttonhole. Geoff and Malcolm arrived in their casual gear and we set about marshalling the remaining exhibits, in between the departures off the depot. The Open Day was staged to celebrate the triple anniversary of the depot and InterCity's Silver Jubilee. In general the exhibit list had been realised: five out of the seven preserved 'Hydraulics' were on hand, as was a cross section of other diesel and electric traction. Tony Mosely had certainly come up trumps; the '25' *John F Kennedy* in two-tone green looked resplendent; the fact that it was positioned inside the depot made it no less alluring. Queues had formed along Embankment Road and the gates were opened before the 11.00 start time. Additional trains were run to get visitors to the event: an 08.40 Bristol to Plymouth HST

Another view of diesel-hydraulics taken on Saturday, 14 September for invited photographers; D1015 *Western Champion*, D1023 *Western Fusilier* and D1062 *Western Courier*, with a partial view on the extreme right of Class '50' D400. Bernard Mills

Classic line-up at Laira 1991 style! Five featured Class 52 diesel-hydraulics are: D1010 *Western Campaigner* (masquerading as D1035 *Western Yeoman*), D1013 *Western Ranger*, D1015 *Western Champion*, D1023 *Western Fusilier* and D1062 *Western Courier* on display at Laira depot. Bernard Mills

arrived in the station with so many passengers that the DMU shuttle service was over-subscribed, and the HST was extended to the Flush Apron where the passengers alighted and walked to the depot; a similar arrangement was already in place for the two railtours. The 07.50 Paddington-Plymouth additional, produced BRC&W Nos. 33042/64; the diesels came to the depot for fuel before working back at 18.10. Courtesy of Network SouthEast the 09.00 Waterloo-Exeter was extended to Plymouth, the proviso being that a Class 50 locomotive was made available to work the train. Of the two railtours, Hertfordshire ran a 07.42 Paddington to Laira with Nos. 58027/41; on arrival the diesels would work the return Pathfinder Rail tour. The latter started from Manchester at 04.37, and en route worked down to Paignton, then from Newton Abbot the train was formed with two Class 56s at the front and two Class 37s on the rear. On arrival at Laira, the 2x56 ran light to Exeter to work the continuation of the Hertfordshire Railtour that was worked from Laira to Exeter by the 2x37s. On reflection, we had insufficient handsignalmen on duty, the DMU shuttle being delayed for some time whilst the handsignalman was in Friary yard with the railtours.

A further factor was that the Movements Supervisor was slow in organising the move back from Friary with the Hertfordshire Railtour. There was an even greater delay to the shuttle in the afternoon when the return Hertfordshire Railtour stood on the single line for over forty minutes waiting a path onto the main line. With hindsight, we could and should have done better.

Each depot/station is located in a TOPS Responsibility Area; in the morning I did the usual Power Report for Exeter. The printout showed the diesels on hand at Laira, Exeter and Penzance and also locomotives arriving on trains bounded by the area Taunton to Penzance. One locomotive missing from the list was 25173, an eleventh hour replacement courtesy of Tony Mosely. A loco enquiry on TOPS revealed the diesel still on hand at Crewe Basford Hall, supposedly arrived on 9 September and still shown out of service and stored. Obviously the move from Crewe had not been reported to the local TOPS office; nevertheless the locomotive should have been claimed by Laira. Under the circumstances though, things were left as they were. To get so many exhibits over such a long distance was a feat

LAIRA OPENDAY '91
TIMETABLE OF EVENTS

- 11:30 Re-railing demonstration,
- 12:30 Re-railing demonstration,
- 13:00 Naming of ARC locomotive 59102 "Village of Chantry",
- 13:30 Re-railing demonstration,
- 14:00 Naming of Intercity 125 power car 43179 "Pride of Laira",
- 14:30 Re-railing demonstration,
- 15:00 Rail magazine rededication of pioneer class 50 locomotive "D400",
- 15:30 Presentation to the Guide Dog for the Blind Association from Pathfinder Railtours,
- 16:00 Draw of the Intercity quiz,
- 16:30 Draw of openday raffle.

SUBJECT TO CHANGE

Timetable of events Laira Open Day in 1991.

The meticulous positioning of the exhibits for the open day was paramount. Area Fleet Manager Geoff Hudson examined varying options in his quest for the perfect line up. Here a Class '08' moves 50033 *Glorious*, 50050 *Fearless* and 50007 *Sir Edward Elgar* on the depot.

Peak diesel 45133 came down from the Midland Railway Society at Butterley on Civil Link services for the 1991 open day at Laira. In the background is English Electric Deltic 55015 *Tulyar*.

D400 was built by the English Electric Company at the Vulcan Foundry, Newton-le-Willows, and was allocated new to the London Midland (Western Lines) in 1967. The whole fleet was transferred to the Western Region from 1972, to displace the non-standard diesel-hydraulics. Looking resplendent for its inclusion at the Laira Open Day in 1991.

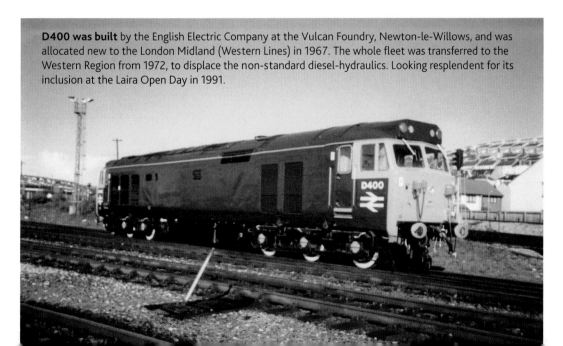

Hertfordshire Rail Tours

LAIRA OPEN DAY - SUNDAY 15 SEPTEMBER 1991

Stock: FSS Set BN91 (13 vehicles)

2 x Class 56: 58 (handwritten: 58 replacing 56)

```
PADDINGTON                d 08.15    No earlier please
Slough                    d 08U35
Reading                   d 08U55    Via Berks & Hants
Exeter St Davids            10/50
Plymouth North Rd Stn     a 12.00    Run round/photo stop
                          d 12.15
Lipson Junction                      Via West Side of Triangle
PLYMOUTH FRIARY           a 12.30
```

Attach Class 08 pilot at rear, to drag into Depot Platform:

```
PLYMOUTH FRIARY           d 12.40
LAIRA DEPOT PLATFORM      a 12.50    Passengers alight
```

2 x Class 56 [handwritten: 58] to be detached, ready to work Pathfinder tour to Bristol.
Break not to be significantly less than three hours please.
After break, train departs with 2 x Class 60 [handwritten: 37] leading (these locos
will have worked Pathfinder tour from Bristol):

```
LAIRA DEPOT PLATFORM      d 15.50    Via 'Depot' (south) side of triangle
Newton Abbot              a 16.40
```

Attach 2 x Class 37 at rear (2 x 60 remain at front):

```
Newton Abbot              d 16.50
Heathfield END OF LINE    a 17.10    No alighting at this point
                          d 17.15
Heathfield STATION        a 17.20    Photo stop
                          d 17.35
Newton Abbot              a 17.55
```

Detach 2 x Class 37: AT EXETER REPLACE WITH 2 × 56. *(handwritten)*

```
Newton Abbot              d 18.00    Via Berks & Hants
Reading                   a xxDxx
Slough                    a xxDxx
PADDINGTON                a 21.00    Not significantly later
```


At some stage, the kitchen car will need tanking for the return journey

It is important that the train traverses all three sides of the Laira Triangle.

In order to secure sufficient seats in FO stock, the set must run with 13
vehicles on.

Hertfordshire Rail Tour specification.

"The Tamar Tart" Railtour — Sunday 15th September, 1991

MILEAGE		TIME		LOCATION	COMMENT	TRACTION
Passenger	Freight					
			0437	MANCHESTER PICCADILLY	Pick Up	ANY
		0846	0448	STOCKPORT	Pick Up	
		0505	0507	MACCLESFIELD	Pick Up	
		0532	0534	STOKE-ON-TRENT	Pick Up	
		0625	0640	NUNEATON	Pick Up LOCO RUN ROUND	
			-	WATER ORTON		
		0721	0724	BIRMINGHAM NEW STREET	Pick Up	
				STOURBRIDGE JUNCTION		
			0814	WORCESTER SHRUB HILL		
		0837	0839	CHELTENHAM SPA	Pick Up	
		0915	0917	BRISTOL PARKWAY	Pick Up	
		0927	0942	BRISTOL TEMPLE MEADS	Pick Up LOCO CHANGE	CI.56x2
			-	WORLE JCT.		
			1008	WESTON SUPER MARE	(ROUTE THIS WAY PLEASE)	
			1024	BRIDGWATER		
			1040	TAUNTON		
			1117	EXETER ST. DAVIDS		
		1134	1148	NEWTON ABBOT	LOCO CHANGE CI.37x2	
		1204	1235	PAIGNTON	LOCO'S RUN ROUND	
		1251	1305	NEWTON ABBOT	RE-ATTACH CL 56 AT WEST END / REVERSE	CI.56x2
			-	TOTNES		
		1350	1355	PLYMOUTH NORTH ROAD (CENTRE ROAD PLEASE)	REVERSE	
			1358	LIPSON JCT.		
			1400	MOUNT GOULD JCT.		
		1407	1412	FRIARY STATION (AS FAR AS POSSIBLE. THANK YOU)	REVERSE	
		1447	1605	LAIRA CARRIAGE PLATFORM	LOCO CHANGE / WATER COACHES	CI.58 x 2
			1607	MOUNT GOULD JCT.		
			-	— VIA SPEEDWAY —		
			1610	LAIRA JCT.		
			-	TOTNES		
			1653	NEWTON ABBOT		
		1703	1706	DAWLISH WARREN	PICK UP BANANA FRITTERS !!	
			1716	EXETER ST. DAVIDS		
			1753	TAUNTON		
			1813	CASTLE CARY		
			1833	WESTBURY		
			1842	BRADFORD JCT.		
		1903	1905	BATH SPA	SET DOWN	
			-	DR. DAYS JCT.		
		1935	1937	BRISTOL PARKWAY	SET DOWN	
		2022	2024	CHELTENHAM SPA	SET DOWN	
			-	BROMSGROVE		
			-	SELLY OAK		
		2114	2116	BIRMINGHAM NEW STREET	SET DOWN	
			-	ASTON		
		-	-	BESCOT YARD		
		2211	2213	STAFFORD	SET DOWN	
		2237	2239	STOKE-ON-TRENT	SET DOWN	
		2304	2306	MACCLESFIELD	SET DOWN	
		2323	2325	STOCKPORT	SET DOWN	
		2334		MANCHESTER PICCADILLY	SET DOWN	

NOTES: The locomotives utilised are also involved with the working of Hertfordshire Railtours Paddington—Plymouth charter.
Class 56 from FAWK pool
    " 58 " FEBN "
    " 37 " FCLL "

STOCK CIRCUIT = LL910/911 (5xTSO/2xBFK/5xTSO)   Revision no.2: 21/08/91   Issue original: 12/4/91   PAGE 1
Issue revision: 20/5/91   OF 1

C. BROOKS 21/8/91

Specification for Pathfinder's 'Tamar Tart' Rail Tour.

```
KD83400 15/09/91 08.15.52 U2935
ON N185 BY POP FROM KD83400,SUNDAY 15/09/91    08.15.50
              POWER REPORT FOR EXETER        A  08.15 ON 15.09.91


MAINLINE          LOCOS OUT OF SERVICE                    ********

LOCO  DP SP T BK    NEXT    NEXT   PREASS O  REA  STOP'D EST OK WTT ALLOC
 NO   AL CH H TY RW EXAM    MAJOR  TOHRDY P  SON  HRDYMO HRDYMO  1    2


LOCATION-83400-RIVERSIDE BR
50019 HQ B M E XA    A  38? F-2544H        R  /ONE 152808 000000
50023 HQ B M E XA    A  39  F  175H        R  /ONE 121510 000000


LOCATION-83403-EXETER SD M&EE
33047 EH   M R XA NH A -19  S  204H EH1410 T N/612 000409 000000
37673 LA   M 0 XA    A  10  D  -72H        F N/600 231309 141409


LOCATION-83632-PAIGNTON  DART VRLY
98455 HQ     A VW    A   5  B 5999H        S  /    142309 000000
98488 HQ     A VW    A   5  B 5999H        D B/XAM 140410 221410


LOCATION-83703-TOTNES    DART VRLY
98238 HQ     A VW    A   6  B 6000H        D B/XAM 140410 100510


LOCATION-84081-TAVISTKJN BR
50003 HQ B M E XA    A  34  B  120H        R  /ONE 210107 000000
50020 HQ B M E XA    C  17  C   17H        R  /ONE 011605 000000
50026 LA B M E XA    A  13  C -297H        R  /ONE 110511 000000
50036 HQ B M E XA    A  16  B -261H        R  /ONE 032703 000000
50040 HQ   M E XA    A   6  B   35H        R  /ONE 192208 000000
50042 HQ B M E XA    A  30  B  250H        R  /ONE 121510 000000
50043 HQ B M E XA RW A  34? E -809H        R  /ONE 063101 000000
50045 LA B M E XA    A  32? D -670H        R  /ONE 012109 000000


LOCATION-84089-LAIRA JN  BRX
50001 HQ B M E XA    A  49  B  169H        R  /ONE 131004 000000
50002 HQ B M E XA    A  48  C -118H        R  /ONE 142208 000000
50007 HQ B M E XA R1 A  19  B   99H        R  /ONE 001007 000000
50010 LA   M E XA    A  12  B  146H        R  /ONE 193007 000000
50017 HQ B M E XA    A  25  B -160H        R  /ONE 080409 000000
50018 HQ B M E XA    A  38  F -186H        R  /ONE 111607 000000
50027 HQ B M E XA    A   8  D  -84H        R  /ONE 111107 000000
50031 HQ B M E XA    A  18  F  -75H        R  /ONE 222107 000000
50037 HQ   M E XA    A  18  B  194H        R  /ONE 081908 000000
50048 HQ B M E XA    A  45  B   -8H        R  /ONE 221506 000000
50049 HQ B M E XA    A  30  D    9H        R  /ONE 010108 000000


LOCATION-84090-LAIRA TMD M&EE
20110 HQ   M 0 XG    A  35  B  205H        R  /ONE 031009 000000
37417 LA B M E XA    A  16? C -459H        T N/100 091209 000000
37674 LA   M 0 XA    A  53? D -789H        D N/612 011608 221709
50046 LA B M E XA    A  23  D -398H        T N/100 030709 223009
50050 LA B M E XA    A  41  B  261H        X N/500 062108 221709
86609 CE P M 0 XH    A   1  C  123H CE1416 T N/SPT 091409 000000
90132 CE P M 0 AH    A -10  B  118H CE1416 T N/SPT 091409 000000


LOCATION-84202-KEYHAMMOD MOD NAVY
47538 HQ B M E XA    A  16  B  -50H        R  /TWO 120507 000000
```

196

```
MAINLINE          LOCOS ON HAND OK                    ********

LOCO  DP SP  T BK     NEXT    NEXT    PREASS O FUEL  TIM-AV WTT ALLOC
NO    AL CH  H TY RW  EXAM    MAJOR   TOHRDY P HRS   HRDYMO  1    2


LOCATION-83000-TAUNTONYD BR
47280 TI B M 0 XA     A  20  B   -8H       N 025 X 221409


LOCATION-83403-EXETER SD M&EE
37671 LA   M 0 XA     A  19? E -956H       N 000?X 121409
37885 CF   M X XA     A  23  B  189H       N 002 X 051409


LOCATION-83421-EXETSTDAV BR
33102 EH QPM P XA     A  38  T  693H       N 005 X 211309 2003
47710 OC PBM E XA     E  18  E   18H       N 009 X 221409 1035 1V17


LOCATION-84090-LAIRA TMD M&EE
31405 BS   M E XA     A  46 B02 141H       N 012 X 191409
35017 HQ     0 XA    ·A   4  B 5998H       N 000 X 151209 7017
35018 HQ     0 XA     A   1  B 5995H       N 000 X 160909 7018
37675 LA S M 0 XA     A  54? D-1369H       N 015 X 071409
42021 HQ     0 XA     A   6  B 6000H       N 000?X 160909 D821
45133 HQ     0 XA     A  55  B  275H       N 000?X 191209 SHOW
47479 CD B M E XA     A  12? F  -79H       N 005 F 101409
47509 CD B M E XA R2  A  28  B    7H       N 000?F 211409 5C02
47829 BR BXM E XA     A  14  E   61H       N 010 X 221409
47975 CD B M E XA     B  23  B   23H CD2020 N 004 X 141309 SHOW
47707 OC PBM E XA     A  55  B   38H       N 017 X 031509 5037 1037
50008 HQ B M E XA     A  20? D -934H       N 000 X 151209
50015 HQ B M E XA     A  55? F -265H       N 000 X 180609
50033 LA B M E XA     A  24? F-1731H       N 005 X 171409 5041 1041
52013 HQ     0 XA     A  -3  B 5991H       N 000 X 211309 1013
52015 HQ     0 VA     A   1  B 5995H       N 000 X 160909 1015
52023 HQ     0 XA     A   6  B 6000H       N 000?X 160909 1023
52035 HQ     0 XA     A   4  B 5998H       N 000 X 151209 1010
52062 HQ     0 XA     A   6  B 6000H       N 000?X 211309 1062
55015 HQ     0 XA     A -29  B 5965H       N 000 X 191209 SHOW
59005 HQ B M 0 AA     A4943  B-3743H       N 000?X 131409
59102 HQ B M 0 AA     A1480  B-1471H       N 000?X 131409 7083
60024 CF B M 0 AA     A -56   -1726H LA2213 N 005 X 201309


LOCATION-84139-PLYMOUTH   BR
47458 CD B M E XA R2  A  33  B  205H       N 004 X 001409
47814 BR XBM E XA     A  55  B -149H BR0715 N 013 X 031509 5M01 1M01


LOCATION-85734-PENZANCE   BR
47449 OC B M E XA     A  30  F  197H       N 000 X 081409 1A70
47476 CD B M E XA     A  24  B   -1H CD1019 N 000 X 061409
47539 CD B M E XA     A  47  B  178H       N 000 X 041409
47624 CD B M E XA     A  55  B   -4H CD1218 N 004 X 131409
```

A list of locomotives in, or due to arrive in, the Exeter TOPS area
on 15 September 1991 – Laira T&RSD Open Day.

```
TRAINS DUE TO ARRIVE WITH LOCOS FOR DETACHMENT          ********

LOCO  DP SP  T BK      NEXT    NEXT    PREASS O FUEL   E.T.A.     TRAIN      WTT A
 NO   AL CH  H TY RW   EXAM    MAJOR   TOHRDY P HRS    +-TIME   IDENTITY     1


LOCATION-83000-TAUNTONYD BR
37092 CF    M X XA     A  28   D   184H          N 000 X  TIME   838Z70A 14


LOCATION-83400-RIVERSIDE BR
37191 CF    M X XA     A  44   B    17H          N 004 X   +15  837Z72A 14
47301 TI B M 0 XA NS A  27   D   143H          N 016 X  TIME   837Z74A 15


LOCATION-84139-PLYMOUTH  BR
58041 TO SBM 0 AA      B  21   B    21H TO1718 N 000 X   +13  731Z981 15
58027 TO SBM 0 AA      A  35   B   355H          N 000 X   +13  731Z981 15


LOCATION-85734-PENZANCE  BR
47812 BR XBM E XA      A   9   B   -62H BR0716 N 000 X  TIME   731C02M 15 0C02


LOCOMOTIVES ALLOCATED TO ARRIVE                        ********

LOCO  DP SP  T BK      NEXT    NEXT    PREASS O FUEL   WTT TO WTT
 NO   AL CH  H TY RW   EXAM    MAJOR   TOHRDY P HRS    ARRIVE ALLOC


LOCATION-83421-EXETSTDAV BR
47708 OC PBM E XA      A  28   B   119H          N 001 X 2L18 2V13
47710 OC PBM E XA      E  18   E    18H          N 009 X 1035 1V17
47712 OC PBM E XA      A  14   B   129H EH2213 N 000 X 1V11
47814 BR XBM E XA      A  55   B  -149H BR0715 N 013 X 5M01 1M01
50030 LA B M E XA      A  14   B  -195H          N 001 X 1V08


LOCATION-84090-LAIRA  TMD M&EE
35017 HQ      0 XA     A   4   B  5998H          N 000 X 7017
35018 HQ      0 XA     A   1   B  5995H          N 000 X 7018
42021 HQ      0 XA     A   6   B  6000H          N 000?X D821
45133 HQ      0 XA     A  55   B   275H          N 000?X SHOW
47509 CD B M E XA R2 A  28   B     7H          N 000?F 5C02
47975 CD B M E XA      B  23   B    23H CD2020 N 004?X SHOW
52013 HQ      0 XA     A  -3   B  5991H          N 000?X 1013
52015 HQ      0 VA     A   1   B  5995H          N 000?X 1015
52023 HQ      0 XA     A   6   B  6000H          N 000?X 1023
52035 HQ      0 XA     A   4   B  5998H          N 000?X 1010
52062 HQ      0 XA     A   6   B  6000H          N 000?X 1062
55015 HQ      0 XA     A -29   B  5965H          N 000?X SHOW


LOCATION-84139-PLYMOUTH  BR
33042 SL    M R XA NH A  44   U    87H          N 000?X 0Z34 1Z34
33064 SL    M R XA NH A  43   L   208H          N 000?X 0Z34 1Z34
47707 OC PBM E XA      A  55   B    38H          N 017?X 5037 1037
50029 LA B M E XA      A  43   B    80H          N 020?X 1V09
50033 LA B M E XA      A  24?  F-1731H          N 005?X 5041 1041


LOCATION-85731-PENZANCSD M&EE
47812 BR XBM E XA      A   9   B   -62H BR0716 N 000?X 0C02
```

A complete list of all exhibits, with the exception of Class 25 *John F Kennedy*.

in itself, and some 11,000 visitors attended the event realising over £23,000; after setting-up expenses, that left approximately £12,000 which was donated to various charities. Many people commented on how well the exhibits were posed, producing some excellent pictures. After the gates closed at five o'clock, with the last of the stragglers on their way home, it was time to tidy up as in a couple of hours trains would begin to arrive for servicing.

The first exhibits to leave the depot should have been the two ARC/ Foster Yeoman Class 59s at around 18.00, followed by the Class 60 going out to Tavistock Junction for the returning empty tanks to Fawley. The Eastleigh driver had come down earlier than expected, which was just as well as it turned out, for he was unable to start his diesel. Meanwhile, the return movement to Crewe was formed up and left at 18.30, Class 31 No. 31405 hauling away 86609, 90132, and gloriously bright *JFK*, 25173. Still with no success regarding the starting up of No. 60024, and eager to get the loco moved out of the way, I had the two Class 59s attached to the front and sent the trio out to Tavistock Junction to work away the Fawley tanks. Other exhibits were towed over to Lipson sidings; some would remain on hand for a few weeks including D821 that required tyre turning. The following day Class 50 No. 50008 hauled away to Bristol East Depot D1013, D1062, 55015 and 45133; from there they would be worked forward on Civil Link Services. On Wednesday, 18 September No. 50008 towed D7018 back to Taunton Fairwater en route to the West Somerset Railway. The next day D7017 and D1035 were hauled into Cornwall for the Bodmin & Wenford Diesel Gala Weekend of 5/6 October. Also that day, No. 50008 took No. 50015 and D1015 to Exeter Riverside from where they would connect into the 16.30 Meldon Quarry to Eastleigh, en route to Brighton for their Open Day. This then left D821 and D1023, which were hauled to Bristol East Depot by No. 50008 on 8 October, the same day as No. 50015 worked D1035 and D7017 from Bodmin back to Taunton Cider Sidings and then onto the West Somerset Railway.

LAIRA OPENDAY '91 CHARITY DONATIONS LIST

• Helping Hand fund,	£1000
• Dawlish railway home,	£1000
• Woking homes,	£1000
• Guide dogs for the blind,	£1000
• Freedom Fields maternity unit,	£850
• Plympton Hospital,	£850
• See - Saw,	£850
• Multiple sclerosis,	£850
• Trengweath,	£850
• St Lukes Hospice,	£850
• Immediate medical support,	£850
• Battered wives refuge,	£850
• Cornwall air ambulance,	£850
• Lord Mayors fund,	£300
• Sutton Trust,	£300
• St Johns ambulance Crownhill,	£300

Proposed charity donation list.

Skirting the sea wall approaching Dawlish is a Penzance to Paddington express in the summer of 1964, hauled by a diesel-hydraulic 'Warship' Type '4' locomotive.

Outstanding then was No. 20110 that had been receiving attention at Laira. The locomotive finally left the depot on 17 October, being hauled to Totnes for the South Devon Railway. So ended what had been an interesting diversion to the normal run of the mill duties.

The demise of the Class 50 fleet continued apace – by late 1991 there were now fourteen locomotives awaiting disposal – this was hindering the working of the depot, particularly on the night turn when stabling room was at a premium. There were no immediate plans for any of them to be worked away out of the south-west and the tender list wasn't going to close for some time. In deciding to send six of the condemned diesels, Nos. 50020/26/40/42/43/45, out to Tavistock Junction in August for outstabling, special dispensation was required from RHQ Swindon. The diesels were all unbraked and Class 9 trains no longer operated in the area.

The Rules and Signalling section was not at its most co-operative and demanded a week or more notice for the moves. This was clearly unacceptable and it was given an ultimatum; if the move was not forthcoming then the performance of services emanating from the depot would be affected. To add further weight to this, I rang Doc Ley in the tower block, firing on all four cylinders, telling him that the position at Laira was approaching a critical point. Although Ken didn't carry all that much weight, he could always be relied upon to make a drama out of a crisis and, to give the chap his due, he was never afraid to jump in, often feet first, which at times could be a little embarrassing. Nevertheless, the veiled inferences had the desired effect and six Class 50s were worked out to the junction, three at a time with a locomotive at either end.

From : Area Fleet Manager
       Plymouth

Ext : 079 2290

o/r : LA01/2.9(GH)

LAIRA OPEN DAY

The Open Day was a tremendous success and we have received
several letters of thanks. In fact so many have come in that I
have held back writing to you until now.

I will arrange to post copies on staff noticeboards, the first
set will be displayed in the foyer.

We took over £23,000 which after setting up expenses means
approximately £12,000 will be donated to charity. We estimate in
the region of 11,000 people attended the event.

From the comments I have received from the Railway press, they
are also receiving very good reports and it is generally felt
that the Open Day was not only the best this year but the best
Open Day that has been staged by a BR depot for the past ten
years. It is a great credit to everyone and has demonstrated
once again that we can be the best in what we achieve.

Events such as the Open Day of course don't just happen, they are
planned, and over eighteen months of hard work have gone into
preparing it. It is not just the staff that were involved in
the event, there were numerous people behind the scenes who
contributed.

Staff who kept the train service running, particularly on the
Friday and Saturday night, when the Depot was overcrowded with
exhibits.

The staff on the Sunday night who had to turn the Depot back to
"normal".

The Movements Supervisor, shunters and traincrew, who had the
difficult task of moving everything and placing the exhibits, not
least with myself standing over them to ensure everything was
exactly where it should be. This was particularly worthwhile as
several people commented how well the exhibits were "posed" and
the ability to photograph them.

I would also like to thank all those staff who were on duty or
volunteered to help on the day. It was hectic to say the least

Letter to staff from the area fleet manager.

The monies raised at the open day would have increased considerably had the event been held on the Saturday, when a more diverse train service would have been realised. In addition, there would have been no movements leaving the complex.

but we have received several comments of the helpfulness and courteous attitude of the stewards - well done !

The apprentices also deserve a mention for helping in setting up the displays and preparation in the run up to the day.

The catering department, both in the mess room and on the train must also be thanked for all their efforts in the splendid job they did in feeding the masses.

Finally I would like to thank all members of the Open Day Committee for all their hard work in planning the event, setting it up and not least all the badgering, persuading and calling in favours, even threatening! that resulted in so many exhibits coming to Plymouth.

We are now starting to hold review meetings to sort out what went wrong and how we can improve. If you have any comments please let me or any member of the Committee know so we can build them into the next Open Day. Certainly we were short of help on the day and if you were not involved on the day but would like to in future please put your name forward.

All in all it was a tremendous success, watch Railway Magazine and Rail Magazine for full coverage.

A line up with condemned Class '50' locomotives waiting assignment to the breakers yards. 50010, formerly *Monarch*, was eventually cut-up on site.

The next event has to be even better - how many preserved Class 50's can we pack in along with the hydraulics, HST's and other exhibits.

G P A HUDSON
Area Fleet Manager,   Plymouth

Three condemned Class '50' locomotives are waiting to be worked away to the various scrap yards. 50036 (*Victorious*) is accompanied by two in NSE livery.

```
To:   Mr G Morgan          From:   Area Fleet Manager
      CP95                         Plymouth
      Swindon
                           Ext :   079 2452
cc:   Mr K Ley
      Safety Manager       o/r :   LA09(RF)
      Plymouth
                           Date:   26 July 1991
      Mr B Clark
      Driver Manager
      Plymouth
```

CONDEMNED CLASS 50 DIESELS AT LAIRA

The latest withdrawals of the class 50 fleet over the past
fortnight has resulted in fourteen of the diesels awaiting
disposal at Laira. The earlier withdrawn diesels have of course
been here for some considerable time with no likelyhood of being
worked away to a breakers yard.

The stabling room at Laira particularly on a Friday and over the
weekend is now at a premium with no less than fourteen trains on
the depot/carriage sidings on Fridays, this together with three
and sometimes four rakes of HST trailer cars on hand makes
shunting extremely difficult.

Earlier this week six of the earlier withdrawn class 50 diesels
were brought into the shed for examination with a view of working
them out for stabling at Tavistock Junction. All efforts to
produce a "brake " on these diesels proved negative as many
components had been removed over their long period of
withdrawal.

As material has to be taken off the later class 50s recently
withdrawn, would it be posssible to have dispensation to work out
the six condemned diesels (possible three at a time) from Laira
to Tavistock Junction with a diesel at either end?

The clearance of these six (50020/50026/50040/50042/50043/50045)
would enable the other condemned locos to be put out in Ocean
Sidings therby releasing a road for stabling coaching stock.

R FOWKES
Movements Planning Manager
for Area Fleet Manager, Plymouth

Memo to RHQ Swindon: Safety Manager and Driver Manager Plymouth outlining the problems encountered on the depot with the number of withdrawn diesel locomotives.

A further request
to RHQ Swindon for
dispensation to move
unbraked condemned
Class '50' locomotives
from Laira to
Tavistock Junction.

```
To:   Mr G Morgan                  From:   Area Fleet Manager
      CP95                                 Plymouth
      Swindon
                                   Ext :   079 2290
cc:   Mr K Ley
      Safety Manager               o/r :   LA09(RHF)
      Plymouth
                                   Date:   6 August 1991
      Mr B Clark
      Driver Manager
      Plymouth
```

CONDEMNED CLASS 50 DIESELS AT LAIRA

Confirming telephone conversation Fowkes/Morgan, owing to the
rapid withdrawal of the Class 50 diesel fleet over the next six
weeks there is a need to outstable further condemned locos at
Tavistock Junction.

Would you please arrange special authority to convey a further
three diesels unbraked from Laira to Tavistock Junction on
Thursday 8 August 1991.

R H FOWKES
Movements/Planning Manager
for Area Fleet Manager, Plymouth

Some four months later, in late November, advice was received from the Director of Procurement regarding the invitation to tender, which was followed by sales acceptances for nineteen Class 50 locomotives. Nos. 50001/20/26/36/40/45 at Laira, along with 50023 at Exeter and 50004/16 at Stratford, were all destined for Booth Roe Metals Ltd, Rotherham. The remainder, Nos. 50003/18/37/46/48, were destined for M.C. Metals at Springburn, Glasgow, whilst 50002/17/27/31/42/43/49 were for private owners. No. 50010 was to be cut up on site at Laira.

The six Class 50 locomotives were brought back to the depot from Tavistock Junction in early December. As each one was unbraked, a 70ft long flexible air-pipe had to be fitted in order that the ensemble could operate under through-pipe conditions. Bill Griffiths, in the freight section at Swindon, requested I arrange to work the Class 50s up to Exeter Riverside on the Civil Link Service, one at a time. From there, a special movement would be arranged to Rotherham or Glasgow, each conveying three locos with the requisite vehicles as brake force.

Paul Furtek, of *Locomaster Profiles* fame, found time out from his day job to video most of the movements and incorporate them into his next video production. Geoff first introduced me to Paul on the stairway to his office a couple of years earlier. Having come off the Midland, I told him that my allegiance lay with the 'Peak' diesels of which I had a video, of not very good quality. 'Oh,' said Paul, 'I made the video of the Class 45s,' and with that promised me another one taken off his master copy.

Operations and Safety Manager,   Operations Manager,
Regional Railways,   InterCity G.W.
Plymouth.   C.P.95
                                                   Swindon.
                                          Ref: TX/2/139.
                                          Date   8.8.91
                                          Ext: 077-3357

MOVEMENT OF DEFECTIVE CLASS 50 LOCOMOTIVES

Reference my letter of 1st August, and subsequent phone conversation
(Ley/Watts) in which an repeat of the authority formerly granted, to convey
defective class 50 locomotives from Laira depot to Tavistock Junction as an
unfitted train, was requested.

I am prepared to authorise the movement providing that the following conditions
are met:

1. The movements will be between Laira Depot and Tavistock Junction
   sidings.

2. The prevailing gradients are generally level and the distance involved
   does not exceed one and a half miles.

3. The composition of the train will be:- locomotive (brake operative),
   dead locomotive, rear locomotive with at least hand brake operative. A
   tail lamp must be conveyed on this locomotive.

4. The rear most locomotive must be manned by someone fully conversant with
   the route and able to apply the brake in emergency and competent to
   carry out emergency protection arrangements.

5. The speed of the movement must not exceed 15 M.P.H. throughout, subject
   to any lower speed restriction currently in force in the route
   concerned.

This authority should not be extended beyond Saturday 10th August. Please note
that further requests will not be considered unless at least seven days' notice
is given; also that all requests for unfitted moves of a non-local nature, e.g.
to Totnes or beyond, should be addressed in the first instance to the Freight
Train Planning Section (C.P.89) and not to the Rules and Signalling.

Please note also that, in view of the short timescale involved, this move is
authorised without the issue of any special instructions to the Plymouth panel
Signalman. I cannot allow a further repetition of this situation to occur.

N.S. Watts

for Rules and Standards Officer

A further request to RHQ Swindon for dispensation to move unbraked condemned
Class '50' locomotives from Laira to Tavistock Junction.

FACSIMILE MESSAGE

British Railways Board
Director of Procurement
Room 196 Derwent House
Railway Technical Centre
London Road
Derby   DE2 8UP

From: Mr Myers

Telephone: Derby (STD 0332) 42442
Extension: 3449

Facsimile: Derby (STD 0332) 386748
Telex: 37367 BRTEK G

Date: 21 - 11 - 91

To: Booth - Roe Metals

Rotherham

Tel 0709 559198
FAO: Mr Sulley

Facsimile number: 0709 - 561859

Total number of pages (including this header sheet): ~~one~~ two

*IF ANY PART OF THIS FAX IS ILLEGIBLE, OR THE NUMBER OF PAGES
SHOWN IS NOT RECEIVED, PLEASE CONTACT US IMMEDIATELY.*

MESSAGE

We have accepted your offers for these locos
sales acceptance follows in few days

Director of Procurement – Invitation to Tender – withdrawn diesel locomotives.

≢ **British Rail**   BR 3/6

from	Item No	Loco No	Lying At
○ Booth Roe			
Sk. 230 -			
5210 -			
295	003	08540	Allerton
	018	08411	March
	019	08438	March
	020	08549	March
	021	50004	Stratford ✓
	022	50016	Stratford ✓
	025	50023	Exeter ✓
	026	50001	Plymouth ✓
	028	50020	" ✓
	029	50026	" ✓
	030	50036	" ✓
	031	50040	" ✓
	034	50045	" ✓
317	003	08808	Carlisle
	009	08688	Allerton
	010	08787	Crewe
	011	08608	Gateshead
	012	08671	Gateshead
	017	08463	BRML Doncaster
320	001	08141	Tinsley

Class 50 locomotives for disposal at Booth Roe Metals Ltd, Rotherham. 50004/16
at Stratford, 50023 at Exeter, and 50001/20/26/36/40/45, all at Tavistock Junction,
requiring to be worked back into Laira.

To: Operations Manager
    InterCity Great Western
    CP 95
    Swindon
    FAO Mr G Morgan

cc: CP 89
    Swindon

From: Area Fleet Manager
         Plymouth

Ext : 079 2452

o/r : LA09/RF

Date: 27 November 1991

CONDEMNED CLASS 50 LOCOMOTIVES

Seven condemned Class 50 locomotives have now been allocated to Booth-Roe at Rotherham for cutting up. Six of these, 50001, 50020, 50026, 50036 , 50040 and 50045 are at present out-stabled at Tavistock Junction and 50023 is on hand at Exeter. In addition, 50042 has been purchased by a group at Bodmin and 50043 similarly by a consortium at Manchester.

The diesels at Tavistock Junction all un-braked now require to be staged back into Laira for preparatory work to be carried out, this will include making each diesel through-pipe only. The movements from Tavistock Junction at Laira can be arranged as soon as possible with forward movements to Rotherham as and when a service is arranged.

50023 will have attention at Exeter and further advice regarding this diesel and also 50042 and 50043 will be advised later.

R FOWKES
Movements and Planning Manager
for AREA FLEET MANAGER, PLYMOUTH

To: Movements and Planning Manager,
    Area Fleet Manager's Office
    Plymouth

From: Operations Manager (G.W.),
      CP.95, Rules & Signalling,
      125 House, Swindon

Copy to:
    Operations and Safety Manager,
    InterCity Great Western
    Exeter

    Area Manager, West of England
                          Freight
    Westbury

Ext: 077-3357

y/r: LA09/RF

o/r: 95/TX/SBI/UNF

Date 29.11.91

MOVEMENT OF DEFECTIVE CLASS 50 LOCOMOTIVES

Reference your letter of 27th November in which a repeat of the authority formerly granted, to convey condemned class 50 locomotives between Tavistock Junction and Laira diesel depot as unfitted trains, was requested.

I am prepared to authorise the movements providing that the following conditions are met:

1. The earliest date for such a movement will be Wednesday 4th December.

2. The movements will be between Tavistock Junction sidings and Laira Depot, and are authorised to operate in either direction.

3. The prevailing gradients are generally level and the distance involved does not exceed one and a half miles.

4. Trains conveying unfitted vehicles must be allocated train numbers in the series 9Z30 to 9Z39.

5. Before such a train leaves Tavistock Junction sidings for Laira diesel depot, the Person in charge of the Yard at Tavistock Junction must contact the Plymouth panel Signalman and advise him in the following terms:

    "Train No. 9Z32 (for example), conveying unfitted vehicles, ready to depart from Tavistock Junction sidings for Laira depot".

The Signalman will signal the Class 9 train in accordance with his special instructions.

Before such a train leaves Laira diesel depot for Tavistock Junction sidings, the "Mobile One" movements supervisor at Laira depot must contact the Plymouth panel Signalman and advise him in the following terms:

    "Train No. 9Z35 (for example), conveying unfitted vehicles, ready to depart from Laira Depot for Tavistock Junction sidings".

The Signalman will signal the Class 9 train in accordance with his special instructions.

=CONTINUED OVERLEAF=

SB3LETTR/8

6. The composition of each such train will be:- locomotive (brake operative), dead locomotive, rear locomotive with at least hand brake operative. A tail lamp must be conveyed on this locomotive.

7. The rear most locomotive must be manned by a person fully conversant with the route and able to apply the brake in emergency and competent to carry out the provisions of Section M of the Rule Book.

8. The speed of the movement must not exceed 15 M.P.H. throughout, subject to any lower speed restriction currently in force in the route concerned.

This authority should not be extended beyond Wednesday 18th December 1991.

<u>Note</u>: All requests for unfitted moves of a non-local nature, e.g. to Totnes or beyond, should be addressed in the first instance to the Freight Train Planning Section (C.P.89).

Rules and Regulations Officer

```
KD83400 02/12/91 17.00.41 U5427                                    hdr

FROM JD83400 VIA N897 BY POP
FROM MOVEMENTS AND PLANNING MANAGER LAIRA
==========================================
PRODUCTION MANAGER LAIRA. MOVEMENTS SUPERVISOR LAIRA.RESOURCES MANAGER PLYMOUTH
==============================================================================
               MOVEMENT OF CONDEMNED CLASS 50 DIESELS
----------------------------------------------
THE FOLLOWING CLASS 50 DIESELS HAVE BEEN ALLOCATED TO BOOTH-ROE AT ROTHERHAM
FOR CUTTING UP = 50001 50020 50026 50036 50040 50045.
IN ADDITION 50042 HAS BEEN PURCHASED BY A GROUP AT BODMIN AND 50043 SIMILARLY
BY A CONSORTIUM AT MANCHESTER. WITH THE EXCEPTION 50001 THE 7 OTHER LOCOS
REQUIRE MOVING FROM TAVISTOCK JUNCTION INTO LAIRA UNBRAKED IN ACCORDANCE WITH
THE SPECIAL INSTRUCTIONS ISSUED BY RHQ SWINDON.
A SPECIAL 8Z40 (TIME TO BE CONFIRMED) LAIRA TO ROTHERHAM WILL RUN ON FRIDAY
07/12/91 COMPRISING OF 47XXX HAULING (50001 50020 50040 UNBRAKED BUT THROUGH-
PIPED) AND BARRIER VEHICLES 9466 9423 17131.
WOULD THE RESOURCES MANAGER PLYMOUTH PLEASE PROVIDE TWO DRIVERS ON WEDNESDAY
MORNING 03/12/91 FOR THE MOVEMENT OF THE UNBRAKED DIESELS FROM TAVISTOCK JCTN.
INTO LAIRA? THANKS:
END




KD83400 03/12/91 09.30.39 U5555                                    hdr

FROM JD83400 VIA N018 BY POP
FROM MOVEMENTS AND PLANNING MANAGER LAIRA.
==========================================
TO YARD SUPERVISOR TAVISTOCK JUNCTION.(COPY TO RESOURCES MANAGER PLYMOUTH)
==============================================================================
*****************************************************************************
WEDNESDAY 03/12/91.
--------------------
MOVEMENT OF UNBRAKED CLASS 50 LOCOMOTIVES TAVISTOCK JUNCTION TO LAIRA:
50008-50015 EX LAIRA 0800 TO TAVI JCTN TO WORK 50020/50040/50042/50043 BACK TO
LAIRA DEPOT,IN ACCORDANCE WITH SPECIAL INSTRUCTIONS ISSUED BY RHQ SWINDON,
IE- LOCOMOTIVE EACH END:
*****************************************************************************
END
```

To   : Freight Office Crewe & York
Copy : Laira TMD
From : Freight Planning Swindon 077 4027

SPECIALLY AUTHORISED MOVEMENT

The following will appear on our WR Notice. Please note that on arrival
Rotherham could a 60 MPH STP special be planned Rotherham to Laira to return
Class 47 and passenger coaches, which are NOT for booths. Note flexible brake
pipes are also required back at Laira and should be loaded in the coaches
unless the M & EE departments agree road movement between them.

THURSDAY 9 JANUARY

MOVEMENT OF CONDEMNED LOCOMOTIVES

8Z50 20.10 Exeter Riverside - Rotherham Booths

Conveys 50001, 50020 & 50040 all piped only and three fully braked vehicles
(expected to be coaches 17131, 9423 & 9466 which must be returned to Laira
along with temporary flexible brake pipes fitted between each class 50).

	Arr	Dep		Arr	Dep
Tiverton Loop	20*42	21*00	Standish Jn	00/44	
Taunton		21/35	Gloucester G.239	00C59	01*12
Bridgwater		22/01	Cheltenham Spa	01/28	
Worle Jn		22/36	Eckington	01/51	
Bristol T.M.		23/12	Abbotswood Jn	02/05	
Stoke Giff.Loop	23*29	23*48	Bromsgrove	02BL33	02BL38
Westerleigh Jn		00/01	Barnt Green	02/52	(Fri)

FABRIC 35

NIWE 47/7 diag O.O.C.80 on arrival Exeter Thurs to work 8Z50 to destination.
Laira will arrange for class 50 to work diag until 47/7 returns.

**Reference Rule Book Appendix 2 page 2.11 item 3. The Director of Operations
B.R.B. has specially authorised this movement of three piped only class 50
locomotives provided the following additional conditions are met : -**

1. The locomotives are coupled together and marshalled at the front of all
   other vehicles.

2. Sufficient other braked vehicles are provided, at least three marshalled
   rear, to meet the brake force regulations specified in table E1 of the
   Working Manual for Rail Staff using 35 MPH column.

3. Must be assisted Bromsgrove Bank whether single engine load or not.

C. ABBOTT

```
              SPECIAL TRAFFIC LOCOMOTIVES            LRX/41

      MONDAY 6TH JANUARY TO FRIDAY 10TH JANUARY
                                  OLD OAK COMMON DEPOT

ZY0601/F/OCLX    /00    DISTRIBUTED ON 08/01/92 AT 14:05:41   PAGE NO. 233
-----------------------------------------------------------------------------
Activity                            :Activity
  Code    Location  Arr    Dep      : Code    Location  Arr    Dep
-----------------------------------------------------------------------------
WTT Dgm OC80                   SX   :
          06/01/92 to 12/01/92      :
Class 47/7              DUAL B ELECTRIC H:
Spl Chars                           :
Sector   NTWE NSE WT OF ENG 47/7    :
====================================:
Off   - OC079 - SUN   OC079 - FSX   :

DAYS RUN:                      FSX  :
Laira TMD        05.45 0C08          :
Laira TMD 05.50 06.10 5C08          :
N.Abbot   06.52 07.12 2C08          :
ExeterStD 07.46 08.10 1034   RR     :
Waterloo  11.40 13.19 0V10          :
Waterloo  13.22 13.40 5Y20          :
(OC081 0/R)                         :
ClaphamYd 13.56 14.45 0V15          :
Waterloo  14.55 15.15 1V15          :
ExeterStD 18.43 18.52 5V15          :

DAYS RUN:                      MTWO :
Exeter NY 18.54 19.22 0V15          :
Exeter HS 19.29 22.30 0F77          :
Laira TMD 23.37                     :
FUEL                                :

DAYS RUN:                      THO  :
Exeter NY 18.54 19.22 0V15          :
Exeter R  19.27 20.10 8Z50          :

DAYS RUN:                      FO   :
TinsleyYd 07.21 07.48 8Z50          :
Booth'sPS 10.00 11.10 5Z51          :
Laira TMD 22E00                     :
FUEL                                :

DAYS RUN:                      SX   :
Works  - OC081  - MX          -     :

------------------------------------:

PAGE(S)    234         NOT USED     :
                                    :
                                    :
                                    :
                                    :
                                    :
                                    :
                                    :
                                    :
                                    :

                     211
```

THURSDAY 23 JANUARY

MOVEMENT OF CONDEMNED LOCOMOTIVES

8Z50 20.10 Exeter Riverside - Rotherham Booths
Conveys 50026, 50036 & 50045 all piped only and three fully braked vehicles (expected to be coaches 17131, 9423 & 9466 which must be returned to Laira along with temporary flexible brake pipes fitted between each class 50).

	Arr	Dep		Arr	Dep
Tiverton Loop	20*42	21*00	Standish Jn	00/44	
Taunton		21/35	Gloucester G.239	00C59	01*12
Bridgwater		22/01	Cheltenham Spa	01/28	
Worle Jn		22/36	Eckington	01/51	
Bristol T.M.		23/12	Abbotswood Jn	02/05	
Stoke Giff.Loop	23*29	23*48	Bromsgrove	02BL33	02BL38
Westerleigh Jn		00/01	Barnt Green	02/52 (Fri)	

FABRIC 35

NTWE 47/7 diag 0.0.C.80 on arrival Exeter Thurs to work 8Z50 to destination. Laira will arrange for class 50 to work diag until 47/7 returns.

Reference Rule Book Appendix 2 page 2.11 item 3. The Director of Operations B.R.B. has specially authorised this movement of three piped only class 50 locomotives provided the following additional conditions are met : -

1. The locomotives are coupled together and marshalled at the front of all other vehicles.

2. Sufficient other braked vehicles are provided, at least three marshalled rear, to meet the brake force regulations specified in table El of the Working Manual for Rail Staff using 35 MPH column.

3. Must be assisted Bromsgrove Bank whether single engine load or not.

A positioning movement: the Class '08' has 'picked up' English Electric 50007 *Sir Edward Elgar* and attached it to 50050 *Fearless*, to be tested for multiple working. The two diesels were featured working together on 11 April 1992, working the 'Carlisle Fifty Farewell' railtour.

B R I T I S H   R A I L W A Y S
LONDON MIDLAND REGION
S P E C I A L   N O T I C E

(PRIVATE and not for publication)
The times shown in this Notice are approximate only.
Times shown with an oblique stroke are passing times.

Tele :   05-32037/32078/32226 Timing/Diagramming - COAL

05-32237/32238/32239 Timing/Diagramming - RFD

05-32087/32228/32230 Timing/Diagramming - METALS/CONST/OIL

05-32229/32240/32241 Timing/Diagramming - DEPARTMENTAL

05-32235 TOPS

TOPS REPORTING

AFC's - This notice includes
additional/altered trains with new/
amended schedules. Make sure these
trains are reported correctly and
currently.
ALL OTHER STAFF AS APPROPRIATE
Current reporting to your AFC is
required for all trains in
this Notice.

DATE : 12.02.1992

FRIDAY 14 FEBRUARY

8Z40 21 05 (THURS) ADDNL STRATFORD TMD TO ROTHERHAM MASBOROUGH MILLMOOR   DL (MM2 MM1)

Luffenham Jn.		01/11	Clay Cross South Jn.		07/00
(from E. Region)			Chesterfield		07/08
Manton Jn.		01/20	(to E. Region)		
Melton Mowbray		01/50	Tinsley	arr	07C42
Syston North Jn.		02/10		dep	08C05
Loughborough		02/26	Aldwarke	arr	08RM38
Ratcliffe Jn.		02/40	Eleven Inch Mill	dep	10RM00
Trent East Jn.		02/44	Rotherham Booths	arr	10 22
Toton Centre	arr	02L55	(25014)		
	dep	06L20			

Conveys: 3 CLASS 50 DEAD DIESEL LOCOMOTIVES ALL PIPED ONLY plus THREE
         FULLY BRAKED VEHICLES.
         Loco Nos. 50004, 50016 and 50023.
         Vehicle Nos. (C1 Coaches) 5308, 9423 and 9466.
         443 TONNES TRAILING.

Max. Speed : 35 m.p.h.

Charge to: D of M & E.E.

/Continued ...

605/DR.R/07534S/FT2/CB/PG.1

1252/26

THE ABOVE FORMAT LINE MUST BE USED
IF YOU USE YOUR OWN FORMAT LINE THE ITEM(S) IN QUESTION
WILL NOT BE INCLUDED IN THE NOTICES

THURSDAY 2 APRIL

MOVEMENT OF CONDEMNED LOCOMOTIVES

8Z50 20.10 Exeter Riverside - Glasgow (M.C.Metals)

Conveys 50003 & 50048 all piped only and three fully braked vehicles
3222,5680 and 5790 which must be returned to Laira along with temporary flexible
brake pipes fitted between each class 50).

	Arr	Dep		Arr	Dep
Tiverton Loop	20*42	21*00	Standish Jn	00/44	
Taunton		21/35	Gloucester G.239	00C59	01*12
Bridgwater		22/01	Cheltenham Spa	01/28	
Worle Jn		22/36	Eckington	01/51	
Bristol T.M.		23/12	Abbotswood Jn	02/05	
Stoke Giff.Loop	23*29	23*48	Bromsgrove	02BL33	02BL38
Westerleigh Jn		00/01 (Sat)	Barnt Green	02/52	

FABRIC 35

C147/7 diag Crewe 116,Light Bristol Exeter and work 8Z50 Exeter to Crewe,
Return light to Bristol

Reference Rule Book Appendix 2 page 2.11 item 3. The Director of Operations
B.R.B. has specially authorised this movement of three piped only class 50
locomotives provided the following additional conditions are met : -

1. The locomotives are coupled together and marshalled at the front of all
   other vehicles.

2. Sufficient other braked vehicles are provided, at least three marshalled
   rear, to meet the brake force regulations specified in table E1 of the
   Working Manual for Rail Staff using 35 MPH column.

3. Must be assisted Bromsgrove Bank whether single engine load or not.

```
LALO                    SUPPLEMENTARY LOCO WORKING (SO)
                        ==============================
                              LAIRA DEPOT
                              ===========
                                              (TEL: 077 3323)
ZS0604/P/LALO    /00      DISTRIBUTED ON 08/04/92 AT 16:18:53    PAGE NO. 651
---------------------------------------------------------------------------
   Train    Working    WTT          : Train    Working    WTT
            Arr    Dep  No RemarksDays :        Arr    Dep  No RemarksDays
---------------------------------------------------------------------------
WTT Dgm LA1                      SO  :
                06/04/92 to 12/04/92 :
2 x Class 50/0  in MULTIPLE          :
                    DUAL B ELECTRIC H:
Spl chars                            :
Sector   NWXA NSE WESSEX CL50        :
===================================== :
                                     :
2 X CLASS 50 SPECIALLY PREPARED.  *  :
------------------------------------ :
                                     :
                                     :
Off    - LA001 - FO          -       :
                                     :
DAYS RUN:                       SO   :
ClaphamYd       07.50 0Z38           :
Waterloo  08.00 08.20 1Z38    EHA    :
(RAILTOUR CHARTER)                   :
Via Earley,Reading,Oxford,Birmingham, :
Carlisle  15.25 15.30 0Z38           :
UpperbyHS 15.45                      :
FUEL                                 :
UpperbyHS       16.20 0Z38           :
Carlisle  16.35 16.55 1Z38    EHA    :
(RTN RAILTOUR CHARTER)               :
Via Birmingham,Oxford,Reading,Earley, :
Waterloo  23.39 00.20 0Z38           :
ClaphamYd 00N35                      :
LOCOS TO RETURN TO LAIRA TMD UNDER   :
CONTROL ARRANGEMENT.                 :
                                     :
Works  - LA001 - SUN         -       :
                                     :
 * SPECIALLY PREPARED LOCOS TO BE :  :
   50007(D407)'Sir Edward Elgar' AND :
   50050(D400)'Fearless'             :
                                     :
WATERLOO CONTOL TO NOTE :            :
------------------------             :
ORGANISORS REQUEST: PLEASE ARRANGE   :
FOR 50007 TO LEAD FROM WATERLOO.     :
                                     :
                                     :
-----------------------------------: :
                                     :
PAGE(S)     652  TO  700  NOT USED   :
```

```
To:  Production Managers              From:  Area Fleet Manager
     HST Supervisors                         Plymouth
     Main Shed Supervisors
     Depot Inspectors               Ext :   079 2290
     Movements Supervisors
     Carriage Cleaning Supervisors o/r :  LA01/1.3.4(GH)
     Stores Manager
     Workshop Staff Notice Board    Date:   15 April 1992
     Apprentices

cc:  Mr M Wishart
     Mr B Smith
     Mr R Dellar
     Mr R Fowkes
     Mr P Kilvington
     Workshop Committee
     Carriage Cleaners Representative
     Shunters Representative
```

RESTORATION OF 50007 "SIR EDWARD ELGAR"

I am pleased to advise you that on 11 April, 50007 successfully
completed its inaugural run from Waterloo - Carlisle and return.
The locomotive along with 50050 (D400) performed perfectly. A
lot of hard work has been put in by many people at Laira not only
the apprentices and workshop staff but also shunters and
operation staff played their part in presenting the locos for the
photo day. The run on the 11 April was expected to be a high
profile affair and it certainly was.

All along the route hundreds of people turned out to see the two
fifties and when we arrived at Carlisle there were over a 1000
people on the platform.

Numerous people congratulated me on the fine work that you have
achieved and the people on the train were absolutely delighted.
You may feel that they are only railway enthusiasts but I would
point out that they paid up to £50 each for the privilege of
travelling behind the fifties and as such they are our customers.

Travelling on the footplate as we climbed Shep Bank and as we
rolled into Carlisle, I was reminded of our quality statement:-

> We are committed to providing a total
> quality product in a way which generates
> for all of us, pride and enthusiasm, so
> that our customers want to use our
> services again, recognising that ours are
> the premier depots.

I felt that we achieved it on the 11 April.

You could feel the pride and enthusiasm, we had produced a total
quality product, everybody recognised we were the best and they
will certainly want to travel again.

In short it was a tremendous day, we achieved a lot and it should
serve to keep the depot in the headlines for sometime to come. I
am only sorry that more of you could not have been there on the
day, but I will try and arrange some free tickets if at all
possible for later in the year. We made a lot of people very
happy and the expression of delight on their faces was reward
enough.

For all of you that contributed and put in a lot of hard work, I
offer my thanks. It has certainly been worthwhile. The
challenge of course is to deliver these standards on our everyday
work and produce a product that meets our customers requirements.

PS. Full coverage is in Rail Magazine issue 172 published on 15
April and subsequent copies will cover the Railtour.

G P A HUDSON
Area Fleet Manager, Plymouth

Letter to staff from the Laira area fleet manager.

216

A surprise awaits those gathered outside No. 6 road at Laira as to what will appear from behind the screen.

English Electric Class '50' 50050 *Fearless* emerges from No. 6 road at Laira T&RSD in 1994 to work 'The 50 Terminator' with 50007 *Sir Edward Elgar*, a 600-mile journey from Waterloo to Penzance, returning to Paddington. Paul Furtek launched a video of the run sponsored by Pathfinder Tours, which was subsequently re-released on DVD.

Getting ready to leave Laira Depot are English Electric 'Type 4s' No. 50051 *Fearless* in multiple with 50007 *Sir Edward Elgar* to work 'The 50 Terminator' railtour Waterloo - Penzance - Paddington, sponsored by Peter Watt's Pathfinder Tours in March 1994.

He was most appreciative of being furnished with the timings for the movements of the condemned Class 50s out of the south-west; unfortunately most were running during the hours of darkness. He was, however, over the moon at being able to video the cavalcade crossing Ribblehead viaduct one afternoon en route to Glasgow. Three years earlier Paul would no doubt have been delighted to have witnessed Nos. 50012/14/22/47 being hauled from Taunton Fairwater to Leicester (Humberstone Road) for Vic Berry.

Earlier, I reflected on the seminar held at Langdon Court for the managers. A year before returning to Laira, there had been a Leadership 5000 course held at Borringdon Hall just outside Plymouth. We were now going to be subjected to a further 'jolly' out on Dartmoor at the Two Bridges Hotel. All very well, the beer flowed in the evenings after the team building exercises of the day, and a change of scenery did us all good. But, what was achieved? As soon as we were back at the depot it was business as usual, nothing had changed. The underlying problem at Laira was the 'them and us' syndrome. It had persisted for years and showed no signs of abating despite being highlighted at many, many meetings. The carriage cleaners and the shunters and, to a lesser extent, the movements supervisors often felt isolated, without recognition; everything was geared around the maintenance department. I told Geoff on a number of occasions that if it wasn't for the movements supervisors constantly chivvying at the maintenance department, then the performance of trains off the depot would be less than acceptable.

B R I T I S H   R A I L
TRAINLOAD FREIGHT
S P E C I A L   N O T I C E

(PRIVATE and not for publication)	**TOPS REPORTING**
The times shown in this Notice are approximate only.	**AFC's** - This notice includes
Times shown with an oblique stroke are passing times.	additional/altered trains with new/
	amended schedules. Make sure these
Tele : 05-32037/32078/32226 Timing/Diagramming - COAL	trains are reported correctly and
	currently.
05-32237/32238/32239 Timing/Diagramming - RFD	**ALL OTHER STAFF AS APPROPRIATE**
	Current reporting to your AFC is
05-32087/32228/32230 Timing/Diagramming - METALS/CONST/OIL	required for all trains in
	this Notice.
05-32229/32240/32241 Timing/Diagramming - DEPARTMENTAL	
	DATE : 12.06.1992
05-32231 TOPS	

MONDAY 15 JUNE

8Z50 ADDITIONAL FREIGHT EXETER RIVERSIDE TO MOSSEND   DL (WM1 WC3 WC4 WC5 WC6)

Exeter Riverside (83400)	dep	20 10 (SUN)	Warrington		arr	11*10
(FROM SWINDON TPU)					dep	11*34
Abbotswood Jn.		02/05	Wigan NW		arr	12C01
Bromsgrove		02/33			dep	12C03
Barnt Green		02/48	Farington Jn.			12/28
Landor St. Jn.	arr	03C15	Blackburn			12/48
	dep	03C17	Hellifield			13/46
Castle Bromwich Jn.		03/27	VIA YORK TPU			
Park Lane Jn.		03/32	Petterill Bridge Jn.			16/32
Walsall		04/07	Carlisle L. Rd Jn.			16/35
Bushbury Jn. DGL	arr	04*30	Carlisle Station		arr	16C40
	dep	04*55			dep	16C42
Stafford		05/20	Carlisle Yard		arr	16L57
Madeley		05/45			dep	18L05
Basford Hall (42159)	arr	06L07	Gretna Jn.			18/22
	dep	09L59	(TO GLASGOW TPU)			
Winsford		10/21	Mossend (07360)		arr	22 01
Weaver Jn.		10/53				

Max. Speed : 35 m.p.h.

Conveys three condemned locomotives Nos. 50018, 50037 and 50046 all Through piped only for Glasgow Works
MC Metals.
Also conveys three coaches Nos. 5753, 5802, 17070 marshalled rear to provide adequate brakeforce and comply with WHFRS White Pages 82/2.

N.B:- Special authority is given for the Three piped only Main line locomotives to be conveyed in a Class 8 Train and Rule Book Appendix 2 Page 2.11 Paragraph 3 Sub-heading Class 6, 7 or 8 trains does not apply.)

Gross Trailing Weight : 455 tonnes.

(SUN)	CD 127 CLASS 47 (PXLC) work 8Z50 20 10 (SUN) Exeter to Crewe BH. LD to Laira.
(MO)	CD 407 CLASS 31 (RCJC) work 8Z50 09 59 Crewe to Mossend. LD to Crewe MS.

TRAINCREWS (SEE OVER)

/Continued ...

605/DR.R/24209S/FT4/CC/PG.1

Paul Furtek of Locomaster Profiles captured this movement crossing Ribblehead viaduct on its way to the scrap yard at M.C. Metals, Glasgow.

Supplementary notice in connection with the forward movement from Taunton to Leicester of condemned Class '50' locomotives 50012/14/22/47, initially from Laira.

Built in 1968 by English Electric at their Vulcan Foundry Works at the Newton-le-Willows Plant, 50014 *Warspite*, with nameplates removed, was the last Class 50 to be refurbished at Doncaster in 1983. It was withdrawn from service in December 1989. 50014 was towed away to Leicester (Vic Berry) in April 1989 along with 50012, 50022 and 50047.

PRIVATE AND NOT FOR PUBLICATION

F.T.N. No. 2|2

3 APRIL 1989

BRITISH RAILWAYS
WESTERN REGION
DAILY (SUPPLEMENTARY) FREIGHT TRAIN NOTICE

WEDNESDAY 5 APRIL

DEPARTMENTAL TRAFFIC

9Z41 10.40 Taunton Fairwater Yd – Leicester (Humberstone Rd)

Special. Hauled by Cl.47 Loco. Conveys Condemned Locos 50012/14/22/47 all brakes inoperative (air piped only) en route Laira to Leicester (Vic Berry). FABRIC 25 mph. Load 515 tonnes gross.

	Arr	Dep		Arr	Dep
Bridgwater		11/13	Charfield	13/32	
Highbridge		11/30	Glos Sig G.339	14C20	14C50
Yatton		12/00	Abbotswood Jn	16/00	
Bristol TM		12/40	Hartlebury	16/45	
Bristol Parkway		12/58			

WEDNESDAY 5 AND FRIDAY 7 APRIL

COAL TRAFFIC (MGR)

7Z02 14.20 Barrow Hill – Didcot P.S. (Arr 19.27)

Specials. Conveys loaded HAA's

6Z62 21.00 Didcot P.S. – Barrow Hill

Specials. Convey empty HAA's

THURSDAY 6 APRIL

OIL TRAFFIC

6Z05 23.30 Waterston – Heathfield

Special. Runs in MAP Serial 247 path

CP61/AME/5201m/1

(bdl)

```
KD83400 18/03/91 10.00.14 U3466                                          hdr
ON N688 BY POP FROM KD83400,MONDAY 18/03/91    10.00.13

TRN ENQUIRY RESPONSE FOR 847Z70A 18. BOOKED ID 7Z70A

0200 MO    LAIRA JN  - OLDOAKCCS

BUSINESS SECTOR M        TRAIN CATEGORY D


DEPT LAIRA JN   0445 18      LATE RSN ZZ EX ORIGIN STN
  09 SETOUT 82100   WESTBURYY
     37098 37 X 1750 105 50 5 080 0 X M CF F13 1410  0030 A 0125 D    13

  09 SETOUT 73221   OLDOAKCCS
     50021 50 X 2700 117 59 6 060 E B M HQ RONE0000  0039 A 0069 D
     50033 50 X 2700 117 59 6£100 E B M LA T1000000500000 F 0000 F
     50028 50 X 2700 117 59 6 100 E B M HQ RONE0000  0039 A 0061 B
     50044 50 X 2700 117 59 6 100 E B M LA RONE0000  0000 C 0000 C
       0 LDS     4 MTYS     468 TONNES    276 FT    0 POTENTIAL  AIR BRAKE FORCE

       0 LDS     4 MTYS     468 TONNES    276 FT    0 POTENTIAL  AIR BRAKE FORCE

       1 UNITS    1750 HORSEPOWER    105 TONS     62 FT     50 BRAKE FORCE

    338 FT-TOTAL TRAIN LENGTH       50 TOTAL TRAIN BRAKE FORCE
END
```

```
KD83400 19/03/91 08.15.06 U3587                                          hdr
ON N818 BY POP FROM KD83400,TUESDAY 19/03/91   08.15.04

TRN ENQUIRY RESPONSE FOR 837Z70A 19. BOOKED ID 5Z50A CHANGED IDS 5Z50A

0500 TO    RIVERSIDE - OLDOAKTMD

BUSINESS SECTOR L        TRAIN CATEGORY D


DEPT EXETER     0500 19
  09 SETOUT 73220   OLDOAKTMD
     50048 50 X 2700 117 59 6£100 E B M LA T1000000LE0044 A 0169 B

  09 SETOUT 73220   OLDOAKTMD
     50028 50 X 2700 117 59 6 100 E B M HQ RONE0000  0037 A 0059 B
     50044 50 X 2700 117 59 6 100 E B M LA RONE0000  0000 C 0000 C
       0 LDS     2 MTYS     234 TONNES    138 FT    0 POTENTIAL  AIR BRAKE FORCE

       0 LDS     2 MTYS     234 TONNES    138 FT    0 POTENTIAL  AIR BRAKE FORCE

       1 UNITS    2700 HORSEPOWER    117 TONS     69 FT     59 BRAKE FORCE

    207 FT-TOTAL TRAIN LENGTH       59 TOTAL TRAIN BRAKE FORCE
END
```

Not all of the movement of condemned locomotives went without a hitch. On 19 March 1991, 50048 failed at Woodborough, hauling two Class '50's to Old Oak Common, as the incident list from RHQ Control at Swindon testifies.

INCIDENT LIST

Ref.: 28174   Category: A CM&EE(LOC)   Type: 03 LOCOMOTIVES
From: 19/03/91 at 0648 To: 19/03/91 at 1135   Serious?:

Location: WOODB WOODBOROUGHION   Speed Restriction: 000
Train Head Code: 7Z70   Set Number:
Vehicle/Equip. Type: LOCOMOTIVE   V/E Number:
Depot/Control Box: LAIRA LAIRA LOCO/HST   Drivers Turn: 0000
Casualty/Follow UP: F.A.O.: AMBT AMRG AMEX AFMPL

Short Description:
  LOCOMOTIVE FAILURES ON 7Z70 0500 EXETER-OLD OAK COMMON (TRAIN OF DEAD LOCOS).
Additional Detail:
  A special train movement, 7Z70 05.00 Exeter - Old Oak Common, at 50 mph, was
  arranged in order to move two condemned Class 50 locos (50028 and 50044),
  using 50048 (LA, NWXA) to haul them. 50048 was itself en route from Laira to
  Old Oak Common for repairs and carried a "Light engine only" restriction
  (applied at 11.04 on Monday 18th March 1991).
  At 06.48 the Driver of 7Z70 reported to Reading Panel from R.819 signal at
  Woodborough that 50048 had failed on the Up Main line.
  Loco 47711 (OC, NWRA), running L/D from Westbury to Old Oak Common for
  repairs, was stopped by signals as it approached Newbury and sent back to
  Woodborough to assist 7Z70. 47711 arrived on the front of the failed train at
  07.48 and 7Z70 went forward into Woodborough loop at 07.59.
Delays:
1F21 06.39 Westbury - Paddington ..67 minutes.
1A21 06.00 Plymouth - Paddington ..10 minutes.

  7Z70, now a train of 3 dead Class 50 locos hauled by 47711, departed
  Woodborough at 08.18, but at 09.03 a member of the Theale P/Way staff
  reported to Reading Panel from RC.105 signal at Midgham that one of the dead
  locos was smoking badly.
  At 09.07 the Driver of 7Z70 reported to Reading Panel from R.881 signal at
  Aldermaston that he was experiencing dragging brakes, and requested to go
  into Theale for further examination.
  7Z70 went to the Theale station end of No. 1 reception siding at Theale (i.e.
  away from the MURCO siding) at 09.15. The Theale RST attended and reported at
  09.27 that there was no requirement for the Fire Brigade to attend and the
  train was in order to proceed.
  7Z70 departed Theale at 09.48 and arrived Old Oak Common at 11.35.
Delays:
1A26 05.21 Penzance - Paddington .. 9 minutes.
6A14 23.35 Robeston - Theale held at Reading until 09.48.
2B17 08.53 Newbury - Reading .. 12 minutes.

On 18 March 1991, 37098 left Laira at 4.45am hauling 50021/50033/50028/50044 to Exeter. The following day 50028 and 50044 were hauled from Exeter to Old Oak Common by 50048.

Unified Depot Management was perceived by the AFM (Area Fleet Manager) as the culmination and solution to problems that were rife between the conciliation staff, shunters, carriage cleaners and shop floor staff. Despite repeated overtures to Geoff, and also voiced at the weekly Board meeting, the acrimony still prevailed. Indeed, I was often accused of perpetuating the 'them and us' syndrome – talk about tunnel vision. Strange really how when a problem is highlighted management choose to do nothing about it, hoping no doubt it will go away or resolve itself; in this case it did neither. There was, however, a very different situation in being at Long Rock Depot, Penzance. John 'Lord' Treloar, a junior supervisor under the Area Manager's umbrella, ran a very extraordinary and expensive set-up as the carriage-cleaning supervisor. Bob Poynter was chairman of a first LDC meeting and wanted to withdraw Treloar's post; it was the Sectional Council representatives who fought to retain the position and had the decision overturned at the next meeting, albeit by a different chairman. Ironically, not only was the post retained, but the staff reps also succeeded in getting it regraded, a decision which no doubt infuriated RJP. John Vinton, off his job as shift maintenance supervisor at Long Rock owing to health reasons, oversaw the BS5750 procedure which Laira had been accredited. He had the task to unify the depot that included the transfer of cleaning and shunting activities from the Area Manager's organisation. The complement of carriage cleaners was reduced and we were amazed to discover some of the activities that prevailed down in the far west. A gang of three, maybe four-carriage cleaners were engaged each night in the changing of seat covers on four Great Western and two CrossCountry HST sets. Now this task is not as straightforward as it would seem, as the covers were susceptible to slight shrinkage after laundering. What astounded us both was that under Treloar's regime no less than 89,000 pieces were sent away for dry cleaning in a twelve-month period; an astronomical figure that was to be quickly corrected. J.V., a mild mannered ex-navy man, handled the changeover at Long Rock extremely well during the transitional period and transformed the archaic working practices there.

John, together with a couple of his team, was instrumental in their contributions to a new Great Western presentation manual for carriage cleaning of which I chaired the working party. Also involved were representatives from Laira and St Philips Marsh depots and Dave Prigmore from RHQ Swindon who drew up the schedules. Periodically, representatives from various firms would visit the depot plying their wares, chemicals and cleaning agents, many of which were expensive and often not particularly effective. One company in Derby did take the trouble to undertake in-house demonstrations of their products; they also rewarded their customers each festive season with a Christmas pudding, which was not, I hasten to add, a cheapish one from the supermarket. The Director of Procurement at Derby drew up guidelines with evaluations being undertaken by the Scientific Services at Doncaster, as each chemical/cleaning agent needed to be carefully

'New manual brings clean sweep' headlined in Great Western News.

The army of train cleaners – who work a variety of day and night shifts to keep Great Western's carriages spick and span – have just completed a major project which improves their working practices and demonstrates a commitment to best practice in customer service. The end result, the new *Great Western Train Presentation Manual*, was implemented at the beginning of February.

"Previously, the cleaners had local codes of practice which were loosely based on the old InterCity manual," explained Dave Prigmore, Industrial Engineering Assistant.

"They needed some sort of recognised standard, so staff at the three main depots – St Philips Marsh, Laira and Long Rock – decided to form a working party and undertake some fact-finding tours."

Led by Laira-based chairman Rod Fowkes, the working group members were Andy Cope, Frank Gronow and Tony Jakeman from Bristol; John Vinton, Nigel Gilbert and Keith Williams from Penzance and Phil Underwood, Ian Cowan, Andy Ralphs and Paul Commander from Plymouth.

Visits

During the summer of '94, they organised visits between the Bristol, Plymouth and Penzance sites, and accompanied by Dave Prigmore and representatives from Old Oak Common and Swansea Landore, took the chance to talk to people about their working methods and cleaning materials.

"It really was an excellent communications exercise," Dave continued. "Everyone had a chance to voice their opinions, either directly or indirectly, and it soon became clear that everyone faced similar problems – and needed me which ones I preferred and why. I think the manual is a great idea, because we all need to strive for the same results."

John Vinton, Production Manager at Penzance, added, "Some cleaners have been doing the job for 25 years, and we relates to HSTs, additional sections are planned and these will outline procedures for people who actually do the cleaning, we've been able to produce a working document which will help us raise and maintain standards," stressed Rod Fowkes. "A variety of people helped to make this project a success and I'd like to thank them for their contribution."

Premier

He concluded, "We need to provide a premier cleaning service throughout the Great Western network – from Old Oak Common to Swansea and Penzance – and thanks to everyone's hard work and commitment, we're well on the way to achieving that goal."

materials appear.

"Because we listened to the

Colleagues from Laira gather round as working group chairman Rod Fowkes (centre), Ian Cowan (back left) and Paul Commander (extreme right) – all members of the Carriage Cleaning Working Group – display the new cleaners' manual.

to work together to find solutions."

John Ryan, Heavy Cleaner, was one of the many who contributed. "At the time, we were involved in a refurbishment programme at Laira," he said. "I was using a variety of cleaning chemicals and the working group asked were able to draw on their wealth of experience. We exchanged a number of ideas – Bristol staff redesigned the brush they use for cleaning the front end of power cars, and Plymouth and Penzance have now taken this innovation on board."

Although the new manual

Penzance's John Vinton (centre) and Nigel Gilbert (immediately behind John, back row) – both members of the working group – also helped to launch the new manual.

COSHH (control of substances hazardous to health) assessed before use. InterCity had gradually been losing its way with carriage cleaning, unlike Regional Railways in Wales and some of the London suburban lines and East Anglia. They had a rolling programme of meetings with the Department of Procurement and Doncaster, the respective firms knowing full well the responsibility for having their products evaluated and assessed by Scientific Services. Each depot appeared to be doing their own thing regarding carriage cleaning. Speedclean was widely used for interior glasswork until a scare at a Midlands depot resulted in the product being discontinued at some locations, and Laira was one of them.

I had a degree of sympathy with carriage cleaning staff, no doubt stemming from when the Edinburgh-Plymouth train came into Laira in the late evening with toilets blocked and smelling. Each turn was repetitious, cleaning up someone else's mess, the only variances being the watering and glasswork duties, but as a supervisor, there was a good deal of satisfaction when inspecting the completed work, many cleaners having a pride in their job. The coaching stock on the Exeter-Waterloo route, particularly during the winter months when the wash plants on the Southern Region were out of action for whatever reason, were externally very dirty, aggravated with deposits of brake dust. The vehicles then had to be cleaned manually as the Laser cleanser at the wash plant only kept clean trains clean. After the coaches had been hand-bashed I made sure that the shunters put them through the wash plant before going into service; they would then have to pass the mess room where the cleaners would see the results of their labours. Laira had an extremely good reputation for its standard of carriage cleaning, and rightly so, despite the withdrawal of the cleaning supervisors. The periodic heavy cleaning programme, every four weeks or so per vehicle, was very robust with both Penzance and St Philips Marsh depots benefiting from the exchange visits of the Laira staff.

'What's going on at Laira for goodness sake?' I was asked that question countless times by sources away from the depot and not necessarily on the parent region. Such was the depth of concern over the continuing failure to meet production targets. The management had created its own abyss. Weak direction going back to the late 1970s had to some extent tarnished the image of Laira. There seemed to be little follow-up concerning the quality of the maintenance work being turned off the depot, which was not up to standard. It would include catering vehicles, where the equipment was not functioning properly, and power cars failing in traffic through lack of the correct procedures being carried out. Even the HST sets off heavy maintenance were not exempt from such problems. Indeed, they had more than their fair share of criticism from train crews, catering staff and the Control, who then had the onerous task of re-allocating sets to cover the delinquents.

A team is only as strong as its leader, and whilst Geoff Hudson's commitment to the depot couldn't be questioned, his direction could. Take

43184 power car is attached to a Western Region Domestic set being serviced, whilst the other is a CrossCountry set with a coach less. There was often criticism levelled at the depot regarding problems with HSTs off maintenance.

nothing away from the Depot Engineer Malcolm Wishart: his dedication to the depot knew no bounds, often visiting the complex late at night and putting in an eleven-hour day, of which he never tired of telling us. The underlying problem was the lack of positive leadership. I always advocated that the art of management was to leave the 'fun of doing' to the level of authority that achieved the most fun out of it. Geoff at one stage would be taking the reins at the daily 9am conference, and was referred to as the fifth Production Manager, such was his imposition. That displeased both Malcolm and the PMs. The underlying factor, of course, was that Geoff had no real confidence in either. Their approaches were different. Having said that, it was he who had made some of the appointments. A more positive lead, with carpeting on occasions, together with a clear concise directive, and not being a strict disciplinarian, were a few attributes that were lacking. The Laira logo of the *Golden Hind* only served to highlight that the ship was rudderless, going round in circles, with no apparent direction. The production managers were the key. To bring out the best in them they had to be set a hard task – one which they could achieve. They weren't, and possibly wouldn't have achieved it anyway; Geoff had stifled any enthusiasm that might have been there. There was no sense of urgency on the part of the maintenance side; and that had been the picture over my seventeen years at the depot, although Laira was not alone, with Toton much the same. In any organisation there is always an exception to the rule, in this case Derek Land – probably the best Depot Engineer Laira never had.

What a line-up! Darren Bignall (Movements Supervisor), the author, Malcolm Wishart, Graham Boot-Handford and Derek Land (Number One!).

The one avenue where Laira did excel was the provision of traction and rolling stock for the special occasion. Power car naming ceremonies were many and each HST set was turned out in pristine condition. So they should have been of course, considering the number of man-hours spent preparing them. The response from the prestige events was always very favourable.

Whilst the presentation standards could not be sustained, for obvious reasons, the depot had for many years been associated with a high standard of carriage cleaning. If the management had shown the same impetus and

D400 (50050) and D433 (50033) are being tested for multiple workings on shed at Laira. 50033 *Glorious* in its latter days became known as *Smokey Joe*. Their next duty was to be 'The Midland Scotsman' to Glasgow in February 1994.

THE CLASS 40 APPEAL
proudly present....

D400   D433

THE
MIDLAND SCOTSMAN

Saturday 5th February 1994

*The final run of Class 50's to Glasgow
outwards via Settle-Carlisle
returning via Shap.*

The Class '50's were built for working passenger services on the West Coast main line (WCML), north of Crewe to Carlisle and Glasgow Central. In original livery, D433 and D400 prepare to do battle in February 1994 for the very last time over their old stamping ground, Shap and Beattock. Sponsorship of D433 was courtesy of Locomaster Profiles, whilst D400 had the backing of Pathfinder Tours.

Area Fleet Manager
Laira T&RS Depot
Embankment Road
Plymouth PL4 9JN

Date: 31 January 1994

Dear Customer

Welcome to the Class 40 Appeal Midland Scotsman Rail Tour. It is now just over 3 years since Laira Depot started marketing its Class 50's, when we ran the "Cornish Centurian" Rail Tour with Valiant and Thunderer and surprised our customers with two different liveries.

For todays Rail Tour we are turning the clock back over 25 years so you can 'ride' behind two 50's in their original livery. 50050 (D400) is now looking a bit tired, after all it is nearly 3 years since its last coat of paint so we have decided to tidy her up for this trip. Old Smoky Joe (50033) has lost her name plates yet again, but don't worry this is for a good cause. She is to become D433 for a very short time and you are privileged to travel behind a pair of 50's not only over Shap and Beattock but also the Settle and Carlisle reviving the scenes of the late 60's. Sponsorship for D433 is courtesy of Locomaster Profiles and sponsorship of D400 is courtesy of Pathfinder Tours.

So why should a modern traction Depot wrestling with the rigours of railway privatisation, bother with such efforts at this time? There are 3 answers:-

1.   It makes commercial sense and is good for our business.

2.   It demonstrates clearly that we care about our customers and try to exceed their expectations.

3.   We have pride in what we do and we want you to enjoy the last few weeks of these machines in service.

My first experience of the class was when I used to spend my Summer Holidays with my Aunt in Penrith and I used to go to Scout Green Box on Shap and see pairs of English Electric Type 4's double heading on the Anglo Scottish Services. Although I was really there for the steam loco's, these machines left a lasting impression on me and little was I to know that 20 years later that I would end up running a depot with nearly 40 of the fleet allocated.

In business terms they were a disaster, I came to Laira in March 1989 and for 2 years struggled with impossible stop lists and loco's frequently requiring major surgery at an unbelievable expense. Having said all that I was aware that the loco's have a tremendous following and with careful planning we could manage the run down with style.

What started as a one off rail tour in January 1991 has continued for 3 years, however, the locomotives will be withdrawn at the end of March. We decided in October 1993 to promote the final runs to the hilt and to take the locomotives over their old stamping ground. Personally this railtour is one I believe is important because the class was built to work between Crewe and Glasgow and they should travel on this route once more before they retire.

I have been conscious that we have had 3 different liveried loco's and that our customers would dearly love to see 2 machines in the same colour and I have been wrestling with this problem for sometime. The answer presented itself when the National Railway Museum claimed 50033 in Network South East colours. Naturally if Laira's workmanship was to be displayed in the museum it would have to be to the highest standard. In preparing the bodywork we decided to rub her down and apply a coat of grey primer. It was then simply a coat of Rail Blue and D433 could reappear. We will then buff off the blue and this will make an excellent undercoat for the NSE livery before she makes her final journey northwards to the Museum.

I hope you have a great day and have as much fun as we have had over the last few years.

Finally I know many people will be excited with this railtour and eager to take photographs please remember that railways can be a dangerous place and would ask you all to take care.

G P A HUDSON
Area Fleet Manager, Plymouth

D400 (50050) and D433 (50033) return for a finale over their old stamping ground, the West Coast main line.

resolve in ensuring that the maintenance of the HST fleet was released to the scheduled timescales, as they did with the presentation of the Class 50s (50007, 50033 and D400) during their last couple of years in traffic, then it would have been better for all concerned at the depot and the Western Region overall.

Admittedly, the railtours hauled by the trio of Class 50s generated a great deal of interest and revenue, but at what cost? The times we sat in on the weekly Board meetings and listened to Malcolm or a production manager reporting yet again that the HST exam programme had slipped. The excuses ranged from the sublime to the ridiculous: a Bank Holiday Monday intervening was cited; the most common cause of course was to blame the stores, which was ineffective anyway. Having said that, it also showed the calibre of the hierarchy at RHQ Swindon, that they could be so gullible in accepting the almost continual lame excuses for the slippages. That aside, the fact of the matter was there was no system; only a bad one with little or no cohesion between the three shifts. All in all it was ineffective management from the top right through to the supervisors, and the shop floor knew this. One person who was not afraid to pillory Laira at every opportunity was Derek Lloyd, a vociferous HST Controller at Swindon. His critical remarks in the daily log rankled both Geoff and Malcolm, and also the production managers. Nevertheless, what was stated was factual. Lloyd was a damn good controller and always made a point of highlighting Laira power cars in

Pathfinder Tours ran a *Cornish Caper* from York to Cornish Branches in March 1994, using D400/50007 from Bristol Temple Meads, with a third diesel, 50033, on the rear from Plymouth. On its return from Penzance, a photo line up of the three Class '50's was staged at Plymouth station before D400 and 50033 worked the train forward to York.

Laira Depot Engineer Malcolm Wishart is in position, about to conduct the 'Laira Concerto', a simultaneous start-up of all three diesels, 50033, 50007 and D400. Did the one on the left jump the gun?

The 'Laira Concerto' is firing on all cylinders and Malcolm Wishart has put away his baton, a sight never to be repeated. On arrival at York, 50033 *Smokey Joe* would make a last run to Scarborough before entering the NRM at York, until the NRM decided to dispose of the locomotive, subject to a suitable home being found. Now at Vintage Trains Tyseley Depot.

Pathfinder THE "CORNISH CAPER" Railtour — SATURDAY 19TH MARCH 1994

MILEAGE Pngose	TIME		LOCATION	COMMENT	TRACTION
			STOCK TO ARRIVE AT YORK BY 22.00 PLEASE.		
O	(Fri) 2315		YORK	PICK UP	ANY
			Swinton		
46	0014	0016	SHEFFIELD	" "	
	0033		Chesterfield		
82	0058	0100	DERBY	" "	
123	0147	0150	BIRMINGHAM NEW STREET	" "	
			Selly Oak		
			Abbotswood Jn		
	0238	0240	CHELTENHAM SPA	" "	
	0318	0320	BRISTOL PARKWAY	" "	↓
213	0300	0330	BRISTOL TEMPLE MEADS	" " LOCO CHANGE	50007 /50
	0500		Taunton		
			Exeter St Davids		
			Newton Abbot		
	0610	0630	PLYMOUTH	PHOTO STOP	50+33 REAR
			St. Austell	PAR	
394	0745	0818	TRURO	ATTACH PAIR 50's 50033/D400	
	0821		Penwithers Jn NEWQUAY		
405	0840	0845	FALMOUTH DOCKS	REVERSE	
	0904		Penwithers Jn	retime 0855 Truro - Falmouth	
416	0907	0915	TRURO	REVERSE/DETACH PAIR ↓	
	0935		Camborne		
	0946		St. Erth		
	0953		Long Rock		
442	0956	1030	PENZANCE	REVERSE/ATTACH PAIR 50033/D400	
448	1040		St. Erth		
452	1050	1058	ST. IVES	REVERSE	
	1108		St. Erth		
462	1118		PENZANCE	DETACH PAIR 50's AFTER 50033 RELEASE ↓	
				BREAK/WATER STOCK	
462		1310	PENZANCE		
			Truro		
			St. Austell		
	1500	1550	PLYMOUTH	PHOTO STOP/LINE UP ALL 50's D400/50033	
	17c		Exeter St. Davids		
	1732		Taunton		
669	1810	1814	BRISTOL TEMPLE MEADS	SET DOWN	
	1824	1826	BRISTOL PARKWAY	" "	
	1908	1910	CHELTENHAM SPA	" "	↓
			Abbotswood Jn		
			Selly Oak		
	2008	2010	BIRMINGHAM NEW STREET	" "	
	2105	2107	DERBY	" "	
			Chesterfield		
	2153	2155	SHEFFIELD	" "	
			Swinton		
882	2258		YORK	" "	↓

Footnote: D400/50033 : follow tour LE N. Abbot-Truro (enter Plymouth station at 0615).
top'n'tail tour Truro-Falmouth-Truro.
follow tour LE Truro - Penzance.
top'n'tail tour Penzance- St. Ives -Penzance, then release
50007 at Penzance, then stand on display (if time) after re-fuelling.
follow tour LE Penzance - Plymouth, with all 50 line up at Plymouth station!
work train north Plymouth to York (utilising Saltley traincrew) so positioning
50033 at York ready for handover to National Railway Museum on the
following day. D400 LE York-Laira on Sunday.

SUBMITTED 29/10/93	STOCK CIRCUIT = CL64/65 (4xTSO/2xBFK/4xTSO) = load 10	PAGE 1 of 1

COULD WE HAVE A 1Z50 HEADCODE PLEASE ?

Cornish Caper was worked by 50007/50050 from Bristol Temple Meads, attaching 50033 on the rear at Plymouth. The itinerary was changed from the Truro to Falmouth branch line to traversing the Par to Newquay line. A photo shoot line up at Plymouth was held on the return from Cornwall.

trouble, in particular those released off repair and exam. He realised that there was a fundamental problem at the depot which was not getting any better.

Geoff, Malcolm, myself, and a couple of production managers and supervisors met with Derek Lloyd, his boss John Reeves and two other controllers; the location a South Devon pub. John Reeves, who was well aware of the problems that existed between the operating and maintenance departments, arranged this Control/Depot liaison meeting in an informal atmosphere. The convivial evening, deemed by some as an opportunity to down a few, did prove useful; it is quite surprising how people loosen up when they've had a couple of drinks, and one of the biggest problems was communication, or lack of it. But I'm pretty sure that in the debriefing that followed, John Reeves would wonder whether it had been money well spent in organising the 'jolly'.

One day Geoff sent down a letter for me to deal with. It was from an 8-year-old boy from nearby Plympton who wanted to know why the colour light signals on the railway were the opposite way round to the traffic lights on the public highway. A very observant lad, whose observation to a number of learned colleagues, me included, was vacillated over. Some hesitancy on the part of the Driver Manager over the matter brought a response from one of his team; the reason being was that the red light was nearer to the driver's eye level. Geoff signed a letter explaining the findings and it was delivered by hand to the boy's home together with some Class 50 memorabilia, crockery and other literature. The lad's grandparents were absolutely delighted and the young lad was over the moon; he responded by promptly writing a letter of thanks to the Area Fleet Manager.

Central door locking on rolling stock was undertaken at various locations, Stewarts Lane and BREL Crewe amongst others, and two of the Ministry of Defence establishments at Rosyth and Devonport. Having been actively involved in the previous Fastrak input of catering vehicles into HM Dockyard, the movements had been relatively straightforward, with a barrier vehicle either side of the catering coach. The move was hauled down to Keyham sidings by a Class '08' shunt loco which then ran round its train, propelled out onto the Down main line and then hauled its train into HM Dockyard. After positioning the vehicles in one of the three short sidings, the shunt diesel then returned to Plymouth station.

To evaluate the movement of a full HST set into and out of the dockyard, a trial run was arranged one Sunday in the presence of representatives from Devonport Management Ltd, a permanent way supervisor, and various members of the technical department who would check the lateral movements on the vehicles at different points. The rake of HST trailer coaches with a barrier vehicle at either end (essential as the HST coaches had no buffers), was hauled down to Keyham by a Class 47 locomotive. A Class '08' shunt diesel would then attach to the rear and draw the complete train into DML towards No. 1 siding, stopping short with the shunt diesel going

towards No. 2 road, with final positioning of the rake being carried out by the Class '47'. The curvature of the track inside the complex with extremely tight clearances would necessitate the use of back-to-back shunt radios. A method of working was set up with Paul Burkhalter of DML; he had total control over movements into and out of HM Dockyard, including the nuclear flasks to and from Sellafield. That move had to be legislated for and was programmed to take place in the envelope between the output and input of HST sets. At the same meeting a further contingency was highlighted, that of a vehicle which would not be ready with the rest of the set and had to be detached to No. 4 siding – not an easy manoeuvre to perform. Laid down working instructions were issued by a representative from Euston who also attended the meeting. lan Bean of DML, would provide the necessary liaison with the on-site BR project engineer in the case of any slippage or other eventualities. On one occasion a HST set went in with the catering vehicle still stocked with beer, wines and spirits; that initially caused a little consternation as HM Dockyard was a dry area. lan saved the day by having the stock placed in a secure store, before being collected by the stores personnel from Plymouth. Each set of HST vehicles was programmed in for a complete week with Friday being the change-over day. The work would be undertaken outside with temporary scaffolding and plastic sheeting providing the necessary cover against the elements. As to be expected, the first rake of vehicles missed the target date for release; instead of the two weeks – a familiarisation period was to be expected – there was a further delay of seven days. That particular Friday I was up the line and, unable to contain my interest, I rang the Duty Manager at Plymouth from the Railway Inn at Sawley at around eight-thirty to enquire how the move was progressing. Mike Smith told me that the two locomotives, a Class '47' and a '08' shunt loco had gone into the dockyard at just after five o'clock and nothing had been heard since then. With that I returned to the card school. At around eleven o'clock I made a further enquiry; Paul Rowe was in the chair and able to tell me that the move out of the dockyard appeared at around nine o'clock and the move back into DML was imminent.

Although Laira's involvement was only to form up each rake of vehicles to go in when the other set had been released, I saw the need to oversee the scheme, although on occasions Geoff told me to desist as he did with the earlier project. I also made sure to check that there was a driver, trainman, shunter and signalman to operate the ground frame, rostered for the trip. For a while a dedicated locomotive, a somewhat ailing Class '47' No. 47851, was allocated to the duty. After a week or two of the operation, it was then decided that the inward working into HM Dockyard had to be altered. When the shunt loco was inside the ground frame at Keyham waiting to go out on the Down main line to haul the train into DML, the ground position signal could not be cleared, and despite a handsignalman from Plymouth panel being in attendance who could authorise the pilot to pass the GPL at danger, it was no longer to be permitted. Quite right, but it certainly slowed down the workings going into the dockyard as the Class 08 shunt diesel had then to be attached to the rear of the rake of HST coaches in Plymouth station, then forward to Keyham just over 2 miles away at 15mph which was funereally slow on the main line. Altogether, fifty-three HST sets were dealt with by DML with relatively few problems being encountered.

A further loss of work at Laira T&RS Depot – the Network SouthEast coaching stock had ceased three or four years earlier – was the Regional Railways DMUs for servicing and exam, supposedly because the price wasn't right. The servicing work went to St Blazey and Exeter with the exams being done at Cardiff Canton. A few said the work would not be missed and that the depot was better off without the railcar work, how absurd; in any climate any loss of work is detrimental. Except for those operating on the St Ives branch, all the Heritage units had been moved out of the south-west, replaced by 150/153 Sprinter units locally, with 158 units on the long distance services between Penzance and South Wales. Bristol Bath Road depot was closing – who would have envisaged that some years previously, when most through trains to the West Country changed locomotives in Temple Meads station? RES, parcels locos, found a new home a short distance away at Barton Hill.

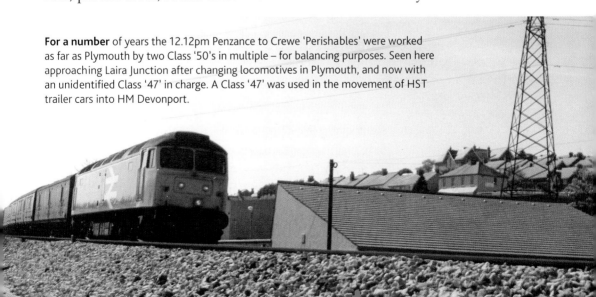

For a number of years the 12.12pm Penzance to Crewe 'Perishables' were worked as far as Plymouth by two Class '50's in multiple – for balancing purposes. Seen here approaching Laira Junction after changing locomotives in Plymouth, and now with an unidentified Class '47' in charge. A Class '47' was used in the movement of HST trailer cars into HM Devonport.

The Way Out

A fleet organisation review team (Fort) had been set up to examine the management structure at RHQ Swindon and the depots at St Philips Marsh and Laira. In the autumn of 1995, Geoff Hudson sounded me out as to whether I wished to consider finishing early under a severance scheme, funded by the BRB. At 54, and with my mother-in-law living with us and her faculties failing, I thought carefully about the offer. At least if I was at home it would allow Maureen more freedom than she was getting at the time. The severance package had actually been available a year earlier, and with more than a little interest I sent off to Stooperdale at Darlington for a pension estimate, and even visited a financial advisor who advised me then to seriously consider the offer. In the end I decided against the move. One man who didn't though was Derek Land; he was slightly older than I was. Ideally, the age of 55 realised the maximum benefit, but with privatisation looming it was a case of make your mind up, as it might possibly be the last severance scheme on offer. Ironically the preferred bidder for Great Western had been Resurgence; they however fell at the first hurdle. That then opened the door again for the management buyout (MBO) led by Brian Scott, whose previous bid had been rejected by the franchise director.

After some more deliberation, all things considered I decided to take the offer of severance and leave the railway after thirty-nine years service. Not an easy decision to have made. However, the industry had moved on; whereby at one time it was a delight to come to work, alas it was now littered with bureaucracy, stifling any enthusiasm one might have had. Decisions were now made for you; the fun had gone out of being a railwayman. Although St Philips Marsh had seen fit to remove their Operations Manager some years earlier, the set up at Laira was completely different to that at SPM. Admittedly more HST sets were serviced at night at the Bristol Depot, but Laira was more diverse in its work and geographically different. In the meantime Geoff wasn't going to be left without an operator as such, no doubt remembering the debacle of the 1990 timetable. Seldom making a decision without clearing it with Ian Cusworth, he tentatively approached Paul Rowe, Resource Manager in Plymouth, himself shortly to be displaced as part of Great Western policy

TRAINCREW LAIRA DEPOT

	OCTOBER 1992	NOVEMBER 1992	MAY 1993	MAY 1994
PL801	0800	0700	0700	0700
PL831	0600	*	*	*
PL832	0600	0600	0600	0600
PL834	0655	0700	0700	0700
PL836	1400	1400	1400	1400
PL837	1400	1400	1500	1500
PL839	1500	1500	1500	1500
PL841	2200	2200	*	*
PL842	2200	2200	2200	2200
PL843	2200	2200	2200	*
PL845	2300	2300	2300	2300
PL846	2300	2300	2300	2300
PL2831	0600	*	*	*
PL2832	0600	0600	0600	0600
PL2834	0700	0700	0700	0700
PL2836	1400	1400	1400	1400
PL2837	1400	1400	1400	*
PL2841	2200	2200	*	*
PL2842	2200	2200	*	*
PL2843	2200	2200	2200	2200
PL2845	2300	2300	2200	2200
PL4831	0600	*	*	*
PL4832	0600	0600	0600	0600
PL4834	0700	0700	0700	0700
PL4836	1400	1400	1400	1400
PL4837	1400	1400	1400	*
PL4841	2200	*	*	*
PL4842	2200	2200	2200	*
PL4843	2200	2200	2200	*
PL4845	2300	2300	2300	2300
PL4846	2300	2300	2300	2300
PL811	0500	*	*	*
PL815	0630	0630	0630	0555
PL817	1400	1400	1400	1355
PL818	2130	*	*	2155
PL822	2205	2205	2205	*
PL705	1810(CS UNTIL 2120)	*	*	*
PL2811	0500	*	*	*
PL2815	0630	0630	0630	0555
PL2817	1400	1400	1400	1355
PL2818	2130	2130	2130	2155
PL4811	0500	*	*	*
PL4815	0630	0630	0630	0555
PL4817	1400	1400	1400	1355
PL4818	2130	*	*	2155
PL4822	2300	2300	2300	*

Rationalisation of traincrew turns at Laira T&RSD.

to withdraw all of those posts and centralise the rostering and the booking on and off of train crews at Bristol, and sounded him out over coming out to Laira to undertake some of my work. That didn't find favour with the Fort team as my post was out of the equation. A leaving date of 15 March 1996 was determined, unfortunate really, as being retained for almost a further four months would have realised a further twenty-seven weeks salary. Maureen's mother had now been admitted into a nursing home from where she would not return. It was then too late to reverse the decision of leaving, particularly with the Fort team in session. The last four years at Laira had been an interesting experience; there was a feeling of satisfaction in my achievements in reducing costs, particularly train crew, although the shunting and carriage cleaning staff did not escape either.

Almost £500,000 had been saved and this would auger well for the new company, Great Western Trains. I had gone as far as practicable with reducing the drivers on the depot. In fact, at the last round of proposed reductions that were put forward for withdrawal, I deliberately highlighted four turns, knowing full well that three was the optimum. Dick Samuels (LDC 'B') came to my office and sat with me and suggested that to withdraw the 22.00 shed turn would create problems. I knew that, but included it as a lever to take out the other turns. Those went through, LDC 'B' was reasonably satisfied, they had saved a turn, or so they thought, but I had achieved my objective. No further reductions could be envisaged with the shunters unless new shift patterns were introduced as had been suggested and there was still a considerable amount to be done on the carriage cleaning front. Malcolm Wishart retired on the same date; a nice enough chap to talk to, he let himself down, however, by his bellowing and choice vocabulary, and was perceived by many in his role as Depot Engineer as a jokey person.

In all of my seventeen years at Laira in various capacities, only once did I refuse to take a train onto the depot. That was during the RMT dispute in 1994. One Thursday in late September (Friday was the strike day), trains had been worked down to Laira in readiness for the final summer Saturday workings out of Cornwall, Plymouth, Torbay and Exeter. The depot was at saturation point, sets being doubled up in the sidings and roads not normally used were pressed into occupation. RHQ Swindon wanted to work into the depot a HST set for retro-fit and I declined it; no way could it be accommodated.

Plymouth panel box had been operating on previous strike days manned by supervisors and managers up until just after midnight. On the Saturday the signalmen reported for duty at 06.00; from then until 09.30 there would be no less than fifteen departures off the depot. With that in mind I arrived on the depot at around 05.30 to oversee the trains departing. Steve was the Movements Supervisor on the night turn; and it was a real dog's breakfast. Little if anything had been pre-prepared despite the shed turners and shunters being on duty throughout the night. The opportunity had been there to go some way towards assisting the train preparer. Jess had failed miserably, and his colleague on the early shift had all the water on the wheel. Delays were inevitable. Out of the nine CrossCountry trains, six were late, and I wrote an apologetic letter to Brian Johnson at CrossCountry Trains that Geoff signed. The regular production manager was on leave that Friday night; had he been there though, it may not have altered the situation all that much.

Geoff Hudson then relinquished his post as AFM Plymouth somewhat unexpectedly, so quick in fact, that at the time, having taken the usual Friday off to go up the line, I'd just arrived in my office on the Monday morning only to be told by Paul Commander that he had left. The depot had stagnated, apathy reigned supreme; as stated previously Geoff, and to a lesser extent Malcolm, had for some time sought to defend the indefensible.

Three views of a line up of both domestic and CrossCountry HSTs in Laira Carriage Sidings on Christmas Day 1993, going nowhere.

On Thursday, 14 March 1996, the day before retiring, a presentation was held at the Duke of Cornwall Hotel in Plymouth for all those finishing under the severance arrangements, together with a few long service awards. Malcolm Wishart didn't attend as Graham Boot Handford was doing the honours after the hurried departure of Geoff. A further presentation for Geoff, Malcolm and myself was held at the BRSA Club at Laira that evening, where, for services rendered, I was presented with a replica nameplate *Fearless*. At a special presentation ceremony the following month in Bath, Malcolm, myself and five others received a solid gold pin bearing the Merlin logo, this being the Great Western badge of excellence, recognising outstanding personal effort.

Brian Scott did the honours over lunch, but what galled me, and still rankled me years later, was that no one bothered to mention the fact that I hadn't had a day off sick for thirty years, which I was extremely proud of. There aren't too many who can match that record.

```
          OFF BOOKED ROUTE REPORTS
PLYMOUTH                07:33  07:38        VIA LIPSON JN

W481700 26/09/94 08.24.40 U0279
TRUST TRAIN ENQUIRY  AT 08:24  26/09/94

831E33M 24 10:01 PAIGNTON  TO YORK     24/09/94 H.S.T. "125" (PLANNED)

           BOOKED       ACTUAL
          ARR   DEP    ARR    DEP
PAIGNTON        10:01          10:35M  34 LATE
TORQUAY   10:05 10:08  10:42M 10:45M  37 LATE
NEWTONABT 10:18 10:20  10:56M 10:58M  38 LATE
TEIGNMTH  10:25 10:28  N/R    N/R
DAWLISH   10:32 10:35  N/R    N/R
EXETSTDAV 10:52 10:55  11:27M 11:30M  35 LATE
TAUNTON   11:16 11:18  11:49M 11:51M  33 LATE
COGLOAD J       11:22         11:56M  34 LATE
BRDGWTRYD       11:26         12:01A  35 LATE
UPHILL JN       11:39         12:08A  29 LATE
WORLE JN        11:41         12:10A  29 LATE
BRISTOLTM 11:56 12:04  12:24A 12:30A  26 LATE
DR DAYSJN       12:06         12:31A  25 LATE
STAPLTNRD       12:07         12:31A  24 LATE
FILTON JN       12:10         12:34A  24 LATE
BRISPKWAY 12:12 12:14  12:38A 12:41A  27 LATE
WESTRLY J       12:19         12:45A  26 LATE
CHARFIELD       12:26         12:50A  24 LATE
STANDISHJ       12:34         13:01A  27 LATE
GLOUCESTR 12:44 12:51  13:09A 13:16A  25 LATE  M LINE
GLOSBARNJ       12:53         13:17A  24 LATE
CHELTENHM 12:58 13:01  13:23A 13:25A  24 LATE
ABBOTWDJN       13:14         13:37A  23 LATE
STOKEWKJN       13:20         13:44A  24 LATE
BARNT GRN       13:25         13:48A  23 LATE  M LINE
K NORTON        13:30H        13:52A  22 LATE
SELLYOAK        13:33         N/R
BHAM NEW  13:40 13:44  14:08M 14:13M  29 LATE
LNDR STJN       13:48         14:17M  29 LATE
WATERORTN       13:53H        N/R
KINGSBRYJ       13:56H        14:26M  30 LATE
TAMWRTHHL       14:02H        N/R
WICHNOR J       14:07H        N/R
BURTON          14:11H        N/R
STENSONJN       14:18         N/R
DERBY     14:23 14:25  14:50R 14:53M  28 LATE
CHESTRFLD 14:46 14:47H 15:13A 15:14A  27 LATE  M LINE
DORESTNJN       14:55H        15:21A  26 LATE
SHEFFIELD 15:01 15:04  15:27A 15:33A  29 LATE
HOLMESJN        15:10         15:38A  28 LATE  M LINE
SWINTON         15:14         15:43A  29 LATE
DONCASTER 15:25 15:28  15:54A 15:57A  29 LATE
SHFTHMEJN       15:32H        16:01A  29 LATE       VIA DOWN
TEMPLHJ         15:37H        16:06A  29 LATE
HMBLTN NJ       15:40H        N/R
COLTONJN        15:47         16:13A  26 LATE  N LINE
YORK      15:54        16:16A         22 LATE
KEY: A,S = AUTO REPORT M,R = MANUAL REPORT N/R = NO REPORT E = EXPECT REP1
 34 PAIGNTON -NEWTONABT        YI INWD STOCK
  2 WORLE JN -BRISTOLTM 014883 ZZ UNEX L/R
  1 FILTON JN-BRISPKWAY 008892 PA PLANND TSR
  1 CHARFIELD-STANDISHJ 013248 PB PLANND COT           STANDISH JN
  2 CHARFIELD-STANDISHJ        TG DRIVER               LOST IN RUN
  1 STANDISHJ-GLOUCESTR 013248 PB PLANND COT           STANDISH JN
  6 K NORTON -BHAM NEW         DA WTG SIGNAL  WTG PLAT. NEW ST
  1 LNDR STJN-KINGSBRYJ 013057 PB PLANND COT
```

The aftermath of the dispute by signalmen resulted in delays to services from Laira, although some of it was our own making. This was the late running 10.01 Paignton-York thirty-four minutes late start – inward stock late from Laira.

On leaving the venue I mentioned to Brian Scott about my attendance and how it had not been recognised, particularly on the day. 'Oh,' he replied, 'when I was DOS at Birmingham I didn't have any time off for...' – what price loyalty? As Maureen often used to tell me, 'you'll get no better thought of going to work when below par.'

Looking back at *From Clerk to Controller* and the varying happenings, readers might conclude that unfair criticism might have been levelled at the maintenance department. It is all too easy on occasions to be devil's advocate, although looking back at Toton and observing Senior Shift Maintenance Supervisors strolling around, decked out in suit and hush puppies only emphasised the situation pertaining on occasions at Nottingham station where they were busy running-round express trains as there was no other Type 4 diesel available to work the train forward. This contrasted markedly with the team at Laira in dustcoat and work boots. Mention has been made of Derek Land through the Laira pages. Of his two colleagues Ivor Cullum was perceived by some as being slightly reclusive and to some extent reticent regarding the release of locomotives when the power position was tight. Unfortunately Ivor, betrayed by his underlings, was removed from the shift by Ian Cusworth and allocated to a position of Riding Inspector. He was supplanted by a supervisor who couldn't handle the subordinates on the shift and who was replaced after a very short tenure. Dear old Ted Lock was of the old school from the steam days, a hands-on person whose appearance bore testimony to his quest of keeping the place afloat. Later, with Ted gone and Derek Land retiring, a fresh band of maintenance supervisors appeared on the scene. Amongst them came Captain Calamity, and a supervisor from the north-east who, when asked one night by the Movements Supervisor how the HST for the early morning Taunton-Paddington service was progressing, promptly laughed and said 'you won't get that for four o'clock' and walked away. Notwithstanding, I mentioned in conversation with the Quality Systems Manager one morning that the HST to work the 9.30 Plymouth to Paddington was in trouble on the depot; his reply, 'there's another one in an hour.' The rot had set in!

The age profile of the Laira footplate staff in the early 1980s realised the transfer to the south-west of an assortment of drivers from depots in London and the south-east. Christened the Lavender Hill Mob, two or three of them were fully paid-up members of the awkward squad and had a rude awakening; they would find out as I did that infiltration from other regions was not all that it seemed.

Retirement presentation at the Duke of Cornwall Hotel by Graham Boot Handford (GBH), who was holding the reins at Laira after the sudden departure of Area Fleet Manager Geoff Hudson.

Epilogue

In 1997, a year after Great Western returned into private ownership, it acquired a second franchise, North Western Trains, a company rumoured to have a significant deficit. Not surprisingly Great Western Holdings had their work cut out delivering the goods. Archaic working practices that were rife on the run up to privatisation had to be addressed across the entire spectrum. It was patently obvious that when First Group stepped in and acquired GW Holdings that heads would roll with the hierarchy – not before some of the Directors had become millionaires overnight though. Brian Scott resigned, others left before push came to shove, the old cliché of too many chiefs and not enough Indians. First Group then wielded the axe on 150 management staff – doesn't that say something about the previous regime on how not to run a railway? North Western Trains' Managing Director resigned, the Manchester-based NWT was laying off 200 workers, slashing services and putting up prices by an average of 10%. Never mind the fare paying public; keep the shareholders happy!

On leaving BR, the Pensions Management office at Darlington sent out, in addition to financial correspondence, other paraphernalia including details of the British Transport Pensioners Federation, which has branches throughout the country. I joined the Nottingham Branch of the BTPF and duly received the quarterly newsletter that included a list of new members along with those deceased. Shortly after, I received a letter post marked Long Eaton, which read: *'I see in the Pensioners Federation Newsletter that we have a new member, R.H. Fowkes from Plymouth, I ask myself can this be the trainspotter supremo and control reporter that used to torment me at Toton Centre? It hardly seems possible that the young lads that worked with me are now retiring.'* So wrote George Bailey. How nice to receive the letter from someone I worked with forty years earlier; I replied immediately. We met at the next BTPF gathering and some weeks later at his home we trawled through all our yesterdays. I was unaware that he had been a signalman at Sheet Stores Junction some years before I went there.

A few months earlier, when visiting Maureen's uncle Bill in a nursing home, the subject of Beyer Garratts came up, as it usually did, such was Bill's fondness for them. He recalled an occasion when the enginemen were both

Signalman George Bailey in Trent Station North Junction box. I was his control reporter at Toton Centre for a spell. He had also been a signalman at Sheet Stores Junction, and when Trent power box was commissioned in 1969, George was accommodated as a Shunter at Toton, before resuming signalling duties at Stapleford and Sandiacre signal box.

scalded when a tube burst on the footplate. After discussing the incident with George Bailey, he must have given the matter some thought and wrote the following:

'While working at Toton East Junction signal box in the winter of 1940, Garratt engine No.7967 was taking a coal train from Toton to Brent on a Sunday night. As the train passed the box, both the driver and fireman could be seen firing the locomotive.

When the train got to Ratcliffe Junction a boiler pipe burst over the fire. Both men were severely scalded. The driver stopped the train and assisted the fireman to walk back to the guard. The two enginemen were eventually taken to Loughborough hospital, but died later. To make matters worse there was a severe frost at the time.'

In the letter he recalled: *'during 1939 the IRA. were attempting to cause disruption on the railways. Instructions were given to signalmen to ask any stranger to sign the train register book. Toton down mechanisation had been completed and a party of officials came into Toton East signal box. I picked up a pen and asked who would sign the book. It was signed by Colonel Watkinson the then Operating Manager of the LMS.'* He went on: *'also during 1939 a trial run was made with two Class 8F engines and 100 coal wagons to London. This was at the time of loose couplings, which apparently had become stretched and no further trials were undertaken that year... A character that used to come to Trent was relief signalman Twink Burrows. The only man I know who could smoke a pipe, eat a meal, and talk on the telephone at the same time.'*

Regional newspapers in the East Midlands periodically produced a special publication on railways. One such edition, of June 1996, was entitled, *The Way We Were - Railways in Notts.* The editorial included, 'Do you have any old pictures of the railways of yesteryear?' Replying to this request, and not hearing anything for well over eighteen months, I was pleasantly surprised to receive a telephone call from the Features Editor of the *Nottingham Evening Post* regarding a further publication, and a meeting then ensued. An article giving an account of working on BR entitled 'Golden Age of Railways' contained nineteen of my photographs, four of which had been printed in reverse. The innocuous reference to my mother who came from a railway family – her father being Stationmaster at Sawley – did not however please Maureen's uncle, Rowland Webb. 'Didn't you tell them that you married into a railway family?' The four Webb brothers were all railwaymen: Rowland (later to become a shift clerk) George and Jack, who emigrated to America, were all goods guards at Toton whilst Bill was on the footplate. Their father was a driver at Toton and his dad a signalman in the Trent area until he was aged 70.

So, from 15 March 1996, I was on permanent gardening leave. Derek Land, Glenys Deighton, a clerical officer, and Morley Crago, a retired guard's inspector were the ones who kept in touch on a semi-regular basis. The train managers, particularly on the CrossCountry route whilst travelling to Long Eaton, were and still are very amiable. Many close contacts were of course in the East Midlands.

One evening in November 1998 the phone rang; it was David Langton, Train Planning Officer of First North Western Trains. After exchanging pleasantries he asked me if I would be interested in examining the operational working at Newton Heath depot. He told me to expect the project to take four weeks to complete. Interestingly, a few weeks earlier on the BBC2 *Working Lunch programme* there was an interview with a representative belonging to an action group in the north-west, which was lambasting First North Western Trains over their performance.

After an initial meeting in Manchester with David Langton and Kenny Scott the Depot Manager at Newton Heath, I set to work spending the majority of the time on the depot on the night shift. Hotel accommodation for the first week was at the Pennine Hotel in Oldham.

I then found myself negotiating three nights for the price of two at the Travelodge in Deansgate, Manchester, for the remainder of the project – old habits die hard. One night at the Travelodge, the fire alarm went off just after 3am. Four fire engines arrived and the hotel was evacuated. Some time elapsed before we were allowed back inside. The cause: a guest taking a shower and the steam activated the fire alarm system.

Newton Heath's allocations of DMUs at the time were:
Class 142 (55), Class 150 (29), Class 153 (12), Class 156 (18), Class 158 (8) + 5 operated by Virgin Trains.

There were forty-two units diagrammed onto the depot from 18.36, the timetabling of which being largely dictated by the passenger service, and the

Three old-timers with almost 150 years service on the railway between them. William Webb, Rowland Webb and George Bailey in the grounds of Mount Saint Bernard Abbey in Charnwood Forest, Leicestershire.

maintenance plan was not robust enough to cope. Although the Manchester North resignalling scheme had been completed in September, the early morning departures of DMUs was in need of a radical overhaul. Some of the timings were totally unrealistic and there were just too many departures in too short a period.

I took the opportunity to visit Blackburn station, where I was proposing to amend the DMU working, and meeting the Station Manager, train crew and driver managers at Manchester Victoria. I also spent time in Rail House with the DMU Controller and the diagramming team. Owing to Christmas and New Year intervening, my report was completed in early January. A meeting was then arranged later in the month to discuss the findings with David Langton and the Depot Manager. Copies of the report had been faxed, but supposedly had not been received at the depot, so on the day in question Kenny Scott could only avail himself for thirty minutes as he had negotiations with a third party, which was most disappointing. I hoped that some of the recommendations in my report, in particular those relating to amendments to both train crew and DMU diagrams, if adopted, could have been instituted as early as the twelve-week cycle in March, or certainly by the start of the summer timetable. There did appear to be at the outset some urgency in the remit. It was in June that year when travelling back to Plymouth from Long Eaton that a train manager, Andrew Thomas, whom I hadn't seen for a number of months, asked me about the Newton Heath project. When he heard that I'd had no further contact with David Langton, I agreed with his sentiments that after all this time it was unlikely that I would hear anything from him now. I then wrote to David Franks, Managing Director FNW Trains, citing the remit as to why no communication had been received and whether any of the recommendations were being implemented, including those appertaining to Newton Heath Depot. On hearing nothing to that letter, a further one was sent in August. A reply from Dave Kaye, Operations Director, apologised and went on to add that some of my ideas had worked well. If I would like further feedback it may be a good idea to speak with David Langton. I wouldn't do that on principle. He was quick enough to ask me to assist sorting out their problems but extremely remiss in acknowledging the outcome of my deliberations.

I had a spell as Coordinator on Rail Replacement with Fraser Eagle Management Services, where engineering work, or an incident on the railway, results in service disruption or suspension. Buses and coaches are then procured to provide a replacement service. Locations included a nine-day block at Hemel Hempstead on the West Coast main line and a week at Kirkcaldy when the Forth Bridge was closed. A couple of days after Christmas in 2004, Mark Croasdale rang asking if I would be available to cover the early turn coordinator at Glasgow Central on New Year's Day; needless to say there were no volunteers north of the border. I replied that I couldn't leave my wife on her own on New Year's Eve; but she could come with me, and did. We stayed at the Jury's Inn (£160 a night) and saw in the New Year in George Square. Great! Fraser Eagle, once the leading rail replacement service in the rail industry, filed for administration in March 2009. The company had been in difficulties for some months. Indeed, many suppliers of the road transport had complained that Fraser Eagle was extremely slow to pay

First North Western
First Floor
Bridgewater House
58 Whitworth Street
Manchester
M1 6LT

Operations Director

First

Mr R H Fowkes
47 Church Road
Wembury
Plymouth
Devon
PL9 0JF

Fax: 0161-228-5909
Tel: 0161-228-4698
Y/R :
O/R : FNW 627498

14 August 1999

Dear Mr Fowkes

Thank you for your letter dated 8 August addressed to David Franks. I am replying on David's behalf as he is currently on leave.

I am sorry that you have not received a reply to your initial letter dated 18 June, please accept my most sincere apologies.

I note your comments about First North Western's service performance and although we did have a very bad period in relation to this last autumn, since the beginning of the year this has significantly improved and we are now amongst the very best in the country for reliability and punctuality.

Although the depot at Newton Heath has undergone significant restructuring, some of your ideas have worked well. If you would like further feedback it may be a good idea to speak with David Langton (0161 228 4061).

I do hope this is helpful and I thank you again for writing

Yours sincerely

Dave Kaye

North Western Trains Company Limited
Registered in England & Wales No 3007946
Registered Office : Milford House
1 Milford Street Swindon SN1 1HL
A First Group **Company**

Reply from Dave Kaye regarding the Newton Heath project.

for their services. The one-time coach company, founded in 1919, expanded into a national operation priding itself on providing bus replacement services for stranded rail passengers. Professional railway men and women staffed a control centre based in Accrington and later much of the control function was transferred to Malta.

In January 2005 I applied for the job of Rail Replacement Manager with National Express; my son-in-law advised me about the vacancy which had appeared in *Rail* magazine. Interviewed by Richard Kirk – whom I had met briefly when at Hemel Hempstead – and David Bloomfield in the Wessex trains office at Exeter, I was appointed to the position.

NX Duty Managers were responsible for the co-ordination and supervision of the pre-planned rail replacement services. They're mobile and roam along the route, liasing with the controllers to monitor the efficiency of the service and keep a record of problems and issues as they arise. They are the first point of contact for operators, controllers and the control centre on the day of operation. With First Group winning the franchise for Great Western and then absorbing Wessex Trains from National Express, there were no opportunities in the south-west, although the Rail Replacement business continued to grow into new areas and expand current operations. At one period National Express had nine UK rail franchises, six of which came up for renewal during 2004 when they lost ScotRail to First; the demise of others followed and were widely documented in the media.

The most interesting time during my three years with National Express – before being advised that I would be coming off their payroll having not worked for thirteen weeks, the penalty for living so far from the action – was during the extremely wet summer of 2007. Staying at my mother-in-law's house in Long Eaton, I had eight weeks on the Erewash Valley block – home from home. Coaches replaced trains between Nottingham, Langley Mill, Alfreton and Chesterfield with the Norwich to Liverpool services diverted via Derby. There had been no let up with the incessant heavy rain and one controller who was making his way to Chesterfield station was caught up in the floods. He was nearing the station in his car when he reported that the water was just above his clutch pedal. The Rail Replacement coaches were then suspended for the remainder of that day with the railway lines at Clay Cross closed due to the flooding. Frequent accidents on the M1 motorway during the blockade also added to the problems of maintaining a schedule. Overall, there was a good-natured rapport between controllers, coach drivers and the passengers, which was good to see. The essence of Rail Replacement is to keep people on the move, it being particularly annoying for passengers arriving on the bus to find their train has already departed; conversely, it was often prudent to hold onto a coach to connect out of a train (within reason) so it was important to maintain a liaison with the station staff.

Now, having just passed 'three score years and ten' I wouldn't have minded continuing with rail replacement duties. Alas – nothing lasts forever!

Postscript

Having been domiciled in the south-west for thirty-three years, we moved back to Breaston in August 2012, a decision Maureen wasn't too enamoured with initially as she would be losing her circle of friends. At the fore was the need to downsize from a four-bedroom property. Alan, my eldest, resides in Brisbane with Kevin a five-hour flight away in Perth. Janet, with her three sons, lives near Midsomer Norton which is almost equidistant from both Wembury and Breaston. Having a brother in the same village and two nephews nearby with a sister at Nottingham, the bungalow we now occupy is a hundred yards from our first home, so it can be said we are now back to our roots.